Glasnost'

American University Studies

Series IX
History

Vol. 103

PETER LANG
New York · San Francisco · Bern
Frankfurt am Main · Paris · London

Montecue J. Lowry

Glasnost'

Deception, Desperation, Dialectics

PETER LANG
New York · San Francisco · Bern
Frankfurt am Main · Paris · London

Library of Congress Cataloging-in-Publication Data

Lowry, Montecue J.
  Glasnost' : deception, desperation, dialectics /
Montecue J. Lowry.
    p. cm. — (American university studies. Series IX,
History ; vol. 103)
    Includes bibliographical references and index.
    1. Communism—Soviet Union—History. 2. Soviet
Union—Politics and government—1917-   3. Soviet
Union—Economic policy—1917-   4. Propaganda, Soviet.
5. Glasnost'. 6. Perestroika.   I. Title.   II. Series.
HX313.L63   1991   335.43'0947—dc20   90-48821
ISBN 0-8204-1522-7   CIP
ISSN 0740-0462

Excerpts from *The Russian Revolution* by Alan
Moorehead. Copyright © 1958 by Time, Inc. Reprinted
by permission of Harper & Row, Publishers, Inc.

Excerpts from *Why Lenin? Why Stalin?* by Theodore von
Laue. Copyright © 1964 by Theodore von Laue.
Reprinted by permission of Harper & Row, Publishers, Inc.

Excerpts from *Perestroika* by Mikhail S. Gorbachev.
Copyright © 1987 by Mikhail S. Gorbachev. Reprinted
by permission of Harper & Row, Publishers, Inc.

© Peter Lang Publishing, Inc., New York 1991

Printed in the United States of America.

TO

THE AMERICAN PEOPLE

TABLE OF CONTENTS

    Hegel
    Marx and Engels
    Lenin
    Marxism-Leninism

    The Summer of 1917
    The October Days
    The Election of November 1917
    The Constituent Assembly

x

LIST OF ILLUSTRATIONS

ACKNOWLEDGMENTS

In writing this book, I owe special appreciation to several individuals. Among these individuals are my teachers, Claude Fike, John Bohon, John Loud, Gordon Smith, and Milan Reban, all of whom provided me with a basic knowledge of Russia and the Soviet Union which enabled me to pursue independent study in this field. I wish to give special thanks to Alan Rehm, a friend who gave me an insight into valuable sources which I might have overlooked.

I wish to express appreciation to my superiors at the Central Intelligence Agency, who, because of security restrictions, must remain anonymous. These individuals, true professionals in every sense, gave me an opportunity to delve into Soviet sources and gain an insight into the Soviet Union which I would otherwise not have had. My brief service with the Central Intelligence Agency was the most intellectually rewarding period of my life, and I received great personal satisfaction from this association. I wish also to thank my fellow analysts at the Agency for the help and support they gave a novice analyst who struggled to catch up in an area shrouded in mystery and secrecy. Special thanks goes to my Russian teacher at the Agency, who must also remain anonymous.

The sources used for this book are not classified and are available to the general public. I have used Soviet sources as much as possible, since the thesis is based on what the Soviets have said. Although some references to *Pravda* are from the Russian language edition, most references to Soviet periodicals and news releases have come from the *FBIS Daily Report* on the Soviet Union.

After studying the Soviet Union for over thirty years and after having taught Soviet history as an integral part of European history and Western civilization, I have attained a repertoire of knowledge which is in my opinion of a general nature. Accordingly, that information which I regard as general knowledge is not cited in the notes.

For permission to use their published material, I extend special thanks to The Academy of Political Science, The *Atlantic Monthly*, *Comparative Strategy*, The Defense and Strategic Studies Program of the University of Southern California, Delphic Associates, Dodd, Mead, and Company, Doubleday & Company, Encyclopaedia Britannica, Harper & Row, D. C. Heath Company, Indiana University Press, *International Journal of Intelligence and Counterintelligence*, J. B. Lippincott Company, The *New Republic*, Prentice-Hall, Inc., Presidio Press, Richardson & Steirman, Simon & Schuster, *Soviet Economy*, Taylor and Francis, The University of North Carolina Press, and Walter de Gruyter, Inc.

I wish to thank Brent Sandy, who read parts of the manuscript. Bullitt Lowry (no relation) and Stephen Livesay receive special thanks inasmuch as they read the entire manuscript. Their comments and suggestions were most helpful; however, the author alone bears the responsibility for any errors which may appear in the text.

I wish to pay special tribute to my family, who endured the year in which I was heavily engaged with this project. My wife Jennifer and my sons Jeremy and Monte II deserve much credit for their patience and moral support.

Montecue J. Lowry

Lynchburg, Virginia
1 May 1990

PREFACE

When J. Edgar Hoover wrote his book *Masters of Deceit*, he portrayed the inner workings of the Communist Party as those of a hard core of fanatical Marxists dedicated to the conquest of the free world by any and every means available, legal and illegal, moral and immoral, peaceful and warlike, of which mankind is capable. *Masters of Deceit*, first published in 1958, went through at least eight printings.[1] The American people were concerned about the Communist threat, and they bought and read Hoover's book.

Since the publication of *Masters of Deceit* the Western world has developed a skepticism about the true nature of Communism. Many people today, even in the United States, view the Soviet Union and other Communists as merely another struggling people who are misunderstood, misrepresented, and mistreated because of prejudices lingering from a misunderstood past. The trend toward minimizing the Communist threat or casting it aside as a myth can be attributed in part to Communist propaganda and in part to a deterioration of American concern for things ideological. Perhaps more important in causing the American public to belittle the Communist threat has been a continuous erosion of traditional American values.

Robert C. Tucker aptly described the Western perception of Communism: "The Western mind has tended to anticipate a mellowing of the Soviet Communist movement in terms of what has been called 'ideological erosion.'"[2] The cause of this erosion of American values can be traced to many conditions, some of the most significant of which are the red scare promulgated by Senator Joseph McCarthy and his subsequent censure, disappointments from the post-World War II period, the permissiveness characteristic of the 1960s, the disillusionments which accompanied United States' involvement in the Vietnam War, and the

Watergate incident.   In general, the American people have been
disappointed in their expectations.

In his book *Perestroika*, Mikhail S. Gorbachëv wrote that he and
his cohorts are "seeking to revive the living spirit of Leninism."[3] Yet,
Westerners so discount the role of Communist ideology that they do not
perceive the degree to which it remains the fundamental driving force
behind Soviet actions.[4]

The Soviets are knowledgeable and shrewd.   They know that
Western analysts spend hours pouring over Soviet writings trying to read
between the lines and discover hidden meanings. United States' analysts
tend to discount open Soviet sources. Consequently, the Soviets do not
hesitate to publish their military doctrine, strategy, and tactics openly.
They do the same with political and other writings with a high degree
of confidence that Western skepticism will serve to conceal their true
objectives.   Accordingly, a close reading of Gorbachëv's writings and
speeches will reveal that, despite his florid and abundant rhetoric, he
adheres to the fundamentals of Marxist-Leninist ideology. He makes no
pretense about Soviet beliefs and objectives.

The Soviets are expending great effort to convince the West that
they have changed their strategy and now sincerely desire to live in
peace and harmony with the rest of the world. Yet, there is much
evidence to indicate that they have not changed their ultimate goal and
are only following a more deceptive path than previously. The Soviets
have a track record - they call it history - which the West should
examine carefully. A careful study of the Soviet past will reveal an
astonishing amount of *déjà vu*.

Mikhail S. Gorbachëv is a highly capable politician who knows
what he wants and how to get it. Gorbachëv is the most audacious
Soviet leader since Vladimir I. Lenin, and he fully understands the
relationship between the Soviet economic, social, and political systems.
Furthermore, he recognizes that all three require reform. The economic
process must come to rest on a better political system, and *glasnost'* and
"democratization" constitute the basis for that better political system.
His strong suit is public relations, he uses the "Madison Avenue"
approach, and he is a master in influencing world-wide public opinion.

Gorbachëv is vastly different in personality, background, and

approach to the West from the traditional Soviet leader. There is a
marked contrast in his personality and that of Leonid Brezhnev, Nikita
Khrushchëv, and Josef Stalin. Historically, Soviet leaders have not
projected an image of "Mr. nice guy." They have projected the image
of an indomitable, irrational, dull boor whose opinion must be accepted
or else they will pick up their things and go home. After World War
II, the Soviets gave the impression that if the West did not play the
game by Soviet rules, the Soviets could solve the problem by walking out
of a meeting or by refusing to meet with the West. Examples include
Marshal V. D. Sokolovskiy's departure from the Allied Control Commission in Germany in March 1948 and the Soviet walk-out from the
UN Security Council in the spring of 1950. In both of these instances,
the long term consequences for the world, as well as for the Soviets,
were negative. Under Gorbachëv's leadership, the Soviets are trying
desperately to reverse their well-earned image.

In their top leadership positions, the Soviets have had a serious
image problem from the inception of the Communist state in late 1917.
Beginning with Leon Trotsky, who thought he could issue a few decrees
and then close the Commissariat of Foreign Affairs, Soviet foreign
ministers have not had the personality, self-confidence, or diplomatic
finesse to win friends and influence Western leaders without arousing
the gravest suspicions. George Chicherin and Maxim Litvinov were
better diplomats than most other Soviet Foreign Ministers, but they still
fell short of engendering international confidence. Soviet Communist
Party leaders have projected the same image.

The Soviets have recognized their image problem since the mid-
1960s, or earlier, and have sought means to solve it; however, until
Mikhail S. Gorbachëv rose to power they had no one whose personality
could mesh with that of Western politicians. The first step in solving
any problem is the recognition and identification of the problem itself,
and apparently the Soviets did this in the late 1950s or early 1960s, since
they began taking measures at that time to overcome their cultural
handicap.

Little by little and step by step the Soviets carefully planned and
carried out a solution to their image problem. They were motivated to
do so for several reasons, one of which was the failure of the Marxist

economy to deliver on the promises made by Marx, Lenin, Stalin, and others of the Communist elite. Another deficiency of Marxism has been the failure of the state to wither away and the people to assume their ultimate role as the dictatorship of the proletariat. In short, Communism has not been working, and this is the theme that Gorbachëv, like his predecessor Lenin, is pushing on the West.

Glasnost' and *perestroika* pose a threat to the West, especially to the United States. This threat has three prongs, one of which is short range and obvious. The others are long range threats and are less obvious since they tend to be obscured by the Western complacency engendered through Gorbachëv's international public relations campaign. The short range threat, which is a more immediate danger and can be countered effectively if recognized soon enough, is the military threat from the Soviet armed forces and the forces of the Warsaw Pact. The long range threats are the more dangerous since they are not readily obvious. The second and more dangerous threat is from the Marxist-Leninist ideology to which the Soviets claim allegiance. In 1987 a defector was asked what he thought of United States' military officers in comparison with Soviet officers. He responded that United States' officers were highly competent professionals, but that in an armed conflict with the Soviet Union the Soviets would win because United States' officers have no belief system. The insidious Marxist-Leninist ideology continues to be important. The third threat is the political system in which one party, the Communist Party, has ruled through an elite oligarchy. The Soviet people have participated in their government by approving the actions and decisions of the Communist Party. It is possible that Gorbachëv's political reforms, proposed in February 1990, will permit more popular participation of the people in the governmental process. Such reform would hasten the withering away of the state and the beginning of the dictatorship of the proletariat.

This book will deal with these three threats. To do so it is necessary to review Marxist ideology and Leninist modifications of Marxism. It is also necessary to review Soviet military doctrine and strategy since World War II. Inasmuch as the Soviets place special emphasis on their history and the role of historical determinism, this book will deal with some specifics of Soviet history which affect

Gorbachëv. This book is not a study in historical determinism, but it will emphasize the importance of studying and understanding Soviet history and the reasons for the importance of this study. To use George Santayana's often quoted observation: "...those who cannot remember the past are condemned to repeat it."

Gorbachëv has talked and written profusely about the traditional Marxist-Leninist arguments, but he presents them in a new package. He is as mendacious as other Soviet leaders, and his use of half-truths is highly convincing to the unsuspecting person who is looking for something new and fresh from a Soviet leader. Gorbachëv has repeatedly referred to Vladimir I. Lenin, his teachings, his attitudes, his methods, and his solutions to problems. Gorbachëv is apparently following the teachings of Lenin, at least that is what he has said. To understand and evaluate Gorbachëv's program, it is necessary to know what Lenin said and did. It is also necessary to know about past Soviet practices. Lenin told Feliks E. Dzerzhinskiy, the CHEKA chief, with regard to dealing with the West: "Tell them what they want to believe." Gorbachëv is doing just that - he is telling the West what the West wants to believe, and indeed it appears that the West believes Gorbachëv.

In the West circulate a plethora of explanations about what Gorbachëv is really trying to accomplish. These explanations include the argument that Gorbachëv is sincerely attempting to bring Western democracy to the Soviet Union, but that in doing so he must of necessity proclaim his loyalty to Marxism-Leninism to provide the credibility to convince the Soviets that his is the correct course. Proponents of this belief argue that Gorbachëv is merely feigning dedication to Marxism-Leninism and that he is indeed a Western democrat who must work within the Soviet system. Closely associated with this view is the rumor that at some vague time in the past Gorbachëv made a profession of faith in Jesus Christ. A further argument in Gorbachëv's favor is the observation that actions speak louder than words, and his reforms, especially in East Europe, tend to "prove" that the Soviets have indeed given up Communism and traditional Communist objectives. These and other arguments do not consider the evidence in the historical context of Marxism-Leninism, nor do they consider all of the evidence. The evidence presented in this book suggests that these and similar arguments are not correct.

One volume is insufficient to deal with all of the flaws in Gorbachëv's "new thinking," especially in view of the rapid changes observed in the Soviet Union and East Europe in late 1989 and early 1990.   Hence, this book will consider only the major facets of Gorbachëv's program.

NOTES

1. J. Edgar Hoover, *Masters of Deceit* (New York: Holt, Rinehart and Winston, 1958), iv.

2. Robert C. Tucker, *The Marxian Revolutionary Idea* (New York: W. W. Norton & Co., Inc., 1969), 213. Reprinted with permission of the publisher.

3. Mikhail S. Gorbachëv, *Perestroika: New Thinking for Our Country and the World* (New York: Harper & Row, Publishers, 1988), 52. Copyright (c) 1987 by Mikhail S. Gorbachëv. Reprinted by permission of Harper & Row, Publishers, Inc.

4. Charles Krauthammer, "When to Call off the Cold War," *The New Republic* (16 November 1987): 18-21. Reprinted by permission of *The New Republic*, (c) 1987, The New Republic, Inc.

LIST OF ABBREVIATIONS

ABM	Anti-Ballistic Missile
CHEKA	*Chrezvychainaya Komissiya*, All Russian Extraordinary Commission for Combating Counterrevolution, Speculation, Sabotage, and Misconduct in Office
CIA	Central Intelligence Agency
CPSU	Communist Party of the Soviet Union
FBIS	Foreign Broadcast Information Service
GNP	Gross National Product
GOSPLAN	State Planning Commission
GPU	*Gosudarstvennoye Politicheskoye Upravleniye*
GUSM	*Glavnoe Upravlenie Strategicheskoy Maskirovka*
ICBM	Intercontinental Ballistic Missile
IMEMO	*Institut Mirovoy Ekonomiki i Mezhdunarodnykh Otnosheniy*
IUSAC	Institute of the USA and Canada
IWWM	Institute of the World Workers' Movement
KGB	*Komitet Gosudarstvennoy Bezopasnosti* (Committee for State Security)

MIRV	Multiple Independently-Targeted Reentry Vehicle
MVD	Ministry of Internal Affairs
NATO	North Atlantic Treaty Organization
NEP	Novaya Ekonomicheskaya Politika (New Economic Policy)
OGPU	*Ob'edinyonnoye Gosudarstzvennoye Politicheskoye Upravleniye*
RSFSR	Russian Soviet Federated Socialist Republic
SALT	Strategic Arms Limitations Talks
SLBM	Submarine Launched Ballistic Missile
SRF	Strategic Rocket Forces
UN	United Nations
USSR	Union of Soviet Socialist Republics
WIN	*Wolnosc i Niepodleglosc* (Freedom and Independence)

I

INTRODUCTION

Beginning when Mikhail S. Gorbachëv became General Secretary of the Communist Party of the Soviet Union (CPSU), 11 March 1985, the world has been dazzled by his promotion of drastic reforms in the Soviet Union and East Europe. His description of this reform movement has been characterized by the words "new thinking," *perestroika*, *glasnost'*, and "democracy," words and concepts which appeared initially as a marked departure from past Soviet policies, practices, and procedures.

The thesis of this book is that Mikhail S. Gorbachëv's "new thinking" is not new but is the implementation of a plan that has been underway since the mid-1960s, that the Soviets have long recognized that there is a serious problem with their socio-economic and political systems, that the solution to these problems is a return to the teachings of Lenin, and that the Soviets perceive that the result of Gorbachëv's program will be a stronger Soviet Union emanating from the working of the dialectic between the opposing forces of capitalism and Marxist-Leninist socialism. *Perestroika*, *glasnost'*, and socialist "democracy" are merely clichés concocted by the Soviets to describe a return to the Leninist way whereby they can consolidate their position in the world and in the long run propagate international, Marxist-Leninist socialism.

Vladimir I. Lenin is the authority whom Mikhail S. Gorbachëv frequently quotes. Gorbachëv claims to base his entire program of "new thinking," *glasnost'*, *perestroika*, and democracy on returning to true Marxism-Leninism. In this regard, he is similar to previous Soviet leaders who have said the same thing. According to Gorbachëv, the

Soviets must return to Lenin's way of doing things. This proposed mode of operation motivates an inquiry to determine Lenin's teachings and Lenin's ways of doing things.

Mikhail S. Gorbachëv has launched the Soviet Union into a "new revolution," the purpose of which is to sort out the theory and ideas of socialism in the spirit of Lenin's heritage and methods.[1] These are lofty words, but the meaning can be understood only in the sense of knowing and understanding the heritage and the methods of Vladimir I. Lenin. A close examination of the heritage of Lenin and Lenin's methods reveals that they were not as humane and honorable as Gorbachëv wants the world to believe.

When Gorbachëv and his cohorts talk and write about socialism, they are talking and writing about Marxism-Leninism in a world where pure Communism has not been achieved. The Soviet Union is a socialist state in the sense of Marxism-Leninism. It is not socialist in the sense of the Social Democracy of Western Europe. West European Social Democracy and Soviet socialism have been bitter foes and are at odds over the methods by which they intend to achieve their objectives. The Soviets are "building Communism," but they have not yet achieved their ultimate goal. Until such time as the Soviet Union is a pure Communist state, the Communist Party will probably be the dominant political power in the state and will "serve the workers" as the vanguard of the proletariat.[2]

Gorbachëv claims that the Soviet democratic process began in October 1917; however, Soviet democracy warrants close study. On 25 October 1917 (old calendar; 7 November new calendar) the Communists (Bolsheviks) seized power in Russia using armed force through a *coup d'etat* to overthrow the Provisional Government. They took control from what the West perceived to be a republican form of government created after the Czarist monarchy collapsed in February 1917 (old calendar).

That first revolution, the one which overthrew the Czar, was in effect a collapse of the old Russian governmental system rather than an organized revolution. The Bolsheviks, whose leaders were Russian intelligentsia, did not participate in the revolution which overthrew the Czar. Most of the Russian intelligentsia of the late nineteenth and early twentieth centuries had taken a radical turn in opposition to the Czar and were dedicated to his overthrow, if not his death. Those Bolshevik leaders accidentally in Russia when the Czar was overthrown had no initiative and were not of sufficient stature to guide revolutionary activity. The leaders capable of influencing revolutionary activity were all in exile. Stalin and Kamenev were in exile in Siberia; Lenin was in Switzerland; the remaining leaders were in various other foreign countries.[3]

Russia was the last country in the world where the Bolsheviks expected to seize power. The overthrow of the Czar was a complete surprise to them, and they had nothing to do with it. In mid-October 1917 Vladimir I. Lenin, the Bolshevik leader, decided that the time was right for the Bolsheviks to seize power by armed insurrection, and he emerged from hiding after having disappeared from public view in July 1917 to avoid being arrested.

To be sure, following the fall of the Czar in 1917 when the Allies recognized the Provisional Government, Russia was not yet a republic. The republican form of government was an open question to be decided by a Constituent Assembly which was elected in November 1917 after the Bolshevik *coup d'etat*.[4] Nevertheless, Lenin and the Bolsheviks began calling Russia a republic before the meeting of the Constituent Assembly. The Constituent Assembly declared Russia a republic in January 1918, but the Soviet Republic came into being only in July 1918 with the formal promulgation of the Soviet Constitution, which incorporated the territory under Soviet control into the Russian Soviet Federated Socialist Republic (RSFSR).[5] Gorbachëv, however, states that the new government which emerged in October 1917 was a republic and the country was called the Soviet Republic.[6]

Initially, when the Bolsheviks were uncertain of their control in Russia, they supported and participated in the one free election which has been held in that country since the Bolshevik *coup d'etat*. The Bolsheviks received less than twenty-five percent of the vote; at the first meeting of the popularly elected Constituent Assembly, Bolshevik armed forces, the Red Guards, surrounded and entered the assembly hall. Failing in their attempt to gain control of the Constituent Assembly, the Bolsheviks walked out of the first session. The following morning, the

Bolsheviks put an armed force around the meeting hall and declared the Constituent Assembly dissolved. Not succeeding in intimidating the delegates, the Bolsheviks seized power under the threat of armed force. Prior to 1990, there has never been another free election in Russia. This Bolshevik action was the manifestation of the democracy to which Gorbachëv so eloquently refers.

Throughout their history, the Marxist Soviets have been highly loquacious in enunciating wonderful goals. They proclaim that they alone have the solution to the world's problems, since everything else has failed. They also have a history which indicates that their actions do not always follow their pronouncements. Numerous Western authors have studied Soviet actions and pronouncements, and some Soviet experts have detected a pattern to Soviet behavior. While this pattern cannot be relied upon to predict Soviet actions, it should be studied as an indicator of what the West can expect in the long term from Gorbachëv and his cohorts. The Soviets, like most other people, are not likely to change their *modus operandi* precipitously with no thought, discussion, and planning; their behavior patterns have become set.

The Soviet Union was born in a milieu of deceit, desperation, and contradiction. Lies, false promises, a failing economy, uncertainty about national security, and ever-present paranoia have been characteristics prevalent in the Soviet Union from its conception. Of these characteristics, those which did not exist naturally were contrived by the leadership to hold the populace in line. The Soviets explain contradictions in terms of the Marxian dialectic, a concept which Marx coopted from Hegel.

There are three primary threats in accepting the Gorbachëv line: military, political, and ideological. In 1947 in his article signed "X," George Kennan pointed to the dangers of two of these threats, the political and ideological. His idea of containment, however, was misconstrued to mean the military threat. Consequently, the idea of military containment of the Soviet Union became United States' foreign policy in the ensuing years.[7] In the immediate past, the Soviet military threat has been a major concern of Western nations. This concern developed after World War II. Prior to World War II and in the years immediately following, there was a widespread fear of the Communist ideology; however, this ideological fear has abated. Today, there is a tendency to treat the military threat in much the same way as the ideological threat. Nevertheless, in the short term, the military threat exists, and there is an ever present danger that someone or some incident will create a situation in which the rational approach projected by Gorbachëv will be overcome by a precipitous act. A study of Soviet history reveals that with the Soviets, reality does not necessarily reflect the rhetoric. Hence, all three threats persist.

Despite the peaceful words exuded by Gorbachëv and Soviet leaders from Brezhnev's days, the Soviets have not changed their global military strategy, and they will not do so until after the West has reduced its armaments to a position from which they are ineffective as a deterrent against Soviet strategic military actions. While the top level Soviet leaders talk peace, Soviet military authors continue to write authoritative books and instructions on the employment of Soviet armed forces, in particular their Strategic Rocket Forces, using the techniques of surprise, preemption, and *Blitzkrieg*.

Gorbachëv argues that over the ages the teachings of philosophers and theologians on the subject of eternal human values are merely scholastic speculation doomed to a utopian dream. He further argues that class interests are the deciding factors in domestic and foreign relations but have been covered up by religious motives or references to universal well being. In his view, only Marxists and other "sober minded" people are convinced that socio-political forces are the determinants of state policy. He asserts that Marxism-Leninism and its role in the universal class struggle to free the working class is the answer to the world's problems.[8]

Soviet society has not assimilated the fundamental Western concepts of constitutionalism, democracy, individual rights, and the free market economy.[9] Politically, the Western concept of democracy is alien to the Soviets. Parliamentary democracy and republican democracy provide a multi-party system in which the people can and do participate to the degree of their preference. Generally, there is no limit to the number of different political views in the West, and within the bounds of constitutional law, anyone can run for public office. In the Soviet Union there has been only one party - the Communist Party.

Although the Soviet Constitution provides for a head of state, the Communist Party General Secretary has held the position of authority in the Soviet Union. According to Marxist-Leninist dogma, the Soviet Union has been ruled not by one man, but by an oligarchy. This collegial body is the Politburo. The head of state and the Party General Secretary have remained in power at the will of the Politburo and the Central Committee, and in some instances both offices have been vested in the same individual. In the West, the tenure of a head of state is subject to the will of the people, either directly or indirectly. A parliamentary prime minister can be removed by his own colleagues at their pleasure; he can be removed by the voters in regularly scheduled elections or sooner. A president can be changed by the people at the end of his constitutionally determined term of office; he can be removed earlier for misconduct. In the past, the Soviets have not tolerated this degree of political freedom and power in exercising the "democratic" will of the Soviet people. In the Soviet Union, the degree of power exercised by the people in the West would be an ever present threat to the Communist Party.

Nevertheless, Gorbachëv continues to talk about democracy in the Soviet Union. He has gone so far as to imply that the Soviets intend to adopt an electoral system whereby the people can elect their own national leader. His immediate question, as he has stated, is whether or not the presidential system will be one of authority or one of administration. He further questions the practicability of adopting a United States' presidential system or a French parliamentary system.[10] Gorbachëv talks about adopting the concept of separation of powers in the Soviet government, and recent articles indicate that the Supreme Soviet must approve a declaration of war. At the Central Committee meeting in February 1990, Gorbachëv proposed political reforms which would permit the organization and operation of political parties which would compete with the Communist Party.[11] In reality, however, there is skepticism about the degree to which the Communist Party will permit these reforms to operate.

In the Western world, military forces are an agency of the executive branch of the government and as such are separate from the other branches, such as the legislative branch. In the Soviet Union, this separation of powers is not distinct, in that active duty Soviet military men serve in the "legislative" branch of the government. In the West, as a general practice active duty military personnel do not run for or serve in public office, because such would constitute a conflict of interests. In the Soviet Union, however, a number of military personnel serve as peoples' deputies on the same basis as other Soviet citizens. In October 1989, eighty-two Soviet servicemen served as people's deputies, and nine were in the Supreme Soviet.[12] These military deputies have formed a club "to help in the solution of the numerous problems which accumulated."[13] Military deputies appear in their seats in the Congress of People's Deputies and in the Supreme Soviet in military uniform, and they represent the Army and Navy and the servicemen who elected them. The military deputies participate in the proceedings of these bodies in the same manner as other deputies. Soviet military deputies include Marshal V. G. Kulikov, Marshal S. F. Akhromeyev, Admiral V. P. Ivanov, and Army General A. D. Lizichev.[14]

Differing from Marxism-Leninism, Western civilization is based on the Greco-Roman culture that was later influenced by other civilizations and movements including Judeo-Christian beliefs, the foundation of which is the Holy Bible. Hence, the roots of Western culture include the Judeo-Christian beliefs of the Bible, and Western culture presently preserves significant vestiges of those Judeo-Christian values. The Bible has been the guide for wise men, philosophers, heads of state, soldiers, and millions of other people who have populated the Western world from the beginning. The Marxists, as practicing, proselyting atheists, treat the Bible as a collection of myths, the appeal of which attracts the ignorant, the superstitious, and the otherwise not too intelligent segments of humanity. Although they talk smoothly and convincingly about human values, freedom of religion, and peace, the Marxists, if permitted to infiltrate and dominate the Western world, would rob Western civilization of its Judeo-Christian heritage as they have done or have tried to do in those countries where they have succeeded in becoming dominant. Although they speak words to the contrary, they would impose their own materialistic, "scientific," atheistic dogma on everyone.

In *The Communist Manifesto*, Karl Marx and Friederich Engels wrote: "Communism abolishes external truths, it abolishes all religion, and all morality, instead of constituting them on a new basis ...."[15] According to Lenin, the Communist Party, the party of the "socialist proletariat," does not consider religion to be a private affair, since their program is based on the "scientific," "materialistic" world outlook. Communist propaganda is of necessity that of atheism. Lenin taught that the yoke of religion is a reflection of the economic yoke in society. In his words: "Unity in this really revolutionary struggle of the oppressed class for the creation of a paradise on earth is more important to us than unity of proletarian opinion on paradise in heaven."[16] He cited this as the reason that Communists did not and should not include atheism in their program; however, according to Lenin, the Communists will always preach the scientific world outlook.[17]

Marxists, like many atheists, know what the Bible says, and they quote the Bible in their contacts with the West in an effort to prove that Christianity does not work. They have studied Western interpretations of the Bible and they use expressions from the Bible as propaganda techniques. For example, Marxists utter phrases such as "an eye for an eye" and "predestination."[18] Occasionally a Soviet writer will refer to God.[19] Some Soviets utter Biblical expressions as a matter of course when communicating with the West. Mikhail S. Gorbachëv talks about the Russian Christian heritage through the Russian Orthodox Church in an attempt to tie the Soviet Union to Western Europe. Gorbachëv does not explain that Christianity came to Russia from Constantinople, not from the West. Yet, Lenin and his Bolsheviks were ruthless, militant atheists who made their fight against the Russian Orthodox Church a fight against all religion.[20] The Marxists have a problem because they want everyone to owe his complete loyalty to the Communist Party and state. The Marxists recognize no authority higher than the Party-state, and in their view, there is no compromise. In this regard they reveal their ignorance of Christianity, since Christianity does not intend to rob the citizen of his duty to the state. The Christian obligation to civil government and authority is quite clear; the Christian is not excused or exempt from civil law.[21]

This book will deal with the military, political, and ideological threats posed by Communism. In so doing, in terms of Gorbachëv's "new thinking," it will discuss the realities of Soviet deception, the desperate, or "critical," status of the Soviet socio-economic position, and the working of the dialectic in what the Soviets perceive to be the class struggle between Marxist-Leninist socialism and capitalism.

Accordingly, this book will present a resume of Marxist ideology, a summary of early Soviet history under Lenin, those aspects of the Stalinist era which plague Gorbachëv, the pattern of Soviet actions in the past, a different approach to Gorbachëv's "new thinking," the Gorbachëv era, an analysis of what Gorbachëv says and what the Soviets have done in the past, and the immediate danger of accepting Gorbachëv's enunciations at face value.

"Tell them what they want to believe."

NOTES

1. Mikhail S. Gorbachëv, *Perestroika: New Thinking for Our Country and the World* (New York: Harper & Row, Publishers, 1988), 31. Copyright (c) 1987 by Mikhail S. Gorbachëv. Reprinted by permission of Harper & Row, Publishers, Inc.

2. Mikhail S. Gorbachëv, "M. S. Gorbachëv's Report at the CPSU Central Committee Plenum 5 February 1990," *Pravda*, 6 Feb. 1990.

3. Leon Trotsky, *The History of the Russian Revolution*, vol. 1, trans. Max Eastman (New York: Simon and Schuster, 1932), 144-145.

4. Leonid I. Strakhovsky, "Kerensky Betrayed Russia," in *The Russian Revolution and Bolshevik Victory*, ed. Arthur E. Adams (Boston: D. C. Heath Company, 1960), 93. Reprinted with permission of the publisher.

5. Theodore H. von Laue, *Why Lenin? Why Stalin?* (New York: J. B. Lippincott Company, 1971), 136. Copyright (c) 1964, 1971 by Theodore von Laue. Reprinted by permission of Harper & Row, Publishers, Inc.

6. Gorbachëv, *Perestroika*, 96.

7. George Kennan, "X," "The Sources of Soviet Conduct," *Foreign Affairs* 25 (Summer 1947): 566-582.

8. Gorbachëv, *Perestroika*, 130-133.

9. Department of Defense, *Soviet Military Power: An Assessment of the Threat, 1988* (Washington: United States Government Printing Office, 1988), 8.

10. Moscow Television Service, 23 Oct. 1989, *FBIS Daily Report*, 24 Oct. 1989, 40-41.

11. Gorbachëv, "Report at the CPSU Central Committee Plenum 5 February 1990," *Pravda*, 6 Feb. 1990.

12. *Krasnaya Zvezda*, 11 Oct. 1989; *Krasnaya Zvezda*, 3 Nov. 1989.

13. *Izvestiya*, 22 Oct. 1989.

14. *Krasnaya Zvezda*, 22 Oct. 1989. Marshal Kulikov is a former Chief of the Soviet General Staff and former Commander of the Warsaw Pact Forces; Marshal Akhromeyev is a former Chief of the General Staff; General Lizichev is Chief of the Main Political Directorate of the Army and Navy; Admiral Ivanov is Commander of the Baltic Fleet. Although some of the high ranking military deputies have received post-career assignments, most remain in an active duty status as full time military personnel.

15. Karl Marx and Friedrich Engels, *The Communist Manifesto*, trans. Samuel Moore (Middlesex, England: Penguin Books, 1977), 103.

16. Vladimir I. Lenin, *Socialism and Religion* (Moscow: Progress Publishers, 1976), 8-9.

17. Ibid., 9.

18. Mikhail S. Gorbachëv, *A Time for Peace* (New York: Richardson & Steirman, 1985), 187. Reprinted with permission of the publisher.

19. *Pravda*, 9 Oct. 1989.

20. von Laue, *Why Lenin? Why Stalin?*, 137.

21. Romans 13; I Peter 2: 13-21.

II

MARXIST-LENINIST IDEOLOGY

Today there is a tendency among many Westerners to denigrate the importance of Marxist-Leninist ideology in establishing long range Soviet objectives and working out the plans for attaining those objectives. This attitude is exactly what the Soviets want the West to accept and adopt. In accordance with Marxist-Leninist ideology, the Soviets perceive themselves to be engaged in a long-term class struggle between two irreconcilable political, social, and economic systems in which they believe that time and history are on their side.[1] Mikhail S. Gorbachëv, in calling for the Soviets to renew their dedication to Marxist-Leninist ideology, is basing much of his new revolution on Lenin's axiom that democracy and socialism are indivisible.[2]

In the Soviet government, individuals do not concentrate on matters of ideology. Moreover, on day to day matters, they are pragmatic and do not talk about Marx, Lenin, or Stalin. On the other hand, in the Politburo, members quote Marx and Lenin, and Politburo members use quotations from the founding fathers frequently in their speeches. Lenin himself, however, "at times carried away by expectations of spreading revolution, never sacrificed practical caution to missionary zeal."[3] Soviet leaders follow Lenin's example in this matter.

In his speech before the 27th CPSU Congress at the Kremlin on 25 February 1986, Gorbachëv repeatedly referred to Marx and Lenin and the role of Marxist-Leninist ideology - the "vitality of Marxist-Leninist doctrine." He said: "Marx's analysis .... has become still more relevant with reference to the bourgeois reality of the 20th century than it was in the 19th." Gorbachëv devoted one entire segment of the speech to a strengthening of the link between "ideology and life":

> In all of its activities, the CPSU takes as a premise that fidelity to
> the Marxist-Leninist doctrine lies in its creative development, on
> the basis of accumulated experience .... Marxism-Leninism is a
> great revolutionary world view .... Above all, in the fact that our
> plans are built on the firm foundation of Marxist-Leninist science
> and rely on the inexhaustible wealth of the ideas of Vladimir Ilich
> Lenin.[4]

Whether or not Gorbachëv intends to follow Lenin's teachings is
a question that only time and his actions can answer. Therefore, it is
appropriate to review the salient points of this ideology to understand
what he is saying and possibly to give the West some idea of what to
expect. The problem with this approach is that Lenin wrote many
volumes (over 300) on every imaginable subject. Hence, historically,
every time the Soviets have inaugurated a new policy they have found
something that Lenin wrote which supports their new objectives.

An understanding of Marxist-Leninist ideology is essential to an
understanding of what the Soviets are saying, but it is of questionable
value in predicting Soviet decisions and actions. In general, the Soviets
write what they mean and they state their views explicitly. There is a
tendency, however, for Western analysts to reject overt expressions by
the Soviets and to search between the lines for some hidden meaning
or innuendo. Such an exercise is fruitless. Soviet decisions are based
on one simple objective: they make decisions based on the Soviet
national interest.[5] This policy is nothing more than the accepted
international practice known as reason of state, on which all sovereign
nations base their foreign and domestic policies.

While certain Soviet writings express new Soviet courses of action,
it is a mistake to collect numerous quotations from Soviet authors,
accept them at face value, and attempt to draw some conclusion from
them without first examining the historical background and the circumstances in which the author wrote. Soviet writings must be considered
in the context of the purpose, target audience, credibility of the author,
historical background, time of writing, and the general circumstances

under which the piece was written.[6] Only then are they useful.

In the recent past, Marxist-Leninist ideology would not be a subject of great concern to the West when a new Soviet leader assumed office; however, Mikhail S. Gorbachëv has repeatedly referred to the works, ideas, and actions of Vladimir I. Lenin, the Bolshevik leader and hero of the Communist *coup d'etat* in 1917. Gorbachëv has pledged the reform and renewal of Soviet Communism, which is based on Marxism-Leninism and has its roots in the philosophy of Georg Wilhelm Friedrich Hegel. (See Figure 1).

The philosophy, or religion, known as Marxism consists of the system of views and teachings concocted by Karl Marx. Marx combined classical German philosophy, classical English politics, French socialism, and French revolutionary ideas to produce what his followers call "modern materialism" and "scientific socialism." This philosophy, Marxism, is the theory behind the proletarian, or working class, movements throughout the world.[7] This is the ideology to which Mikhail S. Gorbachëv adheres.

Georg Wilhelm Friedrich Hegel wrote in depth about the philosophical concept of the dialectic. Several years after Hegel died, Karl Marx studied philosophy and considered Hegel's concept of the dialectic to be nothing short of genius; however, while agreeing with Hegel on the concept of the dialectic, Marx disagreed on the specifics. Accordingly, Marx distorted Hegel's ideas to suit his own purpose, which was to prove that the history of civilization is one of struggle between the exploited and the exploiters - a class conflict. Marx, then, used Hegel's concept of the dialectic as an integral part of his argument for Communism. Marx adopted the Hegelian dialectic and made it his own. In writing Marx's distortions of Hegel in a readable form, Friederich Engels contributed to the Marxian dialectic as a partner with Marx in the formulation of Communist dogma. In the second half of the nineteenth century, the Russian dissident Vladimir I. Ulyanov (Vladimir I. Lenin) read and digested the writings of Marx and Engels and formulated what he considered to be a practical application of Marxist ideology to his concept of the "real world." In his adaptation of Marx, Lenin modified Marx's ideology to the extent that today Soviet Communism is based on Marxist-Leninist ideology.[8] Gorbachëv reports

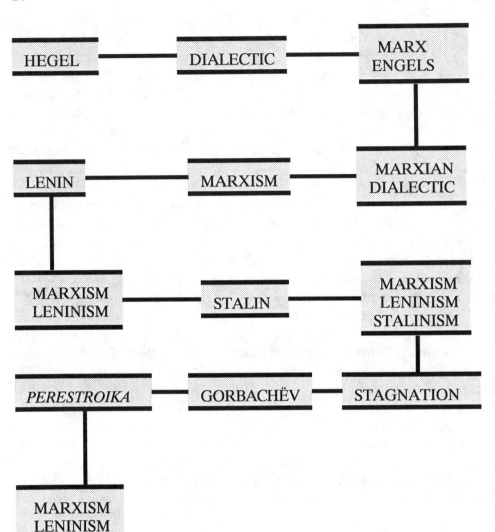

DEVELOPMENT OF COMMUNIST IDEOLOGY
HEGEL TO GORBACHËV

FIGURE 1

that neither Marx nor Lenin had the opportunity to work out the details of the practical application of their ideology, and he has assumed the responsibility for continuing this work.[9]   Inasmuch as Mikhail S. Gorbachëv has repeatedly based his program on a return to the fundamentals of Marxist-Leninist ideology, it is essential to review it.

Karl Marx wrote his doctoral dissertation under the direction of one of Hegel's students.   Although having had no direct contact with Hegel, the philosopher's ideas impressed Marx, who adapted and distorted some of Hegel's ideas to suit his own socialist purpose.   Marx used Hegel to justify class conflict by proving historically that class conflict has been the source of the world's problems from the days of prehistoric man.   Although Marx placed heavy emphasis on the role of history as a determining factor in social events, Hegel observed that both history and experience teach that peoples and governments have never learned anything from history.[10]

Karl Marx was one of the most radical thinkers of all time.   In adapting Hegel's philosophy to his own ends, Marx began with an uncompromising denial and rejection of reality.   Twisting reality, he repeatedly accused the rest of the world, especially the capitalist nations, of not being realistic or of not living in the world of reality.   In Lenin's teachings there is a similar unrealistic attitude toward reality.   Lenin, too, was uncompromising; whoever disagreed with Lenin became the subject of the most rabid vituperation.   Lenin, in his writings and his speeches, repeatedly enunciated the theme that the Bolsheviks were the only realists in the world.   Everyone else lived in a world of fancy. Following Lenin's example and implying that the West is not realistic, Gorbachëv frequently talks about the reality of Communism and its goals.

Marx perceived "humanism" as the essence of the true Communist state.[11]   Today, the Soviets perceive Communism as the only true form of humanism.   To them, Western secular humanism is not the real thing, and Mikhail S. Gorbachëv speaks of Communist humanism as the only true humanism.[12]   In their social policy the Soviets emphasize the humanistic nature of socialism, the qualitative distinction from capitalism, since they allege that socialism abolished man's exploitation of man. The Soviets claim that social justice is a characteristic of Communist humanism, permeates every aspect of social relations, and is supposed to promote popular rule, equality before the law, equality of nations, and respect of the individual.[13]   Accordingly, Gorbachëv has placed his trust in socialist democracy and socialist humanism.[14]   In his speech at the conclusion of his audience with Pope John Paul II in December 1989, Gorbachëv said that Moscow was addressing church issues "in a spirit of democracy and humanism and within the framework of *perestroika*."[15]   This statement does not imply the promotion of Christianity. Moreover, it portrays an attempt by the Soviets to use the church for their own Marxist-humanistic purposes.

Hegel stated as a proven thesis that the Idea or Reason is the only true essence revealed in the world. He wrote that the development of the history of the world has been a rational process and has constituted the course of the World-Spirit, whose nature, always one and the same, unfolds in the phenomenon of the World's existence.   In Hegel's view, the World-Spirit is the ultimate result of History.[16]   Hegel wrote that the History of the World begins with the goal of realizing the Idea of Spirit; the process of history is directed toward making conscious this unconscious impulse.   The Idea advances to an antithesis, that between the Idea itself and its polar opposite.   The two opposites, although acting against each other, in effect cooperate to yield a product.[17]

Hegel argued that the State is the Idea of Spirit in the external manifestation of human will and freedom, and that change in the aspect of history attaches itself to the State. The successive phases of the Idea manifest themselves as distinct political principles.[18]   The mutations produced in history have been characterized generally by progress toward something better, something more perfect. In history there has always been a real capacity to change for the better, or an impulse toward perfectibility.[19]

Hegel said: "This Reason in its most concrete form is God. God governs the world; the actual working out of his government - the carrying out of his plan - is the History of the World."[20]   "Religion is the sphere in which a nation gives itself the definition of that which it regards as true ....   The conception of God ... constitutes the general basis of a people's character."[21]   Marx, Engels, Lenin, and their followers rejected this Hegelian observation and opted for atheism.

Hegel wrote that Universal History shows the development of the consciousness of Freedom on the part of the Spirit and of the consequent realization of that Freedom. This development implies a gradation, a series of increasingly adequate expressions or manifestations of Freedom, which result from its Idea. The logical and the dialectical nature of the Idea is that it assumes successive forms which it successfully transcends, and by the process of transcending its earlier stages gains an affirmative, richer, and more concrete shape. Every step in the process, differing from any other, has its determinate, peculiar principle.[22]

According to the Hegelian dialectic, in time the particular form of Spirit does not merely pass away in the world by natural causes, but it is annulled in the automatic self-mirroring activity of consciousness. Because this annulling is an activity of thought, it is simultaneously conservative and elevating in its operation. While on one side the Spirit annuls reality, it gains on the other side the essence, the universal element of that which it was. Its principle is no longer that immediate significance and aim which it was previously, but it is now the essence of that significance and aim. The result of this process is that Spirit, in rendering itself objective and making its existence an object of thought, on the one hand destroys the definitive form of its being and on the other hand gains a comprehension of the universal element which it includes. It thereby gives a new form to its inherent principle. By virtue of this process, the character of the National Spirit has been altered, and its principle has risen into another and higher principle.[23]

Marx and Engels considered the Hegelian dialectic to be the greatest form of German classical philosophy. They saw in the dialectic an explanation for everything in nature, and to them nature itself was proof of the dialectic, since nature's processes are dialectical. Engels viewed the world as a complex of processes in which there is an uninterrupted change consisting of coming into being and passing away. To Engels, dialectical philosophy was nothing more than a reflection of the thought process. Marx perceived the dialectic as "the science of the general laws of motion." In consonance with Hegel, Marx perceived dialectics to be the theory of knowledge, or epistemology. The idea of evolution, as formulated by Marx and Engels on the basis of the Hegelian philosophy, consists of a development that repeats itself in stages that have already passed, but on a higher level of sophistication. This "negation of the negation" makes progress in a spiral as a development of leaps, catastrophes, revolutions, and breaks in continuity, all of which are imparted by contradiction and conflict of every effect on a given body, within a phenomenon, or in a society.[24]

Marx, although considering himself to be a pupil of Hegel, disagreed with Hegel on the dialectic. Marx, in turn, took it upon himself to turn the dialectic "right side up again."[25] At the time Marx completed his doctoral dissertation in 1841, he belonged to a group of so-called "Left Hegelians" who tried to draw atheistic and revolutionary conclusions from Hegel's ideas.[26] Marx's dialectic is the direct opposite to that of Hegel. Hegel considered the process of thinking, the life-process of the brain, to be the creator of the real world. Hegel referred to the process of thinking as the Idea, and to him the real world was the external form of the Idea. Marx took the view that the idea is merely the reflection of the real world in the human mind.[27]

According to Marx, in the process of social evolution, men form relations independent of their will, corresponding to the stage of their material productivity. The totality of the relations of production constitutes the economic structure of society on which are erected the legal and political systems corresponding to specific forms of social consciousness. Men's social being determines their consciousness. At some point in their development, the material productive forces come into conflict with the relations of production, that is with the property relations in which they have been working. Social revolution ensues, and the entire social system is rapidly transformed. Marx said that the discovery of the materialistic concept of history corrected the two faults of earlier historical theories. In the first place, the earlier theories considered only the ideological motives behind human activity without delving into the origins of those motives. The second fault was that the earlier theories did not consider the activities of the population masses. According to Marx, historical materialism enabled historians to study with scientific accuracy the social conditions of the masses and the changes in those conditions.[28]

Hegel developed the three laws of dialectics as laws of thought: the transformation of quantity into quality, the interpenetration of opposites, and the negation of the negation. All three laws are evident today in Soviet ideology, rhetoric, and writings. Engels accused Hegel of foisting these laws on nature and history as laws of thought rather than being deduced from history and nature. Engels turned it around to suit his own purposes.[29]

In explaining the split in the Social Democratic Party in 1903, Lenin called it a struggle between the revolutionary wing and the opportunist wing, a true enactment of the Marxian dialectic in which the new, more powerful Bolshevik Party emerged.[30] In simple terms, dialectics can be defined as the doctrine of the unity of opposites.[31] Today the dialectic is very much alive in the minds of Communists. In an article in *Pravda* on 9 July 1987, Ye. Primakov, discussing Soviet foreign policy, observed that the 27th Party Congress emphasized the dialectics of the unity and struggle of opposites in the modern world.[32]

Marxism teaches that materialism agrees with natural science and considers matter as primary, whereas consciousness, thought, and sensation are all secondary.[33] Marx concluded that thought, sensation, and consciousness are merely products of a very high state of development. This concept reflects Marx's materialist theory of knowledge.[34] Marxist philosophy is materialistic. Marxists perceive materialism to be the only philosophy which is consistent with the teachings of nature, and it is hostile to superstition, hypocrisy, and other "false" ideas. Marx developed the philosophy of materialism to a higher level by "enriching" it with Hegel's dialectics. Marx's followers perceive dialectic materialism to be confirmed by the most recent scientific discoveries, especially the ideas on biological evolution. Hence, Marxian dialectic materialism completely rejects all forms of idealism.[35] When Marx extended his philosophical materialism to human society, he formulated the concept of historical materialism. Historical materialism applied scientific theory to show how higher systems of social life develop from more primitive forms as a consequence of the growth of productive forces.[36]

The Marxist-Leninist theory of scientific socialism posits that society developed in several distinct stages, the first of which was the primitive

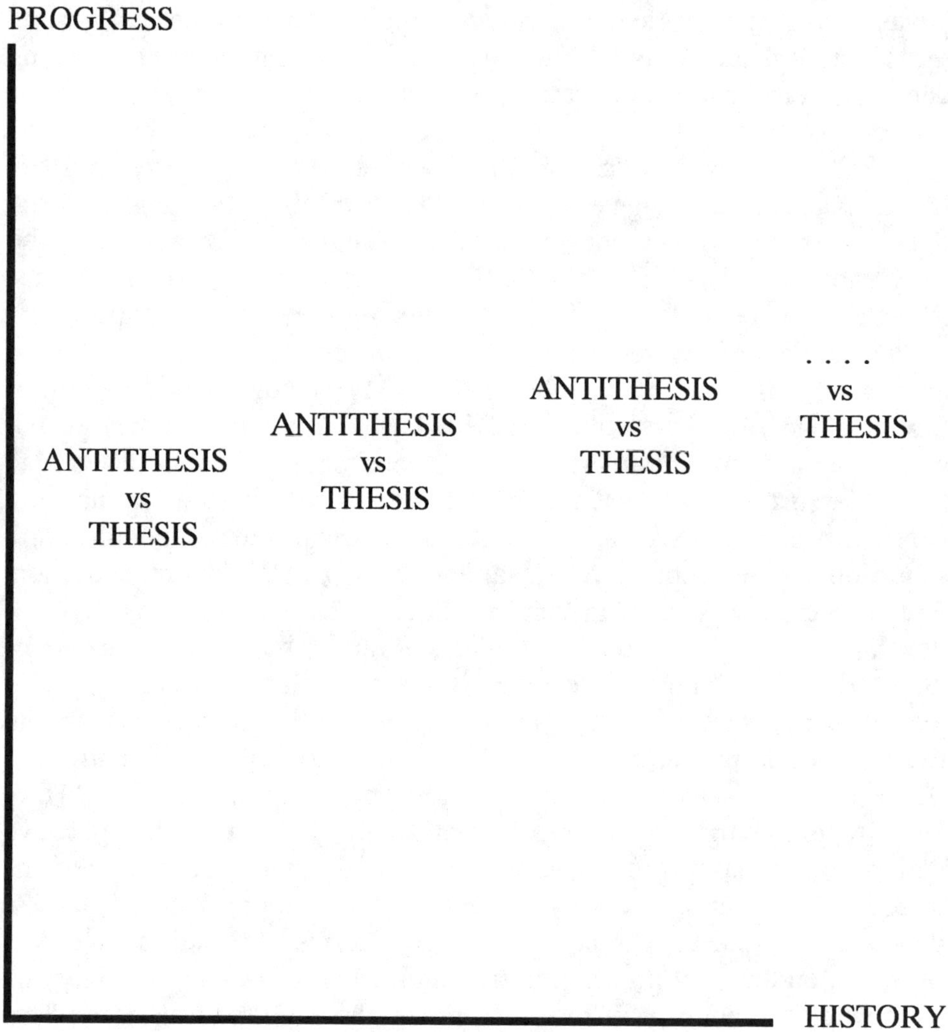

PROGRESS

. . . .
vs
THESIS

ANTITHESIS
vs
THESIS

ANTITHESIS
vs
THESIS

ANTITHESIS
vs
THESIS

HISTORY

THE DIALECTIC
FIGURE 2

society. Primitive society evolved into the system of slave-ownership and then feudalism. Following feudalism, capitalism was to be displaced by socialism. Marxists perceive these phases as the natural unfolding of history, which will decide which system is correct.[37] The final stage in the development of society is to be pure Communism, which can obtain only when the proletariat has emerged victorious world wide.

In summary, the working of the dialectic may be perceived as the struggle of opposites. In Marxian terms, there is at work a thesis which is locked in a life and death struggle with its antithesis. The outcome of this struggle is a new thesis, which is better than the former thesis; but, it, too, must meet its antithesis with which it must struggle. The process continues *ad infinitum* and is an integral part of historical determinism, which always leads to progress. The working of the Marxian dialectic is always onward and upward leading to something better. Marx perceived the thesis to be the struggle of the working class against its historical foes through the stages of history until the final outcome of this struggle will be a world of pure Communism in which the proletariat has defeated all of its class enemies. (See Figure 2).

The first sentence in Chapter One of *The Communist Manifesto* reads: "The history of all hitherto existing society is the history of class struggles."[38] In the Marxist view, revolutions in the Western world, especially those in France, reveal the class struggle as the basis and driving force behind all development.[39] In the *Communist Manifesto*, Marx and Engels wrote: "In short, the Communists everywhere support every revolutionary movement against the existing social and political order of things."[40] The Soviets firmly adhere to this Marxist axiom. "The Communists disdain to conceal their views and aims. They openly declare that their ends can be attained only by the forcible overthrow of all existing social conditions."[41] The Soviets under Gorbachëv's leadership do not conceal their ends, but they have changed their tactics.

Marxist theory approaches history in stages, which Marxists perceive as an evolutionary process moving toward a clear outcome. This perception affects Soviet decisions in domestic and international affairs. Communism, the Soviet version of Marxism, adheres to the doctrine of the inevitably of progress. The Soviets assume that political and economic organizations are transitory. Their emphasis is on materialistic factors, such as modes of production and organization, which influence the nature of social classes. They perceive the basic nature of social classes to be conflict, the process of which is revolutionary change. Marxism teaches the ever presence of crisis which leads to revolution and the overthrow of the old, the net result of which is a new order.

Marx and Engels were concerned with the late nineteenth century break-up of capitalism. They taught that the breakup of capitalism would lead to a socialist society; however, they predicted a vague future society. Property would be nationalized, thus precluding any further class conflict. Society would be egalitarian and people could do anything they wanted to do. Education would develop all skills in everyone and there would be no competition. Marxism would change human nature. Marxism was to develop in two stages: socialism, in which the need for organization dictated that everyone receive in accordance with his work, and pure Communism in which people work freely for the good of society and each receives according to his needs. This was a poor prediction and it has never succeeded. Moreover, Marx and Engels left no details about the process by which their objective of pure Communism would be achieved.

Lenin adapted Marx's and Engels' writings to the Russian situation. As an activist, Lenin formulated a "creative extension" of Marxism. He was not willing to wait for the dialectic to act but wanted to move forward immediately by educating and training the working class - at the time, peasants. Accordingly, he formed a tightly-knit group of professional revolutionaries from the Russian intelligentsia and organized the Bolshevik Party of like-minded followers. Lenin wanted to make the Bolshevik Party ideologically cohesive. Consequently, he wrote profusely and used the newspaper, the *Iskra*, to spread his doctrine. He linked the Russian underground organizationally with the exiled revolutionaries. Lenin organized the Bolshevik Party in cells and controlled it on the principle of democratic centralism. From the Marxist view, Russia was a backward, underdeveloped, peasant nation characterized by a small proletariat. Consequently, Lenin adapted Marxism to the peasant situation in Russia by forming an alliance of the proletariat and the poor peasants.

Under Lenin's leadership, there was an emphasis on the role of ideology. In ideology and practice, Lenin was a very strong willed individual, and he would allow only one solution to any problem - his own. His goal was to develop a nation of a single doctrine, and he would tolerate no difference of opinion. This adamant, single-minded attitude led to a set of conditions that de-legitimized Western values, political ideas, and institutions. This Marxist-Leninist mind set is part of Gorbachëv's heritage.

Marxist theory is hostile toward nationalism. In the Marxist's view, workers, the proletariat, have no homeland, but are international in scope. According to Marx, they are the victims of the ruling classes, the exploiters, and owe their loyalty to no nation. Lenin did not agree with Marx on this point, and the Bolsheviks claimed to defend all oppressed groups, including national groups in their temporary coalition. Lenin introduced national independence with the incorporation of nations into a "free" federation.

Karl Marx gave no guidance on foreign policy. He wrote mostly about the collapse of capitalism. He also spoke and wrote extensively about the dictatorship of the proletariat, but he never did define it. In 1917, Lenin wrote about the dictatorship of the proletariat, and he predicted that the proletarian class would win over the capitalist class. In the Soviet Union, the Communist Party was to be the vanguard of the proletariat. The function of Marxist ideology is to give the Soviet system legitimacy and a rationalization for Soviet policy. It is an analytical tool which gives a world view, setting long term goals for the Communist Party and serving as a form of communication with like minded socialists.

Lenin's interpretation of Marx indicates that the dictatorship of the proletariat is necessary only so long as the class enemy, the bourgeoisie, survives to threaten the new socialist order. The withering away of the state is to begin the instant the class enemy is destroyed in Russia. Since the class enemy was theoretically destroyed years ago, the state and the bureaucracy can no longer be justified in the Soviet Union or any Communist country.[42] Since Gorbachëv proposed the institution of political pluralism in February 1990, the Soviet people, the proletariat, have the opportunity to participate in political activity.[43] With the coming of age of the dictatorship of the proletariat, the withering away of the state may be closer to realization than the founding fathers perceived.

Ideologically, Marxism-Leninism is an important source of Soviet motivation; its impact varies with the time and the leader. It is serving as a basis for Gorbachëv's "new thinking." Conforming to Marxism-Leninism, the 27th Congress of the Communist Party of the Soviet Union (CPSU) underlined the Soviets' commitment to atheism. The Soviets consider atheist education to be an integral part of Gorbachëv's restructuring in the field of Marxist-Leninist ideology. The new CPSU program is dedicated to disseminate as widely as possible the scientific-materialistic understanding of the world and to overcome what the Soviets call religious prejudices. Soviet ideological cadres have been admonished to improve their methods and the effectiveness of their atheist work. Their emphasis is on "scientific" atheism to convince the masses that religion is nothing more than myth based on superstition. In their view, science is the answer.[44]

Lenin was a voracious reader, and he read everything he could obtain regarding politics, economics, and war. One of the books on which he spent considerable time was Karl von Clausewitz's *On War*. Lenin digested Clausewitz and spit it out in bits suitable to his own interpretation of Marxist theory. One of the most frequently quoted Leninist applications of Clausewitz's work is the dictum that "war is a continuation of politics by other means." Since Lenin adapted this dictum to Marxist ideology, it has become a subject of controversy in recent years in the Soviet Union, especially in view of the present Soviet rhetoric on the futility of waging nuclear war. The argument in the 1980s was that nuclear war had negated itself, an idea which emanated from Hegel's third law of the dialectic, the negation of the negation.

In consonance with Lenin's many writings and theories on war, Communist theoreticians early militarized politics which they have long viewed as a form of class warfare. Thus, one can observe the operation of the dialectic in the Soviet political arena, especially when the Soviets deal with Western nations.[45]

According to Lenin, war is an inherent attribute of socialism, and socialists cannot be opposed to all war and continue to be socialists.

Socialists have never been and will never be opposed to revolutionary war. In the Marxist-Leninist view, civil war is war just like any other war, and the socialist who accepts class struggle must accept civil wars, which are the natural and inevitable continuation, development, and intensification of class struggle. A repudiation of civil war would be a renunciation of socialist revolution. The victory of socialism in one country does not in itself eliminate all wars; it presupposes wars. Realistically, Socialism cannot simultaneously achieve victory in all countries. Any attempt by a bourgeois country to crush the victory of socialism in another state is a just and legitimate cause for war, which would be a war of liberation of other nations from the bourgeoisie. Wars will be impossible only when socialism has overthrown and finally vanquished the bourgeoisie of the world. To repudiate the defense of the fatherland of any socialist people or the victorious proletariat against a bourgeois state would be folly. In theory, it would be wrong to forget that every war is the continuation of policy by other means.[46]

Lenin taught that the Bolshevik slogan must be the arming of the proletariat to defeat, expropriate, and disarm the bourgeoisie. Only after the proletariat has disarmed the bourgeoisie will it be able to get rid of all arms without betraying the socialist world historic mission. The primary defect in the Soviet demand for disarmament is the evasion of the question of revolution.[47] Mikhail S. Gorbachëv has studied Lenin's works very closely and accepts this Marxist-Leninist view of revolution.[48]

In the mind of Lenin, the only important character of a war is the class waging the war and the politics which the war continues to propagate. If the belligerents are two bourgeois world groups, it is the duty of the revolutionary proletariat to prepare for the world revolution as the only escape from the horrors of global slaughter. The Communists have the responsibility to argue that they must prepare for, must disseminate propaganda for, and must accelerate the world proletarian revolution. These are the duties of the genuine socialist.[49]

Lenin explained the Bolshevik concept of internationalism, which has two applications in the Soviet Union: external involving the Soviet Union with other nations and internal pertaining to the Soviet nationalities which comprise the Soviet Union.[50] Much of the writing in the Soviet Union which deals with internationalism is in the context of the various ethnic groups which comprise the RSFSR. Although the Soviets have not renounced global internationalism between sovereign states, they appear to be trying to smother this application of international Communism by profuse writings on the Soviet Union as an international state of heterogeneous ethnic groups.

*   *   *   *   *   *   *   *   *   *   *   *   *   *   *   *   *   *   *

Marxism-Leninism is based on the Hegelian dialectic which Marx perverted for his own purposes. The resulting Marxian dialectic posits that history is a record of class struggle in which the working class, the proletariat, is engaged in a conflict with its oppressors, the capitalists. The struggle passes from one stage to another always making progress toward something better. The final result of the dialectic process is to be one world of pure Communism.

Marx taught that the proletariat must overthrow the bourgeoisie and win state power as the first step in world conquest, then use the state power, which he called the dictatorship of the proletariat, as the means for winning the majority of the working people, the proletariat.[51] The proletariat was to seize state power by smashing the state and replacing the state with a new apparatus which would grow from the proletarian class struggle. The proletariat was to win quickly from the bourgeois democrats the masses of people and satisfy their most urgent economic needs in a revolutionary manner by taking it from the landowners and the bourgeoisie. All of these events were to take place quickly in rapid succession.[52]

Marx wrote that classes are to remain intact during the dictatorship of the proletariat, which will become unnecessary when classes disappear.[53] Lenin applied Marx's teaching that the solution to class problems cannot be achieved by voting; the problems must be solved by the class struggle including civil war.[54] Lenin wrote that it is stupid and nonsensical to believe that the transition to socialism can be accomplished by democratic methods. Under the dictatorship of the proletariat, democracy passes into an entirely new phase and the class struggle rises to a higher level.[55]

Every Soviet citizen who has an education has been thoroughly indoctrinated in Communist ideology to include Marxism-Leninism, dialectical materialism, Communist political economics, and the works of Marx, Engels, Lenin, and Stalin. This information, deeply imbedded in the minds of every Soviet, creates an atmosphere, an understanding, and a comprehension of Communist ideology and the limits permitted and not permitted. Mikhail S. Gorbachëv is no exception.[56]

The Communist Party, the vanguard of the proletariat, is to be the guiding force in the Soviet Union until such time as Communism has obtained. The Soviet leadership, however, have not considered the Soviet people ready to proceed to pure Communism. In accordance with Lenin's move to speed things along, Gorbachëv has proposed dramatic political changes which, if successful, will hasten the dictatorship of the proletariat and the withering away of the state. In the meantime, the Soviet leadership wants the Soviet Union to function as a socialist state, a true Marxist-Leninist socialist state. Hence, Gorbachëv has made it perfectly clear that conditions in the Soviet Union have not yet reached the status of Communism:

> Socialism has nothing to do with equalizing. Socialism cannot ensure conditions of life and consumption in accordance with the principle "From each according to his ability, to each according to his needs." This will be under Communism. Socialism has a different criterion for distributing social benefits: "From each according to his ability, to each according to his work."[57]

For the present and the immediate future, the Soviet Union will continue to be a socialist state in which the people, the proletariat, will work toward building Communism under the vanguard of the proletariat, the Communist Party of the Soviet Union.[58]

To accomplish their objectives, the Soviets must win the world ideologically, one aspect of which is the disarming of the bourgeoisie - the capitalist West. Only after the Bourgeoisie - the West - is disarmed can the dissemination of Marxist-Leninist ideology be accomplished unopposed.

"Tell them what they want to believe."

NOTES

1. Department of Defense, *Soviet Military Power*, 8.

2. Gorbachëv, *Perestroika*, 18.

3. Samuel L. Sharp, "National Interest: Key to Soviet Politics," *Problems of Communism*, 7 (March-April 1958): 15-21.

4. *Pravda*, 26 Feb. 1986.

5. Winston S. Churchill, *The Gathering Storm* (Boston: Houghton-Mifflin, 1948), 449.

6. Sharp, "National Interest," *Problems of Communism*, 7 (March-April 1958): 15-21.

7. Karl Marx, Frederick Engels, and Vladimir I. Lenin, *On Dialectical Materialism* (Moscow: Progress Publishers, 1977), 370.

8. Vladimir I. Lenin, *One Step Forward, Two Steps Back* (Moscow: Progress Publishers, 1978), 207.

9. Mikhail S. Gorbachëv, "The Socialist Idea and Revolutionary *Perestroika*," *Pravda*, 26 Nov. 1989.

10. Georg Wilhelm Friedrich Hegel, *The Philosophy of History*, trans. J. Sibree (Chicago: The Great Books Foundation, 1952), 8. Reprinted with permission from *Great Books of the Western World*, (c) 1952 Encyclopaedia Britannica, Inc.

11. Robert C. Tucker, *The Marxian Revolutionary Idea* (New York: W. W. Norton & Co., Inc., 1969), 183. Reprinted with permission of the publisher. Western secular humanists disavow any association with Communism. *Humanist Manifestos I and II* (Buffalo, New York: Prometheus Books, 1976), 15-24.

12. Mikhail S. Gorbachëv, *CPSU Central Committee Political Report, 25 February 1986, FBIS Daily Report*, 26 Feb. 1986, 1-42.

13. Ibid.

14. Gorbachëv, *Perestroika*, 116.

15. Mikhail S. Gorbachëv, Speech at the Vatican, *TASS, FBIS Daily Report*, 1 Dec. 1989, 40.

16. Hegel, *The Philosophy of History*, 11-12.

17. Ibid., 27, 28, 29, 30, 35, 37.

18. Ibid., 49.

19. Ibid., 56.

20. Ibid., 38.

21. Ibid., 52.

22. Ibid., 65-66.

23. Ibid., 79-80.

24. Vladimir I. Lenin, *On the Question of Dialectics* (Moscow: Progress Publishers, 1982), 7-9.

25. Marx, Engels, and Lenin, *On Dialectical Materialism*, 57.

26. Vladimir I. Lenin, *Selected Works*, vol. 1 (Moscow: Progress Publishers, 1977), 16.

27. Karl Marx, *Capital*, vol. 1, ed. Frederick Engels (New York: International Publishers, 1967), trans. Samuel Moore and Edward Aveling, 19.

28. Marx, Engels, and Lenin, *On Dialectical Materialism*, 375-377.

29. Ibid., 122.

30. Lenin, *One Step Forward, Two Steps Back*, 205-207.

31. Marx, Engels, and Lenin, *On Dialectical Materialism*, 380.

32. *Pravda*, 9 Jul. 1987.

33. Marx, Engels, and Lenin, *On Dialectical Materialism*, 208.

34. Ibid., 215-216.

35. Ibid., 364-365.

36. Ibid., 365-366.

37. Gorbachëv, *Perestroika*, 137.

38. Karl Marx and Friedrich Engels, *The Communist Manifesto*, trans. Samuel Moore (Middlesex, England: Penguin Books LTD, 1977), 79.

39. Marx, Engels, and Lenin, *On Dialectical Materialism*, 368.

40. Marx and Engels, *The Communist Manifesto*, 120.

41. Ibid.

42. Richard Pipes, *Survival is Not Enough: Soviet Realities and America's Future* (New York: Simon & Schuster, Inc., 1984), 42. Reprinted with permission of the publisher.

43. Gorbachëv, "Report at the CPSU Central Committee Plenum 5 February 1990," *Pravda*, 6 Feb. 2990.

44. *Pravda*, 28 Sept. 1986.

45. Pipes, *Survival is Not Enough*, 53.

46. Lenin, *Selected Works*, vol. 1, 740-743.

47. Ibid., 743, 746.

48. Andrew A. Michta, *An Emigre Reports: Fridrikh Neznansky on Mikhail Gorbachëv, 1950-1958* (Falls Church, Virginia: Delphic Associates, Inc., 1985), 26-27. Reprinted with permission of the publisher.

49.   Vladimir I. Lenin, *On the Great October Socialist Revolution* (Moscow: Progress Publishers, 1971), 168.

50.   Ibid.

51.   Ibid., 261-262.

52.   Ibid., 262-263.

53.   Ibid., 233.

54.   Ibid., 270.

55.   Ibid., 234-235.

56.   Michta, *An Emigre Reports*, 26-27; Gorbachëv, "Report at the CPSU Central Committee Plenum 5 February 1990," *Pravda*, 6 Feb. 1990.

57.   Gorbachëv, *Perestroika*, 86.

58.   Ibid; Gorbachëv, "Report at the CPSU Central Committee Plenum 5 February 1990," *Pravda*, 6 Feb. 1990.

III

THE BOLSHEVIK *COUP D'ETAT*

Mikhail S. Gorbachëv has said a great deal about Lenin and the Bolshevik revolution. Moreover he, like other Soviet leaders, has always harked back to Lenin as his source of authority, his example, and his inspiration for doing bigger and better things for the Communist world.[1] The Communists revere Lenin and the things he did, and they consider his works as the source of Communist wisdom. The Western world, however, appears to know little about Lenin's works and deeds. Apparently few people have bothered to read his works and discover for themselves what he really wrote. Most people appear content to accept the interpretation of Lenin's works and deeds through the eyes of others.

In this chapter and the next, the Communist heritage will reveal what Gorbachëv is not telling the world about the Bolshevik revolution. It will deal with aspects of the revolution which Gorbachëv calls "mistakes of the past." These mistakes of the past are important to the world because there are similarities between Gorbachëv and Lenin, and if Lenin made these mistakes, it is possible that Gorbachëv or his successors might make the same or similar mistakes.

In the Russian language, the word "soviet" means council, and the name Soviet Union follows from the original meaning of this word. In 1905 the workers in Russia organized themselves into soviets, but the Bolsheviks did not control the soviets in 1905. The workers were joined in the soviets by peasants and the revolutionary segments of the Russian army, also peasants. In 1905, when the revolution of that year reached its peak, the soviets openly vied for power with the Russian monarchy.

With the suppression of the revolution of 1905, the soviets became ineffective and were dissolved, but with the experience gained in 1905 the soviets developed tremendously in 1917 in that they responded to the need for a revolutionary organization capable of gathering the masses and educating them in the techniques of revolution. The Communists allege that the rule of the workers, or proletariat, was realized first in the soviet system.[2] The soviet was a class institution, and in 1917 soviet Russia consisted of the peasants themselves: peasants in uniform, peasants in the factories, and peasants in the countryside.[3] The Bolsheviks did not gain control of the soviets until late 1917.

In 1917 in Russia there were fundamentally three political groupings, one of which had two branches. The Cadets were nationalists who considered Russia to be a Great Power carrying out its historical mission of protecting the Slavic people and participating in world affairs. Politically, the Cadets were followers of Western leadership; however, in science and the arts they looked with pride on Russian accomplishments. Liberal in their views, they expected to receive a greater participation in the new government after the Czar fell.[4]

The Social Revolutionary Party was the successor to the nineteenth century revolutionary organizations and the *narodnik* (to the people) movement.   Organized into a political party in the early twentieth century, the Social Revolutionaries included a number of professional revolutionaries. Consequently, many of their leaders were victims of the Czar's anti-terrorist programs.   In principle, the Social Revolutionary Party claimed to represent the will of the working people, which meant the peasants.   Therefore, they favored seizure of the land from non-peasant owners for distribution to the peasants; the state would hold the title. The peasants were to be the base for rebuilding Russia, but the Social Revolutionaries were vague about how they expected to achieve the new Russia. During World War I they remained passive, but in March 1917 the Social Revolutionaries held a majority since their ranks were swollen by soldiers, peasants in uniform, who believed the propaganda disseminated so long by the Social Revolutionary Party.[5]

Although lesser in number than the Social Revolutionaries, the Social Democrats drew heavily on the intellectual attraction of Marxism. Consequently, the Social Democratic Party attracted numerous Russian intelligentsia whose devotion to the "scientific" laws of history motivated them to treat Marxism as a religion. Marxism's emphasis on the industrial proletariat did not appear to fit Russia where the population was for the most part composed of peasants who did not respond to Marx's ideas. The Social Democrats were not united. Moreover, in 1903, meeting in London, they split into a hard and a soft faction. The soft faction, adhering to the liberal-humanitarian features of Marxism, were willing to adjust to the spontaneity of industrial workers.[6] They would never listen to peasants. They wanted to overthrow the monarchy and establish a liberal-democratic regime.

As a result of the party split in 1903, the soft faction got the label Menshevik, meaning minority. Indeed, the Mensheviks had been in a comfortable majority in London, but being upset over the unrelenting demands repeatedly enunciated by Lenin, walked out in disgust. In their absence, Lenin and his followers declared themselves a majority, quickly approved his demands, and dubbed themselves Bolsheviks, meaning majority. Lenin would brook no disagreement or compromise; his word was law and his ideas were not to be challenged. He was cold-blooded, calculating, and set on one goal - revolution and the establishment of Marxism.[7] In explaining the split in the Social Democratic Party in 1903, Lenin called it a struggle between the revolutionary right wing and the opportunist wing, a true enactment of the dialectic in which the new, more powerful Bolshevik Party emerged.[8]

The monarchy fell so unexpectedly that the opposition leaders were caught with no plans. Suddenly the masses of the people obtained an overwhelming authority in the life of the nation.[9] Quickly and with little cohesion, remnants of the old monarchist order established the Provisional Government. From the middle of May 1917 to the Bolshevik counter-revolution in October (November) 1917, the Provisional Government was the government of a bourgeois-socialist coalition, including representatives of parties which accepted the revolution of February 1917 as final and refused all forms of dictatorship, no matter whether it might be personal, party, or class.[10]

In late spring and early summer 1917, the Russian peasants were restless, they wanted land immediately, and they demanded control of the countryside. The Bolsheviks seized upon the peasant unrest and used it to their advantage. Lenin wanted to establish the dictatorship of the proletariat in Russia, but the proletariat was small. As a result, the Bolsheviks coopted the peasants until such time that they could identify the proletariat. Thus, no matter what the Bolsheviks did to enhance their own position and make Russia a true Communist state, they would do it through or in the name of the people; they never outwardly acted against the people. Inwardly, however, the Bolsheviks remained apart, manipulating the public will as Bolshevik necessity demanded.[11] They systematically identified themselves with the Russian people and "mercilessly exploited the ignorance of the masses".[12]

In addition to issuing a number of decrees on freedom of speech, freedom of assembly, inviolability of the person, and others, the Provisional Government worked out extensive agrarian reform, prepared a law on self-government for the county and town councils on the basis of proportional, universal suffrage, introduced workers' control in factories and workshops, gave great powers to workers' trade unions, introduced the eight-hour work day in all government activities, set forth the principle of cooperative legislation, gave soldiers the rights of citizens, laid down the principles for transformation of the Russian Empire into a federation of free peoples, and drew up the principles of the electoral law for the Constituent Assembly. Unabated and of its own free will, the Provisional Government realized the social and political ideas of the entire Russian liberation movement, liberal and revolutionary, which many generations of Russians had pursued. Moreover, the Provisional Government accomplished all of this work with no pressure from "soviet democracy."[13] Even so, Alexander Kerensky, a moderate Socialist Revolutionary leader in the Provisional Government and a persuasive orator, was unable to resolve the ideological differences between the Provisional Government and the Petrograd Soviet.[14]

The First All-Russian Congress of Soviets met in Petrograd on 3 June 1917 in the Cadet Corps building. There was a total of 820 delegates, most of whom had registered for the congress as socialists. Of the 777 delegates who claimed a party affiliation, 285 were Social Revolutionaries, 248 were Mensheviks, and 105 were Bolsheviks. Thus, the Bolsheviks constituted less than one seventh of the total delegates, even though they claimed to have been much stronger in the countryside than at the Congress. This Congress sanctioned Kerensky's offensive which he had promised the Allies.[15]

The Bolsheviks considered it imperative to their success that they increase their representation in the soviets and thereby gain control of these popular-based organizations. The intent of the Bolsheviks was to seize power, not just in the soviets, but in all of Russia. Gaining control of the soviets was merely a first step. In gaining control of the soviets, the Bolsheviks sought a broad based appeal to the masses. They went before the people with propaganda, promises, and popular slogans, organized militarily, won many members of the armed forces, carried out public protests, refused to cooperate or compromise with any other group, and waited for the appropriate moment to seize power.[16]

During the period February 1917 to October 1917, the Bolsheviks undermined the Russian Provisional Government and seized power through a pattern of actions which they have since repeated in other countries. First of all, Lenin sent the Bolsheviks to the people with instructions to promise the people anything and everything they wanted and thereby recruit a large following for the Bolshevik Party. Lenin's instructions included the caveat not to worry about being able to fulfill the promises. This propaganda campaign promised the people liberty, democracy, social justice, peace, bread, and land - there was something for everyone.[17] Specific promises from the Bolsheviks were immediate peace for the soldiers, land for the peasants, self-determination for the minorities, bread for the hungry, and social justice for the oppressed.[18]

Kerensky's power depended on the support of the soldiers at the front. The Bolsheviks deliberately waged a campaign to change the attitude of the soldiers but at a slower pace than the winning of the Petrograd Soviet. The Petrograd Soviet was the chief center of the revolution, and every increased intensification of the revolutionary spirit in that body tended to undermine Kerensky's strength and increase the strength of the Soviet. The high desertion rate from the Russian Army before the revolution indicated the urgent desire of the soldiers to end the war. Had the leaders of the Provisional Government realized the demoralized state of the army, they might have been able to retain the loyalty of the army; however, they continued to exhort the Russian people to continue the war to ultimate victory in fulfillment of the terms of the treaties with the Allies. On the other hand, the small group of Bolsheviks led by Lenin staked their success on going to the army and calling for an immediate end to the war.[19] The first defeatist propaganda which the Bolsheviks disseminated among the Russian troops at the front was the slogan "peace without annexations and contributions."[20]

Second, the Bolsheviks infiltrated other political parties, the trade unions, soldiers' and workers' councils, and local government. In so-doing, they disrupted the one large political party capable of fulfilling the promises the Bolsheviks were making. The Social Revolutionary Party was dedicated to political democracy and social reform until the Bolsheviks destroyed it from within.[21] In Russia the Bolsheviks, not having a political program of their own, usurped the program of the Social Revolutionary Party, and when the Social Revolutionary Party protested, Lenin made fun of them for being unable to carry out their own program.[22]

The third, and the most effective Bolshevik technique, was the use of armed force. In the one free election ever held in Russia, the Bolsheviks received less than twenty-five percent of the vote. Realizing that they could never expect to win a majority in a free election, the Bolsheviks forcibly seized key positions of power in Petrograd and from there moved to Moscow and into the countryside.[23]

In late summer 1917, Alexander Kerensky was the head of the Provisional Government. There was a psychological fear within the Provisional Government that the Bolsheviks were stirring up trouble. Although there was a provisional authority in Russia, members of the old establishment met, recognized the threat of more revolution, and sought a strong man who could deal effectively with the dissident elements. Consequently, they selected General Lavr Kornilov, a heroic figure who commanded the Wild Division, an elite military unit which was feared by the enemy and many Russians. In August 1917, Kornilov was placed in command of the army to reestablish law and order.

In executing his duties, Kornilov based the Wild Division in Moscow; however, the Germans appeared to be preparing for an attack against Russia. Kerensky panicked and ordered the Wild Division to

Petrograd, and the Wild Division entrained on 8 September 1917. In Petrograd, the news of the imminent approach of the Wild Division created panic among the politicians in the Provisional Government. In their desperation, they looked for someone to organize a defense in Petrograd against the Wild Division as well as the Germans. Leon Trotsky volunteered to organize and lead a defensive force. Since no military leader emerged, he received permission to organize a defense force with commensurate command authority. The resulting organization was the Red Guards, composed of workers and former soldiers - Bolshevik followers.

In preparing for defense, Kerensky opened the government arsenals in Petrograd and gave arms to the workers who later became the nucleus of the Bolshevik Red Guard. After the workers received the arms, the Wild Division was polluted by Bolshevik propaganda and melted en route to Petrograd, Kornilov lost his position, and the German threat disappeared. Following the perceived emergency, the workers were to have returned the weapons; however, Trotsky, the organizer of the so-called defense of Petrograd, knew that the Bolsheviks would need weapons to seize power. Thus, the Bolsheviks did not surrender these arms but retained them and used them against the Provisional Government on 25 October 1917 (7 November 1917).[24]

Because the Bolsheviks had received the blame for the disturbances in Petrograd in July 1917, many Bolsheviks were arrested. Lenin, however, managed to escape the dragnet of the Provisional Government and went into hiding where he remained until shortly before the *coup d'etat* in October 1917. Even though the Bolshevik Central Committee voted to seize power, the plans and preparations of this *coup d'etat* were made by Trotsky, not Lenin.[25]

During his 110 days in hiding, Lenin guided the Party activity and gave instructions on the most important aspects of the *coup d'etat*. From his hiding place, Lenin directed the plans and preparations for the Sixth Congress of the Russian Socialist Labor Party of Bolsheviks, which met in Petrograd from 26 July to 3 August (8-16 August) 1917.[26]

On 12-14 (25-27) September 1917, Lenin wrote a letter to the Bolshevik Party Central Committee and to the Party Committees of Petrograd and Moscow urging them to cause the soviets to revolt, overthrow the Provisional Government, and seize state power. By late September 1917 the Bolsheviks had gained majorities in the Soviets of Workers' and Soldiers' Deputies in both cities. Blaming Kerensky for bungling the opportunity to grant land, democracy, and liberty to the people, Lenin told the Bolsheviks in Petrograd and Moscow that Bolshevik power was great enough for them to seize and retain power by smashing the Provisional Government. He claimed that the majority of the Russian people supported the Bolshevik cause; however, he could point only to Petrograd and Moscow with confidence. He warned the Russian people not to be deceived by election results, since elections prove nothing. Setting himself up as the omnipotent judge of all political forms, he proclaimed that only the Bolsheviks could satisfy the demands of the peasants. He argued further that only the Bolshevik Party, on taking power, could assure the convocation of the Constituent Assembly. He concluded by stating that the task at hand for the Bolshevik Party was to seize power in Moscow and Petrograd and overthrow the Provisional Government by armed force.[27]

On 13-14 (26-27) September 1917, Lenin wrote a letter to the Central Committee describing exactly how the Bolsheviks were to seize power in the "Marxist way." He gave instructions for them to occupy the most important points of the city, to arrest the general staff and the government officials, and move against those armed forces which opposed the Bolsheviks. He ordered the mobilization of the armed workers to wage a "last desperate fight."[28]

In the interim between the revolution and the Bolshevik *coup d'etat* in 1917, the organs of local self-government based on universal suffrage were weakening the authority of the soviets and diminishing their part in local life. The issue of *Izvestiya* published by the Congress of the Soviets on 25 October 1917 said:

> The soviets of soldiers' and workmen's deputies, as a whole organization of proportions, all-Russian as the ground covered, and all-democratic as to their social composition, are passing through an evident crisis. The department of the central executive committee for other towns, at the time of the highest development of soviet organization, reckoned 800 local soviets. Many of them no

longer exist, still more exist only on paper. The net of soviet organization has in many places been broken, in others it has weakened and in others it has begun to decay. The soviets were an excellent organization for the fight with the old regime; they have no specialists, no experience, no understanding of business, and, finally, even no organization.[29]

If permitted, the summons of the Constituent Assembly, scheduled for November 1917, would reduce to nothing the part played by the soviets in post-revolutionary Russian history. Moreover, the slogan of the Bolshevik counter-revolution, "all power to the soviets," in October 1917 appeared initially as a simple, demagogic cover for Lenin's dictatorial plans.[30]

The Bolsheviks knew that all organized and public opinion in Russia opposed any kind of dictatorship and opposed changes in the system of government until the meeting of the Constituent Assembly. Only by conspiracy, by treachery, and by armed force was it possible to break up the Provisional Government and stop the establishment of a democratic system in Russia after the revolution.[31] The Bolsheviks worked feverishly to thwart democracy, and by the time the Second All-Russian Congress of Soviets met in October 1917, they held majorities in the soviets of Petrograd, Moscow, the major industrial cities, and other locations in north and northwest Russia.[32]

Lenin wrote that the Bolsheviks must at all costs on the evening of 24 October (6 November, 1917) arrest the government after having first disarmed the officer cadets and defeating them if they resisted.[33] The seizure of power was the business of the uprising; its political purpose would become clear after the seizure. The people had the right and were in duty bound to decide such questions not by vote but by force; in critical moments of revolution the people have the right and are in duty bound to give directions to their representatives and not to wait for them.[34]

Lenin insisted that the Bolsheviks begin the insurrection before the Second Congress of Soviets in order to get ahead of the enemy, the Provisional Government, which was expecting armed insurrection on the opening day of the Congress. On Lenin's initiative, the insurrection began on 24 October (6 November) 1917. Lenin arrived at the Smolney Institute and took the leadership of the revolt late that evening.[35]

Although the Bolsheviks had a majority in the Second All-Russian Congress of Soviets, they planned the *coup d'etat* for the eve of this conference since they wanted to seize power themselves and not receive it as a gift. A *fait accompli* would maintain the separate Bolshevik identity. Accordingly, early on 25 October 1917 (7 November 1917), the Red Guards occupied the key positions in Petrograd; later in the day, they attacked the seat of the Provisional Government in the Winter Palace. After sporadic firing, they entered peaceably and took the government ministers into custody.[36] On 25 October (7 November) 1917, Lenin announced to the Russian people that the Provisional Government had been overthrown and that the soviets had control of the state.[37]

The Bolsheviks muddled through the take over generally on the schedule they had set for themselves. About a week later, the Bolsheviks took control of Moscow, but they were far from being in control of the country. Control of the country would take several years. Even before the completion of the *coup d'etat* on 25 October 1917 (7 November 1917), Trotsky announced to the Petrograd Soviet that the Bolsheviks had seized power from the Provisional Government. Lenin now reappeared with explanations of events and assumed his new role as head of the government on the night of 26-27 October 1917 (8-9 November 1917). At this point, Lenin began to rule by decree.[38]

Lenin, for this Bolshevik, counter-revolutionary *coup d'etat*, used the military and administrative machinery established by the Provisional Government. Lenin was thorough; he planted militant Bolshevik cells among the Russian troops, in government institutions, in the soviets, and on the town councils.[39] By October (November) 1917 the Bolsheviks had won the Russian Army to the point that it did not offer any resistance to the *coup d'etat*.[40] On the day following the Bolshevik seizure of power, 26 October (November 8), 1917, the Bolsheviks abolished private ownership of land without compensation. They also immediately began the expropriation of all factories, joint stock companies, banks, railroads, and other capitalist businesses.[41]

The Bolshevik *coup d'etat* had no humanitarian objective; it was a power play for the control of Russia and for the establishment of a Communist state with a subsequent propagation of international Communism. Once the Bolsheviks gained control, spontaneity ended and suppression of the opposition began with a vengeance. The suppression began under Lenin's direction, gained momentum as Lenin consolidated his control, and reached the proportions of a reign of terror after the attempt on Lenin's life by Fanny Kaplan. Bolshevik rule was by far worse than anything the Russian people had experienced under the Czars.[42] Lenin had no compassion. For anyone who would not cooperate with the Bolsheviks, compulsory labor and other penalties were waiting.[43] Lenin attributed the Bolshevik victory in October to having an overwhelming majority among the proletariat - not among the population at large; having control of almost half the armed forces; and having an overwhelming superiority of forces in Moscow and Petrograd, the decisive points.[44]

Lenin's opportunism disconcerted his opponents. In the last week of November 1917 the numerous disturbances in Petrograd came to a head in a major brawl in which the mob broke into the wine stores. Drunken soldiers fought drunken Red Guards, and the Revolutionary Committee at the Smolney Institute sent a squad of machine gun soldiers to fire on the rioters. The problem was not entirely due to alcohol since the soldiers had begun to realize that their new Bolshevik masters were no better than their former ones; they also resented the growing strength of the political squads composed of armed workers. As a consequence, the Bolsheviks replaced many of the disaffected soldiers with non-Russian troops, in particular with Lettish soldiers and Estonian and Finnish sailors.[45]

Following the Bolshevik *coup d'etat* in late 1917, based on limited suffrage, the Russian people held the first free elections in Russia to elect delegates to a Constituent Assembly. The Constituent Assembly was to meet in the fall of 1917, and Lenin had to deal with that Constituent Assembly in Petrograd. The elections for the Constituent Assembly began on 25 November 1917, an event for which the Russian people had been waiting since July 1917. The prospect of a freely elected parliament had been the foundation of every political program in every party from the moderate right to the extreme left, including the Bolsheviks, who used the slogan "long live the Constituent Assembly" as a weapon against Kerensky.[46] The fact that the Bolsheviks received less than twenty-five percent of the vote meant that they had no legitimate claim to power. Today the successors to the Bolsheviks, the CPSU and Gorbachëv, appear to be concerned about their legitimacy, since they were not elected to office by the Soviet people in free elections.

Immediately after the Bolsheviks learned that they lost the election, they began proclaiming that the loyalty of the people had changed. They published the results of the election to the Constituent Assembly, but they also published other statistics in an effort to prove that they had the overwhelming support of the people. This effort included the publication of voting results of the various soviets, the membership of which was restricted almost entirely to the industrial areas and did not represent the population in rural Russia. To support their contention, the Bolsheviks argued that the town vote counted for more than the country vote, since the town was superior to the country. Lenin argued that in November 1917 the Bolsheviks were supported by the majority of the proletariat, the town workers. He further argued that since the Bolsheviks had an overwhelming, decisive superiority of forces in Petrograd and Moscow, the Bolsheviks, who represented the proletariat, would succeed in seizing power. The Bolsheviks claimed that capitals, or large commercial, industrial centers mostly decide the future of a state, and the Bolsheviks controlled both major cities in Russia.[47]

When the Bolsheviks learned the results of the elections to the Constituent Assembly, they suddenly discovered that they had no faith in free elections. They promptly adopted and used the slogan: "Down with the Constituent Assembly." Hence, Lenin's major task then was to sabotage the Constituent Assembly and, if possible, prevent it from convening. The opening was postponed from 11 December 1917 to some unspecified date in January 1918; however, the newly elected deputies were already on their way to Petrograd and were not to be deterred. Accordingly, the deputies went to the Tauride Palace on 11 December amid the cheers of thousands of people. The deputies arrived to find the gates locked and guarded by armed, Lettish,

Bolshevik soldiers.   Deputy P. A. Sorokin climbed the fence and addressed the people, who rushed the gates, unlocked them, entered the court yard, and forced the soldiers to open the doors of the hall.   The deputies met and passed a resolution that the Constituent Assembly would open on 5 (18) January 1918, regardless of opposition.[48]

Lenin moved swiftly by seizing all printing presses that published anti-Bolshevik literature.   The CHEKA, the Bolshevik secret police, made house-to-house searches at night and increased arrests.   On 26 December 1917 Lenin stated in *Pravda* that revolutionary interests took precedence over the rights of the Constituent Assembly.   Another Bolshevik decree said that the Russian Republic was vested in the soviets and that every attempt to usurp that authority would be suppressed.[49]

The Constituent Assembly was to meet at noon on 5 (18) January 1918.   The deputies began arriving a few days early, and even within the Bolshevik party there was a large faction which wanted the Assembly to meet.   On 4 (17) January 1918 the authorities at the Smolny Institute ordered the Petrograd garrison to be ready for action, and the Tauride Palace was surrounded by Bolshevik, Lettish guards with artillery pieces deployed in the neighboring streets.   On the morning of 5 (18) January 1918, a large crowd entered the street to demonstrate their support for the Constituent Assembly, but as they advanced toward the Tauride Palace the Bolshevik guards opened fire.   The courageous deputies did not turn back but ran the gauntlet between the jeering Bolshevik soldiers guarding the approaches to the meeting hall.[50]

The Bolsheviks came to the Assembly hall prepared for armed action.   They packed the corridors and galleries of the main hall with Bolshevik, Lettish soldiers and with sailors from the *Aurora* and the battleship *Respublika*.   In their hands, they all carried loaded rifles; they had stacked hand grenades and cartridge belts in the anterooms.   The Bolsheviks were the last of the opposition parties to arrive, and they, including Lenin, came armed.   Ironically, someone stole Lenin's weapon.   The other deputies waited four hours for the Bolsheviks.[51]   Duly elected non-Bolsheviks were in the majority and dominated the Constituent Assembly.

As the senior representative, Right Social Revolutionary deputy

Shvetsov, arose to open the Assembly, the Bolsheviks rushed forward in
an uproar, whereupon one of them seized the speaker's bell and gave
it to Jacob M. Sverdlov, the Chairman of the Soviets' Executive
Committee, who made the opening speech. Following the Bolshevik led
singing of the "Internationale," the deputies elected Right Social
Revolutionary Victor Chernov as chairman with a vote of 244 to 153.[52]

In the ensuing attempt to transact business, the Bolsheviks
continuously interrupted the proceedings with catcalls, jeers, whistling,
and other boisterous behavior. After six or seven hours, the Bolsheviks
made a motion for the Assembly to recognize the Congress of Soviets
as the Russian government; however, the deputies defeated this move
by a vote of 237 to 136.[53] After a recess, the meeting resumed
deliberations at 0100 hours, 6 (19) January 1918.[54] At this point, the
Bolsheviks announced their departure from the Assembly, and some of
them moved to the galleries as spectators. About an hour later, the
Left Social Revolutionaries followed. The Bolshevik guards got out of
hand, whereupon some of them jumped into the hall and tried to break
up the meeting.[55] Others had great sport in aiming their rifles at the
deputies.[56]

The Right Social Revolutionaries and the Mensheviks kept the
meeting alive, and they passed one resolution after another. These
resolutions were of a revolutionary nature, and they disprove the
Bolshevik contention that the Assembly was counter-revolutionary. To
be sure, the Constituent Assembly was almost as revolutionary as the
Bolsheviks. This situation was logical, since the Bolsheviks had stolen
the Social Revolutionary reform program. The deputies approved an
armistice with Germany, passed an extremely radical land decree,
supported the convocation of an international socialist conference, and
declared Russia to be a republic. The Assembly did not acknowledge
the dictatorship of the Bolsheviks.[57]

As Chernov read the land decree, a sailor informed him that the
guards were tired and the meeting must adjourn. Although Chernov
rejected this order, the lights went out, and in the ensuing tension the
deputies managed to escape into the night. The next day, 6 (19)
January 1918, the Bolshevik dominated Executive Committee of the
Congress of Soviets passed a resolution dissolving the Constituent

Assembly. On the authority of the Congress of Soviets, armed guards posted at the Tauride Palace prevented any deputies from returning to the meeting hall. Thus ended the one opportunity the Russian people had for a democratic government. The cycle was now complete from the autocratic Czar to the more autocratic Lenin.[58] On 6 (19) January 1918, Lenin delivered a speech to the Central Executive Committee announcing the dissolution of the Constituent Assembly.[59]

*   *   *   *   *   *   *   *   *   *   *   *   *   *   *   *   *   *

In February 1917, the Bolshevik Party was effete. There was only a handful of Bolsheviks in the Petrograd Soviet, and the Bolshevik leaders were scattered. The Bolsheviks had no blueprint for what they would do after they came to power. They came to power suddenly with no plans. They believed that the revolution in Russia would trigger a world-wide revolution immediately, but Lenin's theory did not work. Initially, they were fixed on the German scene, but when no Bolshevik revolution took place elsewhere, they turned inward.

During the revolutionary clamor in the months following the fall of the Czar, one of the demands from the Russian people was for elections to a Constituent Assembly. As an opportune propaganda ploy, the Bolsheviks participated in the campaign for elections to the Constituent Assembly, and even though they claimed control of the government, their hold on the country was so tenuous that they could not prevent these elections. The Bolsheviks knew that the elections would be held regardless of their wishes; they also knew that their majorities in the soviets did not indicate a Bolshevik majority among the Russian people - they did not.[60] When the election results were in, the Bolsheviks discovered that they had indeed received a sound defeat at the polls.[61] Lenin was powerless to prevent the meeting of the Constituent Assembly, the delegates to which assembled on 6 (18) January 1918 in the Tauride Palace.[62] As the delegates gathered, the Red Guards surrounded the meeting hall.[63] The assembly at once made manifest its anti-Bolshevik orientation; consequently, the Bolshevik delegates walked out.[64] The first session adjourned early the next morning, but when they returned to the hall they found the doors locked by order of the Central Executive Committee of the Second All-

Russian Congress of Soviets.[65] This Congress, under Bolshevik control, declared the Constituent Assembly dissolved.[66] Thus, the Bolsheviks under the threat of armed force destroyed the one attempt by the Russian people to establish a democracy.

Lenin and his cohorts considered the soviets to be superior to any parliament in the world, and they supported that contention with the slogan "all power to the soviets." Being opportunists, when the Bolsheviks sensed that the Russian people truly wanted a Constituent Assembly, they supported it with apprehension; however, when they discovered that they had lost the election, they declared themselves opposed to the Constituent Assembly and to all elected institutions. To the Bolsheviks, handing power to the Constituent Assembly would be a compromise with the hated bourgeoisie.[67]

In the decree announcing the dissolution of the Constituent Assembly, Lenin alleged that the October Revolution had inaugurated a new era in which the soviets now represented the will of the "working and exploited classes." Consequently, the Constituent Assembly had become an obstacle to the October revolution and to soviet power. He argued that the old bourgeois parliamentary system had outlived its purpose and was incompatible with the goal of achieving socialism; only class institutions could lay the foundations for a socialist system. Since the majority in the Constituent Assembly had refused to discuss the proposal of the Central Executive Committee of the Soviets and refused to recognize the October revolution, Lenin claimed that the Constituent Assembly had severed all ties with the "soviet republic of Russia." He further declared that the Constituent Assembly could serve only as a screen for a counter-revolution for the overthrow of the soviets. Thus, the Central Executive Committee dissolved the Constituent Assembly.[68] The Bolshevik *coup d'etat* was complete.

NOTES

1.   Gorbachëv, "Report at the CPSU Central Committee Plenum 5 February 1990," *Pravda*, 6 Feb. 1990.

2.   Trotsky, *The History of the Russian Revolution*, vol. 1, 12-13, 15.

3.   von Laue, *Why Lenin? Why Stalin?*, 104.

4.   Ibid., 81.

5.   Ibid., 82-84.

6.   Ibid., 84-85, 87. For the Bolshevik description of this conference, see Lenin, *One Step Forward, Two Steps Back*.

7.   von Laue, *Why Lenin? Why Stalin?*, 88, 90.

8.   Lenin, *One Step forward, Two Steps Back*, 205-207.

9.   Alexander Kerensky, "Both Left and Right Betrayed the Provisional Government," in *The Russian Revolution and Bolshevik Victory*, ed. Arthur E. Adams (Boston: D. C. Heath Company, 1960), 81. Reprinted with permission of the publisher.

10.   Ibid., 82.

11.   von Laue, *Why Lenin? Why Stalin?*, 107, 110, 111.

12.   Ibid., 111.

13.   Kerensky, "Both Left and Right Betrayed the Provisional Government," in *The Russian Revolution and Bolshevik Victory*, 81.

14.   von Laue, *Why Lenin? Why Stalin?*, 102.

15.   Trotsky, *The History of the Russian Revolution*, vol. 1, 438-439.

16.   Ibid., 442-448, 453-454.

17. William Ebenstein and Edwin Fogleman, *Today's Isms: Communism, Fascism, Capitalism, Socialism* (Englewood Cliffs, New Jersey: Prentice-Hall, Inc., 1958), 39. Reprinted with permission from the publisher, (c) 1958 Prentice-Hall.

18. von Laue, *Why Lenin? Why Stalin?*, 111.

19. Nicholas N. Golovine, "A Demoralized Army Spread Dissatisfaction Among the People," in *The Russian Revolution and Bolshevik Victory*, ed. Arthur E. Adams (Boston: D. C. Heath and Company, 1960), 50-51. Reprinted with permission of the publisher.

20. Ibid., 49.

21. Ebenstein and Fogleman, *Today's Isms*, 39-40.

22. Lenin, *On the Great October Socialist Revolution*, 263.

23. Ebenstein and Fogleman, *Today's Isms*, 40.

24. Strakhovsky, "Kerensky Betrayed Russia," in *The Russian Revolution and Bolshevik Victory*, 94.

25. von Laue, *Why Lenin? Why Stalin?*, 115.

26. Vladimir I. Lenin, *Selected Works*, vol. 2 (Moscow: Progress Publishers, 1977), 14.

27. Vladimir I. Lenin, *Marxism and Insurrection* (Moscow: Progress Publishers, 1980), 7-9.

28. Ibid., 15.

29. Quoted in Kerensky, "Both Left and Right Betrayed the Provisional Government," in *The Russian Revolution and Bolshevik Victory*, 83.

30. Kerensky, "Both Left and Right Betrayed the Provisional Government," in *The Russian Revolution and Bolshevik Victory*, 83.

31. Ibid., 84.

32. von Laue, *Why Lenin? Why Stalin?*, 112.

33. Lenin, *Selected Works*, vol. 2, 415.

34. Ibid., 416.

35. Ibid., 15, 417.

36.   Sergei Mstislavskii, *Five Days Which Transformed Russia*, trans. Elizabeth Kristofovich Zelensky (Bloomington and Indianapolis, Indiana: Indiana University Press, 1988), 119-122, 124, 130.

37. Lenin, *Selected Works*, vol. 2, 15, 417.

38. von Laue, *Why Lenin? Why Stalin?*, 117-118.

39. Kerensky, "Both Left and Right Betrayed the Provisional Government," in *The Russian Revolution and Bolshevik Victory*, 80.

40. Lenin, *On the Great October Socialist Revolution*, 260.

41. Ibid., 232.

42. von Laue, *Why Lenin? Why Stalin?*, 121.

43. Ibid., 114.

44. Lenin, *On the Great October Socialist Revolution*, 260.

45.   Alan Moorehead, *The Russian Revolution* (New York: Harper & Row, Publishers, 1958), 261-263.   Copyright (c) 1958 by Time, Inc. Reprinted by permission of Harper & Row, Publishers, Inc.

46. Ibid., 263.

47. Lenin, *On the Great October Socialist Revolution*, 256-257.

48. Moorehead, *The Russian Revolution*, 263-265.

49. Ibid., 265-266.

50. Ibid., 266.

51. Ibid., 267.

52. Mstislavskii, *Five Days Which Transformed Russia*, 141-143, 146.

53. Ibid., 146-148.

54. Moorehead, *The Russian Revolution*, 267.

55. Mstislavskii, *Five Days Which Transformed Russia*, 148-152.

56. Moorehead, *The Russian Revolution*, 267.

57. Ibid., 268.

58. Ibid., 268-269.

59. Lenin, *On the Great October Socialist Revolution*, 44-48.

60. von Laue, *Why Lenin? Why Stalin?*, 130-131.

61. Lenin, *On the Great October Socialist Revolution*, 252.

62. von Laue, *Why Lenin? Why Stalin?*, 130-131.

63. Mstislavskii, *Five Days Which Transformed Russia*, 137.

64. Ibid., 148-149.

65. von Laue, *Why Lenin? Why Stalin?*, 130-131.

66. Lenin, *Selected Works*, vol. 2, 478-79; Lenin, *On the Great October Socialist Revolution*, 44-48.

67. Lenin, *On the Great October Socialist Revolution*, 46-47.

68. Lenin, *Selected Works*, vol. 2, 478-479.

IV

THE LENIN ERA

The Bolshevik *coup d'etat* in October 1917 did not bring control of Russia to the Bolsheviks. Upon seizing power in Russia, Lenin and the Bolsheviks faced several major problems, the first of which was to end the war with Germany and terminate the external military threat. This necessity led to the Treaty of Brest-Litovsk. Bolshevik political control was not secure in 1917, and the Bolsheviks wrested it by force from the Russian people when they destroyed the Constituent Assembly in January 1918. Inasmuch as they also met domestic opposition, the Bolsheviks had to wage a three-year civil war before they could control the country. The civil war subdued the majority of the Russian people, who did not support the Bolsheviks. Superimposed upon fighting the civil war was the Bolshevik objective of making Russia the first Communist state. The Bolshevik attempt to move directly to pure Communism was a failure, and in March 1921 Lenin replaced War Communism with the New Economic Policy (NEP), a partial reversion to capitalism. Through it all, the Bolsheviks retained control of the economy and the government through their Party. The Bolsheviks eliminated their opponents ruthlessly with terror and fought their enemies with lies, deceit, distortions, and murder. The Lenin years left a legacy of ruthless terror which Mikhail S. Gorbachëv calls democracy.

Mikhail S. Gorbachëv has placed great emphasis on the Leninist period as the time during which the strength of the Marxist-Leninist dialectic proved itself.[1] Accordingly, an understanding of Gorbachëv's program for renewal of the Soviet socio-economic system requires a review of the salient historical events of the Lenin period.

The Russian revolution was in reality a collapse of the monarchist regime in early 1917. In late 1917, the Bolsheviks carried out a counter-revolution and usurped the authority of the Provisional Government. As part of their propaganda campaign, the Bolsheviks initially supported the election of delegates to a Constituent Assembly, which the Provisional Government had planned. On 26 October (8 November), 1917, the Bolsheviks, controlling the Second All Russian Congress of Soviets of Workers', Soldiers', and Peasants' Deputies, established a provisional workers' and peasants' government to rule until the Constituent Assembly could meet. This Bolshevik governing group, the Council of People's Commissars, consisted of fifteen Bolsheviks, with Lenin as Chairman of the Council.[2]

Lenin later wrote that the Constituent Assembly reflected the same popular mood and the same political groupings as did the First All-Russian Congress of Soviets, which met in June 1917. He further claimed that by the time the Constituent Assembly met in January 1918, the Second and Third Congresses of Soviets had met and demonstrated that the people had swung to the left, had been "revolutionized," had passed over to the side of the Bolsheviks, and had joined the proletarian revolution.[3] On the basis of this argument, Lenin gave the Constituent Assembly an ultimatum to reconcile themselves to the proletarian revolution or suffer defeat by the Bolsheviks through "revolutionary means."[4] When they refused the ultimatum, the Bolsheviks executed it.

When the Bolsheviks overthrew the Provisional Government in October 1917, they had no well defined economic policies; they had only general Communist objectives, which were vague and frequently interpreted to suit the views of individual Party leaders. Furthermore, they had no experience in government and did not know how to govern. Consequently, they took over the Czarist bureaucracy and put Bolsheviks in office to force the bureaucrats to conform to Bolshevik desires. This technique of control was the origin of dualism in the Soviet Union. The legislative function was to have been accomplished by a system of soviets at the top of which was the non-functional Supreme Soviet. Parallel to the system of soviets the Bolsheviks created Party institutions from the top to the bottom.

As soon as the Bolsheviks seized power in October (November)

1917, they assumed the responsibility for state foreign affairs. One of the most immediately threatening issues facing the Bolsheviks was the war with Germany and Austria. Although the Russian army had been successful against the Austrians, it always had great difficulty with the German army, and in late 1917 it faced annihilation if it did not defeat the Germans or sign an armistice. The Bolsheviks, not having an effective fighting force that could operate internationally, sought a negotiated peace.

The Bolsheviks, propounding a propaganda of peace with no annexations, were unable to convince the Germans to stop fighting. Leon Trotsky thought that he could merely issue a few peaceful decrees, close the Foreign Office, and go home. The Germans thought otherwise and continued the war. The Bolsheviks and the Germans signed an armistice at Brest-Litovsk on 5 December 1917. Negotiations for peace began between the Russians and the Germans at Brest-Litovsk on 22 December 1917, but because of a deliberate delay by the Soviets - they were waiting for the German revolution which they expected momentarily - the negotiations dragged into 1918.

The revolution in Germany was slow developing.[5] Moreover, the Germans did not subscribe to the Bolshevik slogan of no peace-no war, and at Brest-Litovsk they drove a hard bargain. The Germans sent experienced military officers to negotiate; the Bolsheviks sent some former Czarist officers and "soldiers and workers." Obviously, the Bolshevik representatives were lacking in diplomatic finesse. Years later, German Field Marshal Albrecht Kesselring wrote:

> I conducted the local armistice negotiations on the Duna. Two things struck me: first, the abnormal interest of the negotiators in tactical questions of trench warfare; and secondly the behavior of the soldiers' councils appointed to cover the negotiations. They struck me as callow, uneducated oafs who interfered with practical discussions and peacocked as if they were the officers' bosses.[6]

After intense internal debate, Lenin prevailed and the Bolsheviks decided that their best course of action was to sign the Treaty of Brest-Litovsk, regardless of its humiliating terms. Lenin called this treaty the "unfortunate peace, the exceptionally harsh peace," and he sought to "elucidate" the reasons for it. He presented his rationalization to about sixty Party functionaries in Petrograd on 8 January 1918. He wrote that the peace negotiations at Brest-Litovsk on 7 January 1918 made it clear that the war party controlled Germany and had presented an ultimatum for Russia to continue the war or sign a peace treaty with annexations of Russian territory.[7]

Lenin presented a twenty-two point justification for the treaty. His primary concern was how the socialist revolution could endure until joined by similar revolutions in other countries. He argued with Trotsky against a revolutionary war with Germany at that stage of the socialist revolution. The remnant of the Russian army was in no condition to wage war with Germany; besides, the soldiers would not fight. He further argued that a socialist soviet republic in Russia would be an example to the peoples of all countries and would serve the revolution as a helpful propaganda vehicle. By signing a separate peace the Bolsheviks would free themselves at the moment from hostile imperialist groups and provide the opportunity to consolidate and advance the socialist revolution in Russia.[8] On 3 (16) March 1918, the Congress of Soviets ratified the Treaty of Brest-Litovsk.[9]

In the aftermath of the humiliating peace treaty, the Bolsheviks followed Lenin's rationalization with a resolution on war and peace. Acknowledging that the new Soviet state lacked an army, the Congress of Soviets recognized the fundamental task of the Party, as the vanguard of the proletariat, to be the adoption of the most energetic, most ruthless, and most draconian measures to improve the discipline and self-discipline of the workers and peasants of Russia. The Congress considered the only guarantee of a consolidated socialist revolution to be the conversion of the socialist revolution into a world working-class revolution. The Congress further declared that the socialist proletariat of Russia would support the fraternal revolutionary movement of the proletariat of all countries with all of its strength and with every means at its disposal.[10] This resolve has not changed under Gorbachëv.

The decree on peace put the Bolshevik revolution in a global context. While urging the belligerent governments to sign an immediate armistice, the Bolsheviks simultaneously incited their subjects to revolution. Lenin set the course for Bolshevism: revolution in Europe and in the world-wide European colonial dependencies. Lenin played a dual role internationally. Where diplomatic contact remained, he dealt with other nations as previously; however, at the same time at a subversive level he promoted revolution. To reveal their "imperialist nature," Lenin immediately published the secret treaties Czarist Russia had signed with the Allied governments. In general, the Bolsheviks became the self-proclaimed leaders of a new world order, and they immediately mobilized all world-wide dissatisfaction and bitterness which might serve their political ends. Being past masters in activating and manipulating the fears and hopes of the common people, they drew heavily on the post-World War I pacifism, which was widespread, and they studied in depth the writings of those pre-war authors who had expressed deep dissatisfaction with capitalist society.[11] They even put the pacifist ideal of world peace into their constitution of July 1918.[12] This ploy was the origin of the Communist claim to be peace-loving.

The Bolshevik revolution was effective at first only in Petrograd, then Moscow. The Bolsheviks were not as popular as Gorbachëv would have the world believe. There were large areas in Russia where the people fought fiercely against the Bolsheviks. Consequently, the Bolsheviks had to conquer every area of Russia. The revolution in February 1917 was a revolt against the Czar; it was not an endorsement of Bolshevism, Lenin, or anything for which he stood. In those geographical areas where the Bolsheviks had solid support, the task was relatively easy, but in the rural areas along the mid-Volga, the Ukraine, the south and southeast, in Siberia, and in the outlying areas occupied by non-Slavic peoples there was war. Even in those areas where the Bolsheviks held power, they were confronted with political opposition, disorganization, hunger, cold, exhaustion, anarchy, and backwardness.[13] The people expected Lenin to deliver on the promises of bread and land that the Bolsheviks made in the summer of 1917.

The Bolsheviks responded to the opposition with terror, which included the suppression of the liberal press and summary justice against all "class enemies." To fight their opponents, the Bolsheviks created the political police, the CHEKA, which was the ancestor of the present-day KGB.[14] The head of the CHEKA was Feliks E. Dzerzhinskiy.[15]

Under the urging of Lenin, the Bolsheviks began calling themselves Communists on 8 March 1918 after they seized power in Russia, and at that time they renamed the Russian Socialist Labor Party of Bolsheviks the Russian Communist Party (Bolsheviks).[16]

The Soviet government ruled by decree, the authority for which was a self-proclaimed legitimacy. Only in July 1918 did the Soviets put together a new "constitution," which was a codification of the "socialist transformations" already in place. The laws which emanated therefrom were intended to be administered with no interpretation. The Soviets maintained this intent until Josef Stalin gained control of the Soviet Union.[17] Gorbachëv advocates a return to this Leninist legal policy.[18]

Lenin and his cohorts sought to root out all vestiges of the old monarchist system. They attributed "deviations" from Bolshevik policy to abuses by former government officials, land owners, and bourgeoisie who committed "abominable outrages and acts of tyranny against the peasants." Lenin called for a "terrorist purge, summary trial, and firing squad" to eliminate these "deviationists" from Russia.[19] Lenin made uncompromising demands on the enemies of the revolution, and when "necessary" resorted to ruthless methods in dealing with them. In 1918 Lenin employed the most extreme methods against his Socialist Revolutionary opponents and the kulaks. Lenin repeatedly taught that revolutionary violence is necessary to quell the resistance of the exploiting classes, but he used these extreme methods only against the "exploiting classes, class enemies," - not against other Communists. The Bolsheviks claimed that the use of terror was forced upon them by the "terrorist" methods of the Entente.[20]

From 1918 to 1920, in the reign of terror, the Bolsheviks viciously suppressed their "class enemies" by execution. During the civil war, the Bolsheviks used the newly organized Red Army not only to fight the White forces; they used it in an attempt to overthrow the autonomous national regimes that had formed around the periphery of Russia after the collapse of the Czarist regime.[21]

When the Bolsheviks won the civil war, they completed their domination of the soviets. In 1921 they eliminated the last vestiges of organized opposition when they outlawed the Menshevik and the Social Revolutionary Parties. This act left the Communist Party with a clear monopoly of political power.[22]   Yet, there remained monarchists and anti-Bolsheviks, individuals who continued to oppose the new regime.

The great social and economic upheaval from 1918 to 1921 was the Bolshevik revolution.   During this period, the Bolsheviks fought and won the civil war; it was also the period of War Communism.   Lenin explained that the Bolsheviks could not afford to delay introducing War Communism and moving to the most drastic extremes, measures which imposed on the population prolonged conditions worse than semi-starvation.   In his view, this policy was necessary to preserve the rule of the peasants and workers.[23]

Russia was one of the world's most backward countries where the majority of Russian peasants were engaged in small individual farming. Beginning with the Stolypin Plan in 1910, there had been a gradual conversion to individual farming, a movement that continued after 1917. The Bolsheviks, upon seizing power, immediately set out to apply a program to build a Communist society; however, their methods were beyond the capability of the peasants.   The Bolsheviks justified the excessively heavy demands on the peasants on the basis of the wartime emergency.   To the Bolsheviks, the heavy burdens on the peasants were essential to the successful pursuit of the war and to saving the workers and peasants from the landowners.[24]   Yet, the Communist revolution did not come to the Russian countryside until Stalin's collectivization from 1930 to 1933.

The major objectives of War Communism were to restore large scale industry, organize the direct exchange of goods for the produce of the small peasant farmer, and thereby assist the socialization of the peasants.   To assist the restoration of large scale industry, the state was to "borrow" from the peasants a certain quantity of food and raw materials by requisition.   The state carried out this policy for three years.   The idea was to break up completely the old social and economic systems with one blow, but it did not succeed.[25]   In practice, War Communism consisted of the extreme nationalization of the economy, the seizure of grain from the peasants, and a monopolistic state intervention in all areas of human endeavor.   War Communism was a crash program to achieve the Bolshevik goal of making Russia the first, ideal Communist state.

Lenin explained that War Communism, a makeshift policy, was forced on the Bolshevik regime by extreme want, war, and ruin. Under War Communism, the Bolshevik regime in practice took from the peasants, with no recompense, all of the peasants' surplus, to include their necessities and their seed grain. The purpose of these requisitions was to sustain the workers and meet the requirements of the Red Army. Lenin called War Communism a miracle of heroism performed by the workers and peasants for their emancipation. By the spring of 1921, however, War Communism had outlived its presumed practicality, and the peasants were on the threshold of desperation.[26]

During the period 1917 to 1921, the Russian proletariat and peasants formed a military alliance to defend the revolution and soviet power against foreign invasion and internal enemies. Although this military alliance was the primary bond between the proletariat and the peasants, there was of necessity an economic alliance under the provisions of which the peasants received all of the land and protection against former landowners and kulaks. In turn, the workers were to receive the "loans" of food until large scale industry was restored.[27]

The civil war from 1918 to 1920 aggravated the devastation in Russia, prevented the restoration of production, and depleted the proletariat more than other classes. Upon the civil war, there was superimposed the crop failure in 1920, a fodder shortage, and the death of many cattle. These conditions inhibited the restoration of the transportation system and industry. The economic problems adversely affected the peasants and in the spring of 1921 led to a critical political situation which required an immediate, urgent solution.[28] The serious internal political crisis of 1921 revealed discontent among large segments of peasants and workers. In general, among these groups there were strong feelings against the Bolsheviks. This crisis was one of the factors indicating that a direct transition to pure Communism was beyond attainment.[29]

The first serious opposition to the Bolsheviks came from within the Party. On one side were the syndicalists, the middle class leaders, and Lenin. In opposition were the peasants, political opponents, and the Kronstadt uprising against the authoritarian, anti-democratic Bolshevik practices. The discontented wanted a change in Bolshevik policies.

Lenin's response was the New Economic Policy (NEP) to deal with the crisis. The purpose of the NEP was "to establish a link between the new economy ... and the peasant economy." The Bolsheviks had to prove that they could help the peasants during this period when they were in a state of ruin, impoverishment, and starvation. Otherwise, the Bolsheviks could expect to fall from power by a peasant revolt.[30]

The NEP reversed some major policies of War Communism and included a partial de-nationalization of industry. Yet, the Party retained control of the "commanding heights" - heavy industry, finances, and foreign trade. The remainder, consisting primarily of the retail trade and services, were free to return to private hands, and small businesses could hire up to twenty workers. The Bolsheviks tried to restore confidence in agriculture through a promise to end seizures and restore private ownership. The NEP brought changes in the Bolshevik social policy, but did not deal with the major problem of social differentiation in the countryside. The Soviets consider the NEP to have been one of Lenin's major contributions to the theory and practice of "scientific communism."[31] Introduced by Lenin in March 1921 and running to 1928, the NEP has emerged as the reference point for Gorbachëv's economic revolution. Gorbachëv regards the NEP as the basis for the legitimacy of *perestroika*.[32]

Since the peasants seized power in Russia for the workers, in March 1921, for the Bolsheviks, the first thing to do was to improve the condition of the peasants.[33] Improving the living conditions of the peasants and improving their productivity were the only means whereby there could be an increase in the production and collection of grain and the storage and delivery of fuel. The survival of the regime depended on the well-being of the peasants, and Lenin was well aware of the historical problems the Russian monarchs had with peasant uprisings.[34]

Trade was the only possible link between the millions of small farmers and large scale industry. Existing parallel to the farmers there had to be well equipped, large scale industry with a network of power transmission lines. Soviet industry had to possess technical equipment, organizational superstructure, and other features sufficient to supply the small farmers with the cheapest goods in larger quantities more quickly than before.[35]

The success of Communism in Russia depended not only on the peasants' producing good harvests, it depended on the success of light industry and heavy industry. Heavy industry, however, could not thrive on its own; heavy industry required state subsidies, the funds for which were to come from the sale of excess produce, wheat, from the peasant farms. Wheat would be sold on the international market to establish foreign credits for the purpose of purchasing capital equipment for heavy industry.[36]

The NEP was a different approach to socialism. The new approach in the spring of 1921 was not to break up the old social and economic systems of trade, petty production, petty proprietorship, and capitalism; it was to revive trade, petty proprietorship, and capitalism, using them to restore the economy while simultaneously gaining control over them and subjecting them to state regulation only to the extent necessary for their revival.[37] Lenin explained that there was no danger of the proletariat losing power so long as it held authority and retained full control of transportation and large scale industry.[38] The NEP was important to the Bolsheviks as a means for determining whether or not they were in reality establishing a link with the peasants. The Tenth Party Congress of the CPSU in 1921 approved the NEP with expeditious unanimity.[39]

The linchpin of the NEP was the permission and encouragement of competition between state and capitalist enterprises. The Soviets formed mixed companies using capitalist and socialist methods, since the capitalists knew how to "supply things." The mixed companies included private Russian as well as foreign and Communist participation, the purpose of which was not only to rescue the economy but to teach the Soviets how to organize their economy.[40]

The development of capitalism, controlled and regulated by the proletariat, was necessary in the extremely devastated Russia, since this policy appeared to be the only one capable of the immediate revival of peasant agriculture. The NEP included the granting of concessions to Russian capitalists as well as to foreigners. The Bolsheviks could do this without denationalizing anything, since the proletarian state would lease mines, forests, oil fields, and other natural resources to foreign capitalists for the purpose of procuring the equipment and machinery to restore large scale industry. The price for these concessions was considered unreasonable for Russia, but it appeared to be the shortest course to recovery.[41]

The first step to help the peasants was to change the food policy by replacing the system of surplus appropriation by a tax in kind. The peasants would be left with excess produce which they could sell on the open market, thus inaugurating a free market economy. Lenin explained that the tax in kind was part of the transition from War Communism to pure Communism.[42] Even so, Lenin admitted that the tax in kind marked a revival of the petty bourgeoisie and capitalism on the basis of limited free trade.[43]

The reversion to capitalism was to be temporary; in a few decades, concessions with capitalists would revert in their entirety to the Bolshevik regime.[44] The Bolsheviks dismissed contradictions by referring to the NEP as state capitalism, which they proclaimed to be a step forward from the status of the Soviet economy in 1918.[45] Lenin believed that it was necessary to suppress ruthlessly the capitalists who refused to have anything to do with state capitalism or to consider any form of compromise.[46]

In 1921 a new phase in Soviet rule began. Even though the Soviet state retained control of the commanding heights under the NEP, the Bolsheviks introduced capitalist accounting methods. Again, Gorbachëv recalled this decision by Lenin in his quest to incorporate cost accounting into the Soviet economy. In 1921 there was as yet an insufficient number of real proletarians in Russia, and since Communism was not working, Lenin found it necessary to consolidate the partnership between the peasants and the proletariat. The NEP also brought a relaxation in other areas of life in Russia. In theory, the terror ended, freedom of expression was partially restored, and Soviet foreign policy sought to restore normal diplomatic relations with the West.[47]

The development and modernization of the Russian economic system was the most important and difficult task facing the new Bolshevik regime, and the Bolsheviks made numerous mistakes, which Lenin readily acknowledged. The Bolsheviks laid the foundation for a new economic system on the ruins of the old, and even though they experienced reverses and mistakes, they continued by an iterative process to improve their earlier efforts. The NEP was one means by which the Bolsheviks sought to correct some of their mistakes. Early in their rule they discovered the necessity for flexibility in changing their approach to solving problems, especially if the first effort did not work. Initially, they expected to achieve their economic goals in the same manner they had solved the political and military problems: they expected to overcome obstacles by intimidation, the use of excessive force, and unprecedented enthusiasm. They found quickly, however, that these methods, although they might serve to bluff a timid opponent, did not work in economics. They expected to organize state production and distribution on Communist lines as directed by the proletarian state. They learned that the economy did not respond to proletarian enthusiasm; it required people with knowledge and experience in economic matters. Accordingly, the Bolsheviks changed their approach to the ideal Communist state by inaugurating the NEP, which was "two steps back." The NEP meant a partial reversion to capitalism, which was the only reasonable way for the proletarian state to survive. They realized that personal incentive was an essential ingredient in increasing production at all costs, which was the first and foremost necessity. There was no other way to motivate the peasants, unite them, and spur them to greater effort with a corresponding increase in output. The Bolsheviks were determined to make the NEP work, no matter what the cost or how severe the hardships.[48]

The NEP was a political promissory note with no redemption date.[49] For survival, the Bolsheviks had to pass the economic test in competition with private competition or fail completely.[50] In their quest to revive the economy by forming companies jointly with Russian and foreign capitalists,[51] the Bolsheviks sought to build Communism with non-Communist assistance.[52]

Under the NEP there was accommodation to the realities of the international situation. The Soviets restored the Foreign Ministry and established political ties with European states. Following the Treaty of Rapallo at the Genoa Economic Conference in 1921, there was direct cooperation between the Soviets and Germany. On the subversive level, the Soviets established the Comintern in 1919 to promote the international aspects of Marxism while the Foreign Ministry conducted foreign policy along the traditional lines. Yet, domestically, Lenin was troubled by problems with corruption, control, and the bureaucracy, the same harvest of troubles which Gorbachëv is reaping.

The NEP was a retreat from pure Communism, and that is the way Lenin described it. War Communism had become unworkable, and the fragmented centralism characteristic of War Communism had led to paralysis by 1920. There were numerous attempts at evasion, a prime example of which was the growing black market in Russia. Lenin's solution to the myriad problems of War Communism was a relaxation, with the term to be left open. In politics, Lenin permitted limited pluralism, or "socialist pluralism." During the period of the NEP there was also much repression, especially of the non-Communist parties, which were completely eliminated by March 1921. Although Gorbachëv proposed political pluralism, as late as February 1990, the Communist Party was the only political party permitted in the Soviet Union.

With the initiation of the NEP, the Bolsheviks began a tightening within the Party by which they eliminated all formal factions. There was a simultaneous growth of government and Party institutions and the corresponding bureaucracy associated with each. There are some parallels between the NEP and Gorbachëv's program; however, there is one major difference. The NEP was intended to be temporary whereas Gorbachëv announced that his reforms are permanent. When Lenin decided to launch the NEP, there was an element of desperation present. Moreover, Gorbachëv described desperation (criticality) and crisis in the economic status of the Soviet Union.[53]

The NEP, although a nominal reversion to capitalism and a relaxation of the restrictions on expression, did not signify a relaxation of the innate Communist drive. One of the major problems facing the new regime was that of the non-Russian nationalities, which had looked with anticipation to the new ethnic prominence, self-determination, promised by the Bolsheviks before the *coup d'etat*. Although Marx had taught that nationalism was a bourgeois phenomenon destined to disappear in the socialist order, Lenin found it expedient to promise self-determination to rally the minorities to the Bolshevik cause. Lenin argued that the revolution would hasten the disappearance of nationalism. Consequently, when the Bolsheviks seized power they created the

People's Commissariat for Nationalities, under Josef Stalin, to contain this explosive force. Yet, in the acid test of reality, the nationalities along the western border used self-determination to escape Bolshevik control. The other minorities pressed for the promised federal autonomy. When the civil war ended in Russia, Finland received full independence, and Lithuania, Latvia, and Estonia escaped Soviet rule due to German and, later, British assistance. The other minorities had no choice but to submit.[54]

To control nationalism the Bolsheviks made two concessions, both of which violated Marx's teachings: cultural autonomy to the nationalities and an element of federalism in the formal state structure. Cultural autonomy meant the transaction of internal affairs in terms of national tradition and in the native language. For some groups, this nationality policy meant a new alphabet for people who had never possessed a written language. Regardless of the intent, national autonomy did not cause the nationality problem to wither and die.[55]

The Communist order, the Soviet Republic, became a formal reality when the Bolsheviks promulgated the first Soviet Constitution in July 1918. Those geographical areas which the new regime controlled were embodied in the Russian Soviet Federated Socialist Republics (RSFSR). The Constitution created a hierarchy of soviets in which the workers were overly represented in a system of indirect representation. At the top of this structure was the All-Russian Central Executive Committee, elected by regional councils and which theoretically had its source of authority in popular sovereignty. Although representation proceeded upward from the people, governmental authority applied unilaterally downward. The Council of People's Commissars, the real executive authority in this system, acted with celerity, and its decisions were binding on the executive committees at all subordinate levels. The Central Executive Committee had no voice in decisions; it merely approved the actions and decisions of the Council of People's Commissars.[56] According to Lenin, the soviet system provides the maximum democracy for the workers and peasants.[57] This system constituted the democratic process for which Gorbachёv praises Lenin.

In the new Soviet state, the federalism granted by the Soviet Constitution of 1918 was merely a matter of form. Autonomous soviet socialist republics were permitted to conduct their own business under appropriate supervision, and the border nationalities were given the right of secession. Yet, the primary sources of power and control - the armed forces, foreign policy, communications, economic planning, and the political police - all remained under central control. In 1923 a new Constitution of the Union of Soviet Socialist Republics (USSR) extended the soviet form of government to the entire country. The USSR, known as the Soviet Union, incorporated the RSFSR, Byelorussia, the Ukraine, and the Transcaucasian Federation. The All-Russian Congress of Soviets became the All-Union Congress of Soviets and the Central Executive Committee became a bicameral institution with a Council of the Union and a Council of Nationalities. Soviet federalism was a façade since the rigidly centralized regime was under the tight control of the Communist Party. The Russian Communist Party (Bolshevik) was the party for all Soviet territories regardless of nationality.[58]

The peasants were strongly religious, but the Bolsheviks were anti-religion - in fact they were officially atheists. Moreover, the Bolsheviks wanted to destroy the old system and the old culture. This goal included the emancipation of women, an attack on the family, and the destruction of the school system. Thus, the Bolsheviks needed workable social policies to solve their social problems.

Marxists believe that the world revolution can and must solve all problems in a revolutionary manner under all circumstances and in all spheres of action.[59] The Bolsheviks solved the problems of religion, inequality of women, and the oppression of the non-Russian nationalities by the "legislation" of the October Revolution. They considered these "reforms" to be a product of the revolutionary class struggle. Yet, they continued to fight religion in earnest and eliminated the state religion.[60] The dictatorship of the proletariat did not indicate the end of the class struggle; moreover, it indicated the continuation of the class struggle in a new form and with new weapons.[61]

Even though Gorbachëv talked about the Russian Christian heritage through the Orthodox Church in an attempt to tie the Soviet Union to Europe, Lenin and his Bolsheviks were ruthless, militant atheists who made their fight against the Russian Orthodox Church a fight against all religion. The alleged link between Russian Christianity and Western Europe is historically inaccurate. Realizing the role of martyrs in Christian history, the Bolsheviks were cautious in their persecution of religion and religious leaders.[62] The apparent religious toleration expressed by Gorbachëv reveals the same cautious approach toward the church. Nevertheless, the Soviets pursue an active program to convert to atheism those believers who remain in the Soviet Union.

As the membership of the Communist Party grew, the Central Committee soon became too large to be efficient. Accordingly, a small group, the Politburo, became the ruling body in March 1919. The Politburo initially consisted of five members: Lenin (Chairman of the Council of People's Commissars), Trotsky (Commissar for War), Stalin (Commissar for Nationalities), Kamenev, and Zinoviev. This group sat continually during the critical years and made decisions on matters of urgency, a category into which most, if not all of their decisions fell. In 1922, the Communist Party established a permanent secretariat with Josef Stalin as the General Secretary.[63]

Although the Bolsheviks seized political power and eliminated their opposition, the Russian people were far from being the ideal socialists which Marx predicted. Thus the Bolsheviks sought to educate and train the Soviet citizens by providing an ideal Communist environment where they could breed the ideal Soviet man. The Communist Party supervised this scheme of colossal social engineering, and they supervised it in its every aspect.[64]

* * * * * * * * * * * * * * * * * * *

The tactical retreat from War Communism effected by the inauguration of the NEP merely delayed the dialectic process; it in no way entailed a relaxation of the goals and fanaticism of Communism. The NEP provided the opportunity for Lenin and his cohorts to make the administrative and political adjustments necessitated by the whirlwind of events which broke loose in 1917.[65] Within the Party there were proponents of an early termination as well as those for an indefinite extension of the NEP. Nicholai I. Bukharin believed that the NEP could be indefinite, and Gorbachëv early mentioned Bukharin in his speeches. Gorbachëv perhaps agreed with Bukharin on the indefinite feature.

Writing in January 1923, Lenin opined that it would take a historical epoch to get the whole Russian population into cooperatives through the New Economic Policy. He estimated that the most optimistic time required for this achievement would be ten to twenty years.[66] Gorbachëv's goal for the renewal of Soviet society was the year 2000, fifteen years from the initiation of *perestroika*.

The Party managed everything and expanded its problems. Even so, there were differences in the orientation of Party members, and the Bolsheviks had no confidence in the workers' ability to manage. The Bolshevik controlled Supreme Economic Council (later the GOSPLAN) was to regulate and make allocations for the entire economy. There was a problem with agriculture because the Bolsheviks looked down on the peasants and were hostile to them. The Bolsheviks wanted big business agriculture with giant farms managed by the state, but Lenin had promised to redistribute the land to the peasants.

"One step forward, two steps back ...." Lenin explained that this phenomenon occurs in the history of nations, in parties, and in the lives of individuals. Generally, an individual cannot win all of the time, but in the end he can triumph. He further explained that in the power struggle the only weapon available to the proletariat was organization, which it must develop thoroughly. In the end, the proletariat would triumph despite backward steps and zigzags.[67] The Bolsheviks made a backward movement in 1918 when they signed the Treaty of Brest-Litovsk and again when Lenin inaugurated the NEP in 1921.[68] In the 1980s, especially in 1989, it appeared that Gorbachëv was walking backward at a rapid pace.

Marxists are rabidly anti-capitalist, and as followers of Marx, the Bolsheviks stooped to the lowest levels in their attempt to discredit capitalism. Their propaganda was harsh, and they attacked the West with half-truths, lies, deceit, innuendo, and an air of arrogant superiority that revealed a feeling of Bolshevik inferiority. Underneath the façade of Communist superiority and false confidence, they sought to replicate Western technology in the Soviet environment; however, Marxism-Leninism was not the philosophy most conducive to producing creativity, efficiency, and initiative among Soviet citizens.[69] The new Soviet man had not yet emerged.

NOTES

1. Gorbachëv, *Perestroika*, 12.

2. Chairman of the Council, Vladimir Ulyanov (Lenin); People's Commissar of the Interior, A. I. Rykov; Agriculture, V. P. Milyutin; Labor, A. G. Shlyapnikov; Army and Navy Affairs, a committee consisting of V. A. Ovseyenko (Antonov), N. V. Krylenko, and P. Y. Dybenko; Commerce and Industry, V. P. Nogin; Education, A. V. Lunacharsky; Finance, I. I. Skvortsov (Stepanov); Foreign Affairs, L. D. Bronstein (Trotsky); Justice, G. I. Oppokov (Lomov); Food, I. A. Tedorovich; Posts and Telegraph, N. P. Avilov (Glebov); Chairman for Nationalities Affairs, J. V. Jugashvili (Stalin). Nogin, Rykov, and Milyutin resigned on 4 November 1917. Lenin, *Selected Works*, vol. 2, 444.

3. Vladimir I. Lenin, *Selected Works*, vol. 3 (Moscow: Progress Publishers, 1977), 51-52.

4. Ibid., 49.

5. Ibid., 530-531.

6. Albrecht Kesselring, *The Memoirs of Field-Marshal Kesselring* (Novato, California: Presidio Press, 1989), 17. Reprinted with permission of the publisher.

7. Lenin, *Selected Works*, vol. 2, 480-487.

8. Ibid.

9. Ibid., 584-585.

10. Ibid., 550-551.

11. These authors included Sorel and Spengler. von Laue, *Why Lenin? Why Stalin?*, 128.

12. von Laue, *Why Lenin? Why Stalin?*, 128.

13. Ibid., 129-130.

14. Ibid., 130.

15. P. A. Goluba, Yu. I Korableva, and M. I. Kuznetsova, eds., *Encyclopedia of the Great October Socialist Revolution* (Moscow: Soviet Encyclopedia Press, 1987), 148.

16. Lenin, *Selected Works*, vol. 2, 563.

17. Gorbachëv, *Perestroika*, 92.

18. Gorbachëv, "Report at the CPSU Central Committee Plenum 5 February 1990," *Pravda*, 6 Feb. 1990.

19. Lenin, *Selected Works*, vol. 3, 548.

20. Nikita S. Khrushchëv, "Khrushchëv's Secret Speech," (Washington: United States Department of State, 1956).

21. Herbert J. Ellison, "United Front Strategy and Soviet Foreign Policy," *Problems of Communism* 34 (September-October 1985): 45-64.

22. von Laue, *Why Lenin? Why Stalin?*, 168-169.

23. Lenin, *Selected Works*, vol. 3, 545.

24. Ibid., 610-613.

25. Ibid., 587-588.

26. Ibid., 537-538.

27. Ibid., 562, 563.

28. Ibid., 536.

29. Ibid., 663.

30. Ibid., 610-613.

31. Ibid., 14.

32. Gorbachëv, *Perestroika*, 19.

33. Lenin, *Selected Works*, vol. 3, 555.

34. Ibid., 536.

35. Ibid., 591.

36. Ibid., 666-668.

37. Ibid., 587-588.

38. Ibid., 555.

39. Ibid., 610.

40. Ibid., 614-616.

41. Ibid., 563.

42. Ibid., 537.

43. Ibid., 538.

44. Ibid., 542.

45. Ibid., 660.

46. Ibid., 533-534.

47. von Laue, *Why Lenin? Why Stalin?*, 160-161.

48. Lenin, *Selected Works*, vol. 3, 582-586.

49. Ibid., 616-617.

50. Ibid., 618.

51. Ibid., 623.

52. Ibid., 630.

53. Mikhail S. Gorbachëv, "Holiday Reception in the Kremlin," *Pravda*, 8 Nov. 1989; Mikhail S. Gorbachëv, "Promoting the Economic Reform," *Pravda*, 30 Oct. 1989; *Die Welt*, 31 Oct. 1989; Gorbachëv, "Report at the CPSU Central Committee Plenum 5 February 1990," *Pravda*, 6 Feb. 1990.

54. von Laue, *Why Lenin? Why Stalin?*, 163-165.

55. Ibid., 165-166.

56. Ibid., 136.

57. Lenin, *Selected Works*, vol. 3, 582.

58. von Laue, *Why Lenin? Why Stalin?*, 166-167.

59. Lenin, *Selected Works*, vol. 3, 588-589.

60. Ibid., 581.

61. Ibid., 565.

62. von Laue, *Why Lenin? Why Stalin?*, 137.

63. Ibid., 170-172.

64. John Kosa, *Two Generations of Soviet Man: A Study in the Psychology of Communism* (Chapel Hill: The University of North Carolina Press, 1962), 15. Reprinted with permission from the publisher, (c) 1962 University of North Carolina Press.

65. von Laue, *Why Lenin? Why Stalin?*, 163.

66. Lenin, *Selected Works*, vol. 3, 700.

67. Lenin, *One Step Forward, Two Steps Back*, 209-210.

68. Lenin, *Selected Works*, vol. 3, 592-593.

69. von Laue, *Why Lenin? Why Stalin?*, 177-182.

V

STAGNATION: FROM LENIN TO GORBACHËV

From the death of Vladimir I. Lenin in January 1924 to the accession of Mikhail S. Gorbachëv in March 1985, the Soviet Union experienced many excruciating trials, the most severe of which occurred during the twenty-five year rule of Josef Stalin. The Stalin legacy is one with which Gorbachëv had to contend most rigorously, for it was during the Stalin era that the seeds were sown for the crop of troubles in the Soviet Union that plagued Gorbachëv. The myriad "un-Communist" deeds committed by Stalin are well known, having been aired first by Nikita S. Khrushchëv in February 1956 at the 20th Party Congress. There are several Stalinist policies, goals, objectives, and programs which caused Gorbachëv especially severe headaches. Therefore, it will be worthwhile to sketch the "sins" committed by Stalin as a prerequisite to understanding the necessity for *perestroika*.

At the time of Lenin's death in January 1924, the Communist Party was securely ensconced in Russia although the retreat from pure Communism continued under the NEP. Upon Lenin's passing from the Russian scene, the struggle for control of the Party began, and the factions within the Politburo fought it out as one group after another discredited or destroyed the others. When the dust settled in 1928, Josef Stalin was firmly in control, and he took up the problem of Soviet economic development with a "revolutionary" fervor that made Lenin appear to be a moderate. Upon gaining control, Stalin pledged the Party to lead the fight for modernization; the Soviet Union had to catch up with the West and time was short.[1]

When Stalin died in March 1953, there was an interim period in which it appeared that the Soviet leadership had returned to the collegial principle. Indeed, by 1956 the power struggle was over and Nikita S. Khrushchëv had emerged as the leader. Following a number of foolish schemes, Khrushchëv fell victim to the Politburo, which removed him in October 1964 and emplaced Alexei N. Kosygin whom Leonid I. Brezhnev shortly pushed out. Brezhnev's long tenure attained the reputation for being an era of stagnation. Brezhnev's death in 1982 brought to the fore two General Secretaries whose tenure was curtailed by death shortly after their accession to power. Neither Yuri V. Andropov nor Konstantin U. Chernenko served long enough to make a lasting impression on the Soviet body politic.

*   *   *   *   *   *   *   *   *   *   *   *   *   *   *   *   *   *   *

By 1924, the NEP was an accepted economic program; however, it was not the final solution to Soviet socio-economic ills. There was a genuine crisis with the NEP, and by the late 1920s the Soviet economy was in trouble. There was unrestrained press criticism of the NEP, many Communists, especially young Party members, viewed the NEP as a "sell out," and certain parts of the NEP irritated other Communists. Furthermore, the peasants withheld their grain if the price was not right. Finally, in 1927 and 1928 the government retreated and used the Red Army to force the NEP on the peasants. In this setting, there was great pressure for conformity and uniformity.

War Communism did not work, and its successor, the NEP, did not work either. By the end of the 1920s, after Stalin had succeeded Lenin as Party chief, his power was firm. Stalin was committed to economic planning and rapid industrialization, and he abolished the NEP. With Communist zeal, Stalin waged a civil war against the peasants in a reign of terror which victimized millions of Soviet citizens over a period of twenty-five years. By the mid-1930s a post-revolutionary regime was in place which lasted almost unchanged until Stalin's death in 1953.

In 1928 when Stalin finally consolidated his power, the Soviet Union had recovered economically to a level approximating that in 1913. This level of economic attainment was not sufficient to bring the Soviet Union fully into the twentieth century and insure the continued economic and social advance of the world's first socialist state. To achieve the desired level of economic development required a tremendous investment in capital construction and equipment, which could not be achieved merely by throwing in more workers and more raw materials.

Stalin, being a perceptive despot, was realistic enough to understand that the Soviet Union had many enemies, especially in Western Europe, and he feared the day when those enemies, in particular Germany, would rise against the Soviet Union, invade the new state, and tear out its roots. To defeat any such attempt by the West, either real of imagined, Stalin knew that the Soviet Union had to be prepared militarily. The answer was that the Soviet Union had to create a large, modern armed force capable of defending the motherland of socialism. The Soviets had to act expeditiously; they might have only a few years in which to build this formidable armed force.

Stalin also wanted to achieve Marxist-Leninist goals in the milieu of a true Communist state. This objective required that the entire Soviet Union be converted completely to Communism, economically, politically, spiritually, militarily, and socially. Nevertheless, there was resistance to the socialization of Russia. Many peasants, especially the kulaks, did not want to participate in this community of interests.

To bring the Soviet population into the Communist order of things, Stalin inaugurated several far reaching programs, all of which demanded great personal sacrifice by the people. First, the Soviet economy had to provide heavy machinery for the purpose of improving the industrial base. A modern industrial base was essential to Soviet success in building a large armed force as well as providing the country the means to compete economically on world markets.

Second, the Soviet armed forces had to be modernized, enlarged, trained, and equipped to meet any external threat. Stalin perceived that the Soviet Union was about fifty years behind the West militarily and that the new regime had a very short time in which to achieve a modern, well trained, first rate military machine if the Soviet Union expected to survive a future war of aggression.

A third goal was world trade. Since the Soviet Union had an antiquated industrial base and no means for producing heavy equipment, it was mandatory that industrial equipment be purchased abroad. A major stumbling block to foreign trade was the problem that the Soviet currency, the ruble, was not accepted as a medium of exchange on the international market. This meant that the Soviet Union had to export products for the purpose of establishing foreign credits to purchase the much-needed heavy machinery.

In summary, among his numerous other problems, Stalin had to formulate some plan and program whereby he could acquire the heavy machinery to modernize the Soviet industrial base, modernize and enlarge the Red Army, and obtain foreign credits to make possible the first two objectives. At the same time, he had to feed the population. As a simultaneous, ideological objective, he wanted to inculcate the principles of Marxism-Leninism into the entire population, and make the Soviet Union the permanent home of world Communism.

The solution to these problems was the inauguration of a series of Five Year Plans whereby the Soviet Union would modernize under a crash program. The resulting command economy, planned centrally by the State Planning Commission (GOSPLAN), was to be the panacea for Soviet economic problems. The Five Year Plans were designed to regiment the economy in agriculture and industry; the primary emphasis was on building an industrial base. Agriculture was to support and finance the acquisition of heavy machinery for industrial modernization. The plan was for the agricultural sector to produce an excess of wheat, which would be exported and sold, and the credits thereby gained would be used to purchase heavy machinery in the West. This plan meant that the burden would be heaviest on the peasants, who must raise huge crops, surrender their excess, and survive on the remainder.

The Soviet command economy instituted under Stalin pushed the people into a position of secondary importance where they had very little if anything to say about the management of the Soviet economy.[2] In this command economy, the Communist Party displaced the soviets.[3]

The highly centralized management of the Soviet economy had its roots in the extensive economy directed from above during the Stalinist era. Stalin perceived the young Soviet Union to be alone in a world of enemies, a capitalist world waiting for the first opportunity to smash Communism once and for all. Moreover, the country was backward socially, economically, and militarily. In this situation Stalin perceived an urgent requirement to overcome economic backwardness and build a modern industrial base from practically nothing. He accomplished these objectives with amazing speed; however, the cost was great. The Soviets allocated the bulk of their national resources to heavy industry, especially the defense industry. This extreme effort was supported by the sacrifices of the Soviet people. To obtain these objectives in the shortest time, the Soviets planned and regulated everything in minute detail. Although the Soviets made many mistakes in this process, they succeeded. The Soviet economic problems of the 1980s were the legacy of the mistakes in Stalin's crash program for industrialization.[4]

Fundamentally, the Communists had no use for peasants. Marxism was based on the dictatorship of the proletariat, and peasants did not enter the Marxist scheme. The alliance between the proletariat and the peasants in the early days of the Soviet Union was a "marriage of convenience." Stalin proceeded to eliminate the peasants as such by moving them to huge state farms, or collectives, and organizing them as an "agricultural proletariat" who would raise the requisite crops as proletarians. Many peasants, however, did not want to be agricultural proletarians, and they resisted.

Stalin's solution to the peasant problem was forced collectivization, which had varying degrees of success, but it never did succeed entirely. In the process, the Red Army and the secret police entered the countryside to force peasants to the collectives. In total, about twenty million people died in the forced collectivization.

Stalin's program of rapid industrialization was based on the extensive mode of development of the Soviet economy. This meant that huge amounts of raw materials, which the Soviet Union had in abundance, and large numbers of workers, proletarians, would be thrown into the system to meet huge production goals. The emphasis was on quantity, not quality. The prolonged, continuous expenditure of human and natural resources had a deleterious effect on the Soviet economy. Since their economy under Stalin developed in the extensive mode, the Soviets placed little if any emphasis on modernizing the industrial base. Consequently, heavy equipment became obsolete, raw materials were running out, the introduction of new technology was slow, labor became inefficient, and products were of excessively poor quality. These were some of the problems from the Stalinist legacy which Gorbachëv had to solve in his effort to revive and renew the faltering Soviet economy.

Stalin's program did succeed in improving the Soviet economy quantitatively. The Five Year Plans were successful, although not to the extent of Soviet expectations. Under Stalin, the Soviets did build a formidable military machine which succeeded in defeating Germany. In the area of military production, because more capital was invested in building an industrial base and modernizing with new technology, the Soviets have been able to compete on a par with the West. Their competence in building military hardware has enabled the Soviets to build a modern, well-equipped armed force with modern weapons, especially intercontinental ballistic missiles (ICBM). The success in the military industrial area has not, however, spilled over into the civilian economy. One of Gorbachëv's goals was to use some of the military industrial capacity to improve the civilian base.

By the time Gorbachëv became the Party General Secretary, the Soviet economy was degenerating rapidly, and the inertia from the years since Lenin's death could not be overcome easily. The years of extensive economic development had not only worn thin the economic resources of the Soviet Union; they had eroded the attitudes and the desire of the Soviet people to excel. The emphasis was on gross output, a quantity oriented objective that could be reversed only with difficulty. Whereas the economic output was based on an extensive mode of development, the input was cost-intensive. In addition to a substandard quality of output, there was a shortage of food and consumer goods.[5] The stagnation induced by the Stalinist economy is ingrained in the Soviet culture, and it will require a major transformation to change it.

Many young Communists accepted Stalin's views and the sacrifices endemic to the development of an industrial base. To insure that all Soviet citizens accepted Communism, would willingly obey the Party, and would eventually become good proletarians, the Soviets developed an elaborate program for indoctrinating the Soviet people in the fundamentals of Marxism-Leninism and creating men in their own mold.[6]

The development of the ideal Soviet man began on the demand of Lenin immediately after the Bolsheviks gained control of Russia. Following a general blueprint, the program proceeded on a trial and error basis nationwide. The Soviets produced the first generation of the ideal Soviet man between 1917 and 1945. Beginning in 1946, they evaluated their success and began developing the second generation. The first generation of Soviet man lived, worked, and was educated under the Communist system. The breeding of the ideal Soviet man involved psychological manipulation which was a major human engineering program directed toward changing the human psychological make up in accordance with Marxist-Leninist ideology.[7]

Lenin and Stalin directed the development of the first generation of the ideal Soviet man through the medium of terror. The second generation experienced different methods. After 1946, the development of the ideal Soviet man followed the theory of conditioned response based on the experiments of Ivan Pavlov. Applying Pavlov's experiments socially in the Soviet Union, the Soviets sought to establish an ideal Communist state wherein the people would be taught, would understand, would accept, and would learn the precepts of Marxism-Leninism.[8] The theory went to the extremes with the idea that such traits, once acquired, could be inherited. Thus, if the Soviets could establish an ideal Communist environment, they could breed a new generation of Communist man. Obviously this erroneous theory could never work, and Gorbachëv suffered the consequences in the form of drunkenness, absenteeism, apathy, and the other social ills about which he so loudly complained.

After Nikita S. Khrushchëv became General Secretary, the development of the ideal Soviet man appears to have incorporated individual psychological needs.[9] The Communist Party program for 1961 was clear that to breed the ideal Soviet man the Party would educate "... a new man who will harmoniously combine spiritual wealth, moral purity, and a perfect physique." The moral code of this individual would include devotion to the "Communist cause, love of the socialist motherland, collectivism and comradely mutual assistance, human relations, and mutual respect between individuals."[10]

An integral part of developing the new Soviet man was ideological indoctrination. Marxists are atheists, and they mince no words about their opposition to religion; however, they have generally accepted Lenin's attitude toward the suppression of religion in Russia. Lenin realized that any mass repression of religion could easily provoke a new revolution and undo all that the Bolsheviks achieved in 1917 and thereafter. Lenin considered the religious issue to be a third rate problem and he so treated it. His philosophy was to confiscate church property, control what the people heard by requiring the clergy to preach a watered down religion, and do nothing to promote or provoke a religious revival. Under Lenin, the Bolsheviks permitted the church to endure.

Beginning with Peter the Great, the Russian Orthodox Church was under the authority of a government office which answered to the Czar, and this system remained in the Soviet era. Prior to Gorbachëv's reforms, under the Soviet Constitution and according to Soviet law, all clergymen in the Soviet Union were Communists and worked for the KGB or for the Central Committee of the Communist Party. Under the Communist regime, the clergy was administered through a special committee responsible for church affairs and which answered to the Soviet Council of Ministers.[11]

When Stalin came to power, he suppressed most religious activity. Under his regime, the Soviets arrested and executed some clergymen and in general launched a program against religion. They closed most churches and permitted religious activity only under strict state control. Under Stalin, however, in times of national stress and emergency, the church was permitted more freedom. In general, the Soviets grant more or less religious freedom to the people depending upon the necessity to gain public support for their policies, since for Soviet citizens of strong faith the church is an institution to which they can turn in adversity.

Under Gorbachëv, the Soviets pay lip service to religious freedom, but in reality they attempt to use it to further the Communist cause. The nominal relaxation of restrictions on religious practices could be intended to influence Western religious groups to believe that the Soviets have changed. In effect, however, their relaxation in the religious realm has created an air of suspicion, especially among Western fundamentalists, who do not believe it is permanent.

Stalin tolerated no collegiality in leadership. In practice, he was dominant, a dictator who practiced brutality, violence, and terror. He demanded absolute submission to his ideas; otherwise, the dissenter was eliminated. Those who sought to reason with him or prove their own point of view were damned to removal and subsequent moral and physical annihilation. During the Stalin era, common practices used against "enemies of the state" included mass repression administered through state agencies. The victims of mass repression were loyal Communists, often men who had been instrumental in bringing the new order to Russia. These men were in many cases Old Bolsheviks, whose loyalty to the Soviet Union and to Communism had been true. They were men who had worked with Lenin, had fought in the civil war, had fought internal enemies, and had helped in collectivization and industrialization. Even those who were merely suspected of being enemies of the state were marked for elimination.[12]

Mass suppression of Stalin's "enemies" began in the early 1930s. Through fabrication of evidence, from October 1932 through April 1933, thirty-eight people were arrested. On 16 April 1933, the United State Directorate sentenced thirty-four Soviet citizens to various terms of imprisonment on the grounds that they had participated in counter-revolutionary organizations. Thereafter, a number of other people, falsely accused, were sentenced by the military collegium of the Soviet Supreme court and were shot.[13]

During the mid-1930s, Stalin took drastic measures to rid the Soviet Union of his enemies. Mass repression was especially severe during the years 1936, 1937, and 1938, the years of the Moscow show trials, in which the accused were convicted on the basis of their own "confessions," the only proof of guilt. Other forms of repression were mass arrests, torture, deportations, execution without a trial, fear, and a state of tension. According to Khrushchëv, seventy percent of the members and candidates of the Party Central Committee, elected at the 17th Party Congress, were arrested and shot, mostly in 1937 and 1938.[14]

To the shock of the world, in 1936 the Soviets held the first show trial in which Soviet officials were accused of crimes against the state. The accused openly confessed treason and sabotage. In apparently voluntary confessions Stalin's former cohorts, Old Bolsheviks who had assisted Lenin in bringing about the Bolshevik *coup d'etat*, admitted in open court that they had deliberately committed crimes worthy of the most severe punishment. The defendants were convicted and executed.

The Western press coverage of these trials was detailed, and no one has given a satisfactory explanation for those persons' confessing to crimes they obviously had not committed. Additional public trials followed in 1937 with the trial of seventeen Old Bolsheviks and in 1938 with the trial of twenty-one Old Bolsheviks. All trials followed the same pattern: Old Bolsheviks confessed, the court found them guilty, and the state executed them.

In 1937, Stalin ordered the secret trial of a number of military officers, among whom were three of the five Soviet marshals. Marshal Mikhail N. Tukhachevskiy, and Generals Yona Yakir, Jerome Uborevich, and A. I. Kork were accused, tried, and shot for the alleged crime of plotting a military *coup d'etat*.[15] Estimates of the number of officers eliminated in the military purge reached as high as seventy percent of all officers above the grade of major and thirty-five to fifty percent of the entire Soviet officer corps. Marshal Konstantin K. Rokossovskiy, who rose to high military command during World War II, was tried, imprisoned, and later released after having been tortured and relieved of his teeth.[16] The public purge trials represented only a small percentage of the total Soviet citizens eliminated during the 1930s. This milieu of terror constituted the social and cultural environment in which Mikhail S. Gorbachëv and his cohorts were born and grew to be adults.

In 1953 at the time of Stalin's death, there appears to have been another purge in the making. The occasion was the case of the "doctor plotters," who were alleged to have conspired to murder certain Soviet leaders. The evidence against them was based on one letter from a female doctor accusing her colleagues of improper medical practice. This letter was all the "evidence" Stalin needed to act. The order for the arrest of these prominent Soviet medical specialists went out, and shortly the Politburo received "confessions" of their guilt. When after Stalin's death no evidence could be found to support their guilt, the doctors were released and rehabilitated, alive.[17]

The Soviets have tried to disassociate themselves from Stalin's domestic policies, but in the realm of foreign affairs they generally maintain that they are the successors to foreign policy back to the time of Ivan the Terrible. Yet, under *glasnost'*, some prior foreign policy decisions are becoming an embarrassment. On 23 August 1939, the

Soviets signed a non-aggression pact with the Nazis. The Soviets long denied the existence of secret protocols which were part of this treaty and even tried to prove their non-existence.[18] In 1940, as part of these secret protocols, the Soviets annexed Estonia, Latvia, and Lithuania, all of which had been independent since the revolution. The West has questioned the validity of these annexations, and the people in these Baltic countries are restless for their independence.[19] As part of Gorbachëv's *glasnost'*, in September 1989 the Soviets admitted the existence of these protocols.[20]

A consequence of the Ribbentrop-Molotov pact of 23 August 1939 was the Soviet invasion and occupation of eastern Poland on 17 September 1939. In Gorbachëv's attempt to dissociate the Soviet present from the past, Soviet and Polish historians met in 1989 in an effort to "establish the truth" about those events. The purpose was to improve Soviet-Polish relations.[21] The Soviets partially justify their invasion of Poland in 1939 on the basis that they lost Western Byelorussia in 1920 and that the Poles forcefully annexed the Western Ukraine. The Soviets were "liberating" their brother Slavs and the workers of Poland.[22]

Stalin abused the various Soviet nationalities in violation of the Leninist principles for dealing with the Soviet nationalities. Under Stalin's direction, there were mass deportations of entire nations, including members of the Communist Party, from their native lands. Included in these deportations were the Crimean Tatars, the Volga Germans, the Karachai, the Kalmyks, the Chechens, the Ingush, the Meskhetian Turks, and the Balkars.[23]

In 1953 in the power struggle following Stalin's death, the Soviets executed Lavrentia Beria, the former head of Stalin's secret police. Beria was accused of murdering thousands of Soviet citizens on the order of Stalin. Beria appears to have been the last Soviet leader to be removed by execution. From the power struggle following Stalin's death in 1953, Nikita S. Khrushchëv emerged as the Party General Secretary. Khrushchëv and his successors tried to repair the damage which Stalin did; however, their efforts were little more than superficial attempts to solve a fundamental economic problem. Their efforts in some cases led to temporary improvement in certain economic sectors, but the improvement did not endure. Khrushchëv's effort to reduce the bureaucracy was largely unfulfilled. Gorbachëv, whether or not he personally recognized the problem, in 1985 assumed the responsibility for righting the wrongs of the past.

In a closed session of the 20th Party Congress, 25 February 1956, Nikita S. Khrushchëv exposed Stalin, his methods, and what he did to the Soviet Union. Khrushchëv's speech was the first step in what has been called "de-Stalinization," a process in which the Soviets tried to rectify many of the evils committed in the name of the Party during the twenty-five years that Stalin reigned supreme. In this endeavor, they had some successes and some failures.[24]

In his speech, Khrushchëv strongly condemned the cult of the leader, a veneration of the Party chief which the founders of Marxism-Leninism had sought to avoid. Marxism-Leninism from the beginning emphasized group leadership, the collegial principle, which is the underpinning of the authority of the Politburo. The collective leadership, an oligarchy, is intended to survive only so long as there is a necessity for the vanguard of the proletariat. Once Soviet society advances to pure Communism, all leadership groups will be disbanded and the proletariat will rule as a cooperative body.[25]

To the Soviets, the shock on learning of Stalin's deeds was severe. Consequently, the Soviet leadership since the death of Stalin has reverted to the collegial format specified by Marxism-Leninism. The Soviets appear to depend on their collective leadership to prevent the rise of another leader like Stalin who might aspire to emulate the man of steel. For this reason, it is not likely that Mikhail S. Gorbachëv, or any other individual, will govern the Soviet Union on his own initiative. Gorbachëv, or any other Soviet leader, must have the support of the majority of the Politburo and the support of the majority of the Central Committee. Therefore, Gorbachëv did not appear as a single autocrat deciding Soviet policy to be imposed on the Soviet Union. As part of the collective leadership, Gorbachëv was selected as the front man for the "new thinking" policy.

The period from 1953 to 1956 has been dubbed the "thaw," even though the major period of the "thaw" began after Khrushchëv exposed Stalin in February 1956.[26] Following Stalin's death there was a relief from the tension that had gripped the Soviet Union since 1928. This relief was real due to the relaxation of many restrictions imposed during the Stalin era. Upon his ascendancy to power, Khrushchëv continued the "thaw," and permitted some freedom of expression. As a result Soviet writers such as Vladimir Dudintsëv, Boris Pasternak, and Alexander Solzhenitsyn wrote with a freedom that had been suppressed since the mid-1920s. While some of these literary works created a reaction among the Party elite and were suppressed, they did represent a relaxation from the Soviet norm. One result of the "thaw" was the Hungarian uprising in 1956, which appears to have been stimulated by unwarranted expectations on the part of the people of East Europe. Even though this period has been described as the "thaw," there remained a great deal of censorship in the Soviet Union.[27]

Khrushchëv abolished the Machine Tractor Stations on the collective farms and converted some collective farms to state farms. His proposal to decentralize most non-military industry was approved by the Supreme Soviet in May 1957; however, the members of the Politburo disapproved Khrushchëv's changes in the economy, which led to an unsuccessful attempt to remove him in June 1957. Khrushchëv, supported by a vote of confidence in the Central Committee, survived this crisis and immediately removed those members of the Politburo whom he considered his enemies. Hence, Mikhail S. Gorbachëv was not the first Party General Secretary to hold power by virtue of support of the Central Committee when the support of the Politburo was in doubt. Upon securing their positions, both restructured the Politburo.

Later, the Politburo and the Central Committee opposed Khrushchëv's attempts to restructure the Soviet economy and the bureaucracy. Consequently, when Khrushchëv returned from a vacation in October 1964 he discovered that he was no longer the Party General Secretary and that Leonid I. Brezhnev was the new leader.

Although Gorbachëv referred to the Brezhnev era as a period of stagnation, Brezhnev attempted some innovations which Gorbachëv sought to emulate and exceed. One such innovation was Libermanism, a return to limited capitalist methods. Libermanism made its debut under Khrushchëv when in mid-1964 it was tried experimentally with success in two textile centers. Instituted in October 1965 in the economic sector producing consumer goods, Libermanism allowed a partial return to a market economy for individual enterprises to launch on their own a program regulated by the law of supply and demand. The idea was to allow the people to produce what they wanted with a price flexibility that would permit them to make a profit.

In 1967 during the early years of the Brezhnev era, state farms were made economically self reliant with the major emphasis on profit. Under Brezhnev, the decentralization inaugurated under Khrushchëv was "corrected," and attempts to improve the standard of living were accompanied by emphasis on greater discipline among workers. The economic reforms of 1965 were significantly reduced in application, primarily by the proponents of pure Communism. The final years of Brezhnev's eighteen year reign were characterized by bribery, stealing from the state, increased alcoholism, black market activity, and a general lackadaisical attitude on the part of the workers. There was great slippage in the ideological indoctrination of Soviet citizens. Hence, the quality control in developing the new Soviet man appears defective.

In 1968, following the Soviet intervention in Czechoslovakia, Brezhnev described the Soviet action in terms of protecting the gains of international socialism. In declaring Soviet opposition to interference in the internal affairs of another state, he pronounced that in the event a threat should arise against the cause of socialism in any Communist country, the threat was a problem of concern to all socialist countries and therefore Soviet armed forces would cross the borders into any Communist country if the Soviets considered the situation to be a threat to Communism.[28] Brezhnev's enunciation of this Soviet policy became known as the "Brezhnev Doctrine," which on 27 October 1989 Foreign Minister Eduard Shevardnadze alleged never existed.[29] The Soviets justified their action and the action of other Warsaw Pact countries in 1968 against Czechoslovakia as a manifestation of socialist inter-nationalism, an act of assistance to the security of the entire socialist community.[30]

Brezhnev's final years produced no improvement, and were in reality years of stagnation. The successful Soviet foreign policy of the 1970s did not continue. In December 1979 the Soviets sent their armed forces into Afghanistan, supposedly on the invitation of the Communist government of that country. The Soviets found themselves on the defensive as a result of Western policies and developments in the 1980s, and they were not able to block the Western deployment of intermediate range nuclear weapons in Europe. Later, neither Yuri V. Andropov nor Konstantin U. Chernenko was able to reverse these trends.[31]

In Gorbachëv's words, the Brezhnev era was a period of serious stagnation. The heavy legacy left to the Soviet Union by this period of stagnation has been a detriment to the efforts at economic reform. In 1989 there was still a declining return on investment capital, which indicates that the Soviets had not succeeded in breaking the cost-based nature of their economy. They were still using physically outdated and obsolete equipment, a situation that continued to have a deleterious effect on the entire country. For example, at the end of 1988 over eleven percent of Soviet equipment was twenty or more years old. To make matters worse, much of the new equipment was inferior to the best available in the world or in the Soviet Union.[32]

When Mikhail S. Gorbachëv became General Secretary of the CPSU in 1985, the Soviet Union was in the planning stage of the Twelfth Five Year Plan. Gorbachëv tried to incorporate his revolution into this plan, but in late 1989 the Soviet economy did not appear to be responding to corrective measures. Learning from experience in the Lenin manner, Gorbachëv exerted a greater effort to insure that the Thirteenth Five Year Plan incorporated all of his reforms.[33]

* * * * * * * * * * * * * * * * * * *

The Soviets evaluate the period from Lenin to Gorbachëv as an era of disaster, since the period of Stalinism and the years of stagnation subjected their socio-economic and political systems to serious deformations and retarded the development of socialism and the ultimate building of Communism. It kept the people, the proletariat, from exercising their rightful power.[34] Yet, Gorbachëv did not throw away these years of experience even though they were considered to be years of "mistakes and deformations." Moreover, he had no intention of turning the clock back to 1917 and starting over.[35] Gorbachëv admitted that the acute economic problems with which the Soviet Union is afflicted have grown so bad as to have an adverse effect on the social, political, cultural, and ideological mood of the entire Soviet society.[36]

The death of Brezhnev in 1982 marked the end of an era of relative domestic prosperity and a dramatic increase in Soviet military power and international political influence. Yet, regardless of these accomplishments, the last years of the Brezhnev regime witnessed growing problems in domestic and foreign affairs. There was an alarming slowdown in the Soviet economic growth. The annual average national income fell from a growth rate exceeding eight percent in the 1960s to five or six percent in the 1970s to one or two percent in the 1980s.[37]

In October 1989, Foreign Minister Eduard Shevardnadze, in an apologia for Soviet military action against its neighbors, admitted that the Soviets made a mistake in sending troops into Afghanistan in 1979. Even though the Soviets made the decision on their own, they did not think through the situation properly. On the other hand, Shevardnadze refused to admit a Soviet mistake in entering Czechoslovakia with armed forces in 1968. He adhered to the claim that the action in 1968 in Czechoslovakia was taken as joint action by the leaders of the Warsaw Pact states and had the concurrence of the Party leaders, the Defense Councils, and "elements" within Czechoslovakia.[38] Contradicting the Foreign Minister, in terms of the "new thinking," on 4 December 1989, in concert with the Warsaw Pact states, Gorbachëv condemned the 1968 Soviet action and declared an end to the "non-existent" Brezhnev Doctrine.[39]

Gorbachëv's abrupt *volte-face* on the Czechoslovakia incident of 1968 exemplifies the rapidity with which the Soviets responded to what they think the West wants to hear. This type of declaration indicates that the Soviets were in much more serious difficulty than they want to admit. The years of stagnation impressed the Soviets that their old *modus operandi* did not succeed. Their international reputation is so bad, however, that to convince the West they are serious in the "new thinking" they must take actions which appear to be irreversible. Otherwise, one failure to accede to Western expectations will nullify their entire program of *glasnost'*.

"Tell them what they want to believe."

NOTES

1. von Laue, *Why Lenin? Why Stalin?*, 174, 193, 195.

2. Gorbachëv, *Perestroika*, 97.

3. Ibid., 98.

4. Ibid., 31-33.

5. Ibid., 257-258.

6. Kosa, *Two Generations of Soviet Man*, 15, 186; Mikhail S. Gorbachëv, "The Cause of *Perestroika* Needs the Energy of the Young," *Pravda*, 16 Nov. 1989.

7. Kosa, *Two Generations of Soviet Man*, 15, 17, 25.

8. Ibid., 187.

9. Ibid., 188.

10. *New York Times*, 1 Aug. 1961, sec. 1, 13-20.

11. Oleg Penkovskiy, *The Penkovskiy Papers* (Garden City, New York: Doubleday & Company, Inc, 1965), 236. Reprinted with permission. AFP, Paris, 30 Nov. 1989, *FBIS Daily Report*, 30 Nov. 1989, 68.

12. Khrushchëv, "Secret Speech," 4 June 1956.

13. *Pravda*, 25 Oct. 1989.

14. Khrushchëv, "Secret Speech," 4 June 1956.

15. Sergei Fedorovich Akhromeyev, Interview, Moscow Television Service, 9 Oct. 1989, *FBIS Daily Report*, 13 Oct. 1989, 95-105. Other Soviet generals who died in the purge included Primakov, Feldman, Eideman, and Putna.

16. Penkovskiy, *Penkovskiy Papers*, 46fn.

17. Khrushchëv, "Secret Speech," 4 June 1956.

18. "Radio Soyuz," Moscow Domestic Service, 30 Sept. 1989, *FBIS Daily Report*, 2 Oct. 1989, 35-36.

19. Paris, AFP, 2 Oct. 1989, *FBIS Daily Report*, 2 Oct. 1989, 72-73.

20. "Radio Soyuz," Moscow Domestic Service, 30 Sept. 1989, *FBIS Daily Report*, 2 Oct. 1989, 35-36.

21. *Krasnaya Zvezda*, 3 Oct. 1989.

22. *Krasnaya Zvezda*, 17 Sept. 1989.

23. Khrushchëv, "Secret Speech," 4 June 1956; *Pravda*, 27 Sept. 1989; *Sovetskaya Rossiya*, 24 Nov. 1989.

24. Khrushchëv, "Secret Speech," 4 June 1956.

25. Ibid.

26. Moscow World Service, 29 Oct. 1989, *FBIS Daily Report*, 1 Nov. 1989, 6-8.

27. Ibid.

28. *Krasnaya Zvezda*, 13 Oct. 1989.

29. Eduard Shevardnadze, Prague Domestic Service, 27 Oct. 1989, *FBIS Daily Report*, 30 Oct. 1989, 22-23.

30. *Krasnaya Zvezda*, 13 Oct. 1989.

31. Department of Defense, *Soviet Military Power*, 8-9.

32. *Izvestiya*, 10 Oct. 1989.

33. Gorbachëv, *Perestroika*, 47; Mikhail S. Gorbachëv, "Concluding Remarks," *Pravda*, 6 Nov. 1989; Mikhail S. Gorbachëv, Moscow Television Service, 12 Dec. 1989, *FBIS Daily Report*, 13 Dec. 1989, 51-55.

34. *Krasnaya Zvezda*, 7 Oct. 1989.

35. Mikhail S. Gorbachëv, "The Socialist Idea and Revolutionary *Perestroika*," *Pravda*, 26 Nov. 1989.

36. *Pravda*, 30 Oct. 1989.

37. Department of Defense, *Soviet Military Power*, 8.

38. Prague Domestic Service, 27 Oct. 1989, *FBIS Daily Report*, 30 Oct. 1989, 22-23.

39. Moscow Television Service, 4 Dec. 1989, *FBIS Daily Report*, 5 Dec. 1989, 2; *TASS*, 4 Dec. 1989; *Pravda*, 5 Dec. 1989.

VI

DECEPTION: SOVIET STYLE

Deception has been an inherent characteristic of Communism since the Bolshevik *coup d'etat* in 1917. The Soviets have made a science of deception and have formulated intricate components of this science to be practiced depending upon the specific target and the ultimate objective. Soviet deceptive measures are many and varied; however, four of the more frequently practiced Soviet deception methods are: *maskirovka*, *dezinformatsiya*, *demonstratsiya*, and *stimulirovniya*. This chapter will deal with these four deception methods, discuss Soviet deception, and describe some of the more widely known Soviet deception operations.

The Soviets have a record of disseminating disinformation. They have been the authors of numerous forgeries and lies directed primarily at the United States. Moreover, they are masters at media manipulation, primarily by placing fabricated stories in the foreign press. This activity is widespread. The Soviets make a point to cultivate foreign journalists, publish low-cost newspapers, and supply numerous books to the third world.

An understanding of Soviet deception requires a knowledge of past Soviet practices. In the study of political leaders and decision making, the operational code reveals that the Communists pursue their goals by following three maxims: 1. push to the limit, 2. engage in pursuit, and 3. know when to stop. Pushing to the limit dictates that maximum energy must be exerted to attain the objectives. Pressure should be maintained even though there is no sign of success and even though the opponent may exert more effort. Once there is a weakening of the opponent's resolve, it is essential to maintain the pressure and exploit every sign of weakness. The Communists have shown sufficient discretion to know when to stop, a brake which prevents the exhilaration of success from clouding the judgment and allowing the overextension of their forces.[1]

In studying Soviet behavior since 1917, scholars have detected certain patterns to Soviets actions. The study of these behavior patterns may not lead to an accurate prediction of the next Soviet move, but a knowledge of what they do in certain situations can aid in an understanding of the general nature of what to expect in the long term. Indeed, the study of Soviet history indicates that past practices are a good indicator of what the Soviets may do, provided conditions are similar to those associated with past practices. Furthermore, the study of Soviet motivation can assist in understanding Soviet actions. The Soviets place great reliance on the study of history, and their beliefs in historical determinism are well known. These observations underline the necessity for being familiar with Soviet history, and it will serve the West well to study Soviet history.

The Soviets have conducted deception at all levels and in varying degrees. For example, the Trust, associated with the NEP, is an example of Soviet deception on a global basis. Accordingly, Mikhail Gorbachëv's insistence that his program is similar to Lenin's NEP should be a signal for the West to be wary. The WIN operation in Poland from the period 1947 to 1952 is another example of a successful Soviet deception in East Europe, and the myth of the missile gap in the early 1960s illustrates a Soviet attempt at global deception. Since the Soviets are "scientific" about everything, including deception, the West should approach Soviet deception with great caution.

For their carefully planned deception operations, the Soviets have developed an elaborate theory of command and control over the forces of an enemy or a prospective enemy. They call this system reflexive control, the premise for which states that control (*upravleniye*) is the ultimate objective of Soviet military and political decision making. Sub-elements of this control theory include four methods for control of an opponent: 1. *maskirovka* (denial and concealment), 2. *dezinformatsiya* (disinformation), 3. *demonstratsiya* (demonstration), and 4. *stimulirovniya* (provocation). This theory and the application have a great potential for Soviet manipulation and disruption of Western decision making.[2]

Reflexive control is a means for changing the behavior of people whose interests and beliefs are different from those of the controlling agent. It consists of conveying to the controlled system the motive and bases for a desired decision.[3] To be effective, the controlling agent must intentionally change incoming information and transform it from a cognitive to a controlling role. Thus, reflexive control causes the desired action indirectly. The controller attempts to change the beliefs and objectives of the controlled in such a way to produce the desired results. There are differences in the form of reflexive control. It may be conscious and free as a result of the necessity for joint action, or it may be forced by strongly suggestive stimuli. It is a highly sophisticated form of persuasion in which the victim permits himself to be manipulated. The Soviets, however, have traditionally assumed an adversarial relationship and have traditionally employed deception rather than persuasion. This does not mean that the Soviets have not or will not attempt reflexive control through persuasion.[4] For example, Gorbachëv's expressed necessity for joint action in the prevention of nuclear war may have been the stimulus for conscious reflexive control in which the West chooses to be manipulated.

The Soviets are devoting more effort to the forced or exploitive form of reflexive control in which they employ these four methods for manipulating an adversary's belief system. The purpose of *maskirovka* is to deny correct information to the opponent. In employing *maskirovka* the Soviets use camouflage, concealment, and a plethora of other techniques for disguising reality. These techniques may be passive or active and are intended to promote uncertainty in the enemy's perspective.[5] For example, the rapid changes in East Europe in 1989 created uncertainty in the Western perspective of Soviet motives.

Dezinformatsiya consists of the deliberate projection of an incorrect image of the situation. Its goal is to project an image of false reality. Although they are similar in methods and techniques, *maskirovka* and *dezinformatsiya* have important differences. *Maskirovka*, or concealing reality, is easier to accomplish than *dezinformatsiya*, or fabricating a credible falsehood. Merely concealing or disguising one's activities is easier than persuading an enemy to believe a false story. The latter requires careful planning, preparation, and coordination. In military strategy and in political conflict, there is sufficient time to construct, promulgate, and exploit false images of oneself, an adversary, or of the world.[6] The Marxist "peace loving" rhetoric is an attempt to promulgate an incorrect image of an ideology based on class hatred and warfare.

Dezinformatsiya, employed strategically, assists the Soviets in the execution of national objectives and is directed to mislead the enemy in matters of state policy. They employ it in peacetime as well as in wartime as an instrument of policy. Strategic disinformation, being inseparable from state policy, is formulated at the highest level in the Soviet Union. The Politburo approves long term, global disinformation plans which are projected into the future fifteen years and more.[7] Gorbachëv's "new thinking" has the earmarks of *dezinformatsiya*.

Lenin enunciated the guiding principle of disinformation when in the early 1920s he told the chief of the Soviet security service (the CHEKA), Feliks E. Dzerzhinskiy, to tell the West what the West wanted to believe. Furthermore, Lenin instructed Dzerzhinskiy to build a Soviet disinformation campaign around the theme that Communism was failing, since that was apparently what Western leaders wanted to hear from Russia. Openly, Lenin built a credible base for the disinformation campaign when in March 1921 he announced the New Economic Policy (NEP) in which pure Communism, War Communism, would be replaced by a mixture of state socialism and private capitalism. Lenin also invited foreign businessmen to the Soviet Union where he offered them concessions in mining and manufacturing. Lenin told these Western businessmen that Communism was not working.[8] Gorbachëv's actions resemble those of Lenin, and he has told the West what the West wants to hear.

The Soviet Union propagates a plethora of disinformation themes, some of which are: The Soviet Union is no longer Communist. Soviet military doctrine is defense oriented. Communist ideology is dead. The individual, not the Party, counts in the Soviet Union. The Soviet Union has changed. The United States is not under attack. International Communism no longer exists. The United States' military threat and

Soviet insecurity work together to cause the Soviet Union to maintain a formidable military force.[9]

Another Communist technique which the Soviets have used on a large scale is the "big lie," a flagrant example of disinformation. The theory is that if the deceiver delivers a false statement in a convincing manner and if he repeats it frequently, people will eventually believe the lie no matter how preposterous it may sound at first and no matter how much evidence exists to refute it. Closely associated with the big lie is the use of half truths. Frequently the Soviets will combine a lie with enough truth to convince the audience that the entire message is true. Gorbachëv's rhetoric is replete with half-truths.

The Soviets, especially Gorbachëv, strongly emphasize the Yalta and Potsdam Agreements as the basis for the post-World War II East European settlement. They express a one-sided view: they continually claim that the problems in East Europe are Western in origin, especially the fault of the United States. They habitually fail to relate, however, that at Yalta the United States went to great lengths to satisfy President Roosevelt's idea of legitimate Soviet interests in East Europe. Amid great criticism, Roosevelt succeeded in getting the Western Allies to acknowledge East Europe as a Soviet sphere of influence. He was also instrumental in facilitating for the Soviet Union the annexation of territory in the Far East which belonged to China and Japan. Furthermore, the United States sponsored the award of double United Nations representation to Byelorussia and the Ukraine. The big lie, repeated often enough, tends to be accepted as truth.

In contrast to *maskirovka* and *dezinformatsiya*, *demonstratsiya* involves the use of deceptive operations. *Demonstratsiya* consists of deceptive maneuvers which promote false impressions of the controller's real plan of action. Although *demonstratsiya* are intended to serve as a form of communication, they are interpreted by the controlled as evidence of behavior. They are in practice disinformative messages disguised as behavior. Whereas messages sent to an enemy are habitually received with a great deal of doubt, an enemy will treat actions differently. Actions, unlike words, require the expenditure of effort and their consequences are reversible only with the expenditure of greater effort. Although *demonstratsiya* may be highly effective, they are also very expensive.[10] Gorbachëv's declaration that *perestroika* is irreversible fits this description. Examples of apparently irreversible actions include the relaxation in East Europe in 1989, and in particular, the opening of the Berlin wall.[11] Drastic reductions in Soviet military forces would be reversible with a great expenditure of effort. Most of Gorbachëv's reforms fit the criteria for *demonstratsiya*.

The fourth method of reflexive control is stimulation, or *stimulirovniya*, which is the art of provoking the adversary to make precipitous, ill-considered decisions or to take hasty actions. The purpose is to short-circuit the decision process of the opponent. *Stimulirovniya* employs the techniques of *maskirovka*, *dezinformatsiya*, and *demonstratsiya*. Of the four techniques, *stimulirovniya* is the most risky, since it may provoke an unreasonable response.[12] "New thinking," *perestroika*, *glasnost'*, and democracy may come back to haunt Gorbachëv, the Politburo, and the Central Committee if the relaxation goes too far. For example, a breaking away of the Baltic states from the Soviet Union could ensue as an unreasonable response.

Reflexive control can be either destructive or constructive.[13] To exercise constructive reflexive control most successfully, the controller must have an accurate and complete model of the adversary's beliefs and decision making process. Governments which have powerful, assertive leaders have the type of command and control structure readily susceptible to Soviet penetration and manipulation. Constructive reflexive control may have several specific targets depending upon the Soviets' most critical need at the moment. Employed with skill and care, reflexive control can be a most useful device for influencing an opponent. Hence, reflexive control is an integral part of the political and military policy-making procedure in the Soviet Union.[14]

One major Western weakness which the Soviets exploit to the fullest degree is the idea of convergence. Many Westerners believe that the Soviets are becoming more like Westerners. This eagerness to believe that the Soviets are people "just like us" with the same desires, the same likes, the same dislikes, similar problems, and the desire for success, only with a different political and economic system, enables the Soviets to succeed in massive propaganda campaigns and to dupe innocent Westerners into accepting their mendacious disinformation.

There are many examples of Soviet deception operations. In general, Soviet citizens who become involved in any type of opposition to the regime are susceptible to being used by the secret police against other opponents. The practice has been for Soviet counterintelligence agencies to organize phony organizations opposing the Soviet regime and which have the same purported objectives as the dissidents. The secret police sponsor this "subversive" organization, encourage the dissidents, use them to identify other dissidents, and at an opportune time arrest the unsuspecting opponents of the regime.[15]

A prime example of Soviet strategic deception was The Trust, a deception of international scope, which operated between 1921 and 1927. Although Lenin outlawed all opposition political groups in March 1921, he did not eliminate individual opponents who went underground. In an attempt to identify the opponents and ferret them out, the secret police, under CHEKA chief Feliks E. Dzerzhinskiy, organized The Trust in 1921 to entice Russian dissidents to reveal themselves.[16] The CHEKA established The Trust in conjunction with the NEP.[17]

The CHEKA assigned a name to the phony organization. It was the Monarchist Association of Central Russia, and the Soviets made it authentic by assigning a cover name, the Moscow Municipal Credit Association, from which the organization received the name "The Trust." Operating under the authorization of the NEP, the state security service directed The Trust at the highest levels.[18]

The alleged purpose of The Trust was to assist monarchists and anti-Bolsheviks in Russia by encouraging, organizing, and coordinating their activities. The real purpose, however, was to identify opponents of the regime so that the leaders of The Trust could decide which of these people should be manipulated, incarcerated, or liquidated. Targets of The Trust included the monarchists and anti-Bolsheviks who escaped the Bolshevik reign of terror in the period 1918 to 1920.[19] The Trust was to discover the opponents of the Communist regime and lure the leaders into the hands of the *Ob'edinyonnoye Gosudarstzvennoye Politicheskoye Upravleniye* (OGPU), which replaced the CHEKA in the winter of 1921-1922. The Trust was a superbly planned and executed intelligence operation led by agents of the *Gosudarstzvennoye Politi-*

cheskoye Upravleniye (GPU). The GPU authenticated The Trust by deliberately orchestrating anti-Bolshevism in Russia and organizing fake counter-revolutionary activity and monarchist conferences to attract even a few authentic anti-Communists. GPU agents, playing the dominant role, called for help from Bolshevik forces before events got out of control.[20]

During the period 1922 to 1924, The Trust expanded its network and its disinformation activities, one objective of which was to influence capitalist governments to recognize the Soviet Union and open their countries to Soviet trade. Another objective of the disinformation campaign was to convince the West that the Soviets would be reliable and respectable business partners. Soviet disinformation, after recognition by France and Britain in 1924, resolved to demonstrate to the West that the Soviet Union was becoming a bourgeois state, that a new spirit of moral revival was developing, that Stalin was in reality a Russian nationalist whose objectives were limited to the geographical confines of the Soviet Union, and that the Communists were rapidly losing their ideological convictions. The Trust further tried to convince the West that their previous perception of the Soviet Union was distorted.[21]

Through The Trust the Soviet security service identified, exposed, and neutralized opponents inside Russia. The Soviets permitted many of these opponents to continue operating for several years prior to apprehending them, and the CHEKA used The Trust to prevent the organization of any real anti-communist underground inside Russia. Outside Russia the state security service penetrated the White para-military organizations which served as a conduit for disinformation to unsuspecting Western intelligence organizations.[22]

The Trust sponsored and approved the writing of fabricated accounts of underground activities which were intended as disinformation to convince the West that Communism was on the wane in Russia, Soviet leaders were really a new breed of nationalists, and that outside intervention would be counterproductive.[23]

As the NEP was being emplaced openly, on the covert side the CHEKA organized a conduit to Western intelligence organizations for providing disinformation coinciding with the theme of the NEP.

Nominally, The Trust was an anti-Communist resistance group inside the Soviet Union, but in reality it was deception. Trust representatives made contact with the leading anti-Soviet organizations in exile in Europe and offered to help steal Soviet secrets and arrange the escape of relatives and associates from Russia. The Trust could fulfill all of its promises, and it easily convinced the émigré groups that it represented a powerful anti-Communist organization whose agents infiltrated the entire Soviet government.[24]

After The Trust was accepted as a credible organization, it disseminated bits of secret information - disinformation - to different anti-Communist groups, which sold that information to Western intelligence organizations. Since the Soviet security service very carefully managed this issue, the bits of disinformation fit together and formed an easily corroborated, logical pattern. The theme of this disinformation was that the Soviet government retained power solely because Western intervention had caused the Russian people, in a spurt of nationalism, to rally around the government to expel the foreign invaders. When Western governments accepted this theme, they withdrew their troops, removed the economic blockades, and stopped other forms of harassment. In the final analysis, the Trust was highly successful in its disinformation function.[25]

After the Soviets consolidated their regime and brought about stability, they brought both the NEP and The Trust to an end. In 1927, after they discontinued the NEP and nationalized almost all of the foreign concessions, the Soviet security service terminated The Trust by sending a phony defector to Helsinki with the message exposing The Trust as a fraud.[26] When the Soviets exposed The Trust they did as much damage in its demise as it had caused during its lifetime. The exposure of The Trust disorganized emigration from Russia, created mistrust among émigré groups, destroyed their credibility as Soviet experts, and compromised them as effective intelligence sources.[27] Within the geographical limits of Russia, the Soviets prosecuted many of their opponents and intimidated the remainder. Externally, the Soviet intelligence service blackmailed Trust supporters, tried them in absentia, and ridiculed them.[28]

The Trust created a feeling among some Western Soviet watchers that no internal resistance was possible in the Soviet Union. It also created the idea that the Soviet regime was mellowing and was willing to do business with the West, both governmentally and commercially. The disinformation disseminated by The Trust reinforced the activities of the NEP, the manager of which was the same individual as the manager of The Trust: Feliks E. Dzerzhinskiy, in the years from 1921 until his death in 1926, operated in a dual capacity as chief of the Soviet state security service and chief of the Supreme Economic Council.[29]

When Lenin and his Communist cohorts reorganized the Soviet economy in March 1921 by introducing the NEP, the openness created permitted travel to the West and allowed Soviet representatives to gain personal contact with Western businessmen. The NEP also provided the Soviet Union an opportunity to send its intelligence agents into the West under cover as salesmen or purchasing agents. In general, Soviet intelligence officers believe their Western targets to be naïve and accept at face value any lie used to conceal the truth.[30] The gullibility of many Westerners supports this belief.

A more recent example of Soviet deception is the WIN operation which took place from 1947 to 1952, and which bore many of the earmarks of the earlier Trust operation.[31] During the early post-World War II period, Soviet disinformation was directed to undermining United States' attempts to organize opposition to Soviet rule in East Europe.[32] In Poland, WIN (meaning Freedom and Independence) was the underground successor to the World War II Polish Home Army. The plans for the WIN movement were betrayed to the security services almost from inception.[33]

Through Polish exiles in London, WIN made contact with the United States' Central Intelligence Agency and the British Intelligence Service. The attraction was that WIN represented thousands of armed guerrillas in Poland. Double agents under Soviet control corroborated these claims. Furthermore, Western interceptions of police and militia radio broadcasts in Poland indicated that Soviet and Polish units were under harassment by guerrillas.[34]

Both British and United States' intelligence services accepted WIN for what it was purported to be, and for more than a year delivered by parachute large quantities of weapons, electronic equipment, and gold bullion. They also sent their own agents and Polish dissidents to make contact with WIN officials. Finally, in December 1952 after arresting the agents and dissidents who made contact with WIN, the Polish security service announced that WIN was a fraud, organized and manipulated to entrap dissidents and dupe the West.[35] The effect in the West was similar to the exposure of The Trust in 1927.[36]

Both the Polish government in exile in London and the Western intelligence services suffered a tremendous loss of prestige and morale. There was one important difference between The Trust and WIN; whereas WIN began as a genuine opposition movement, The Trust was deception from the beginning.[37]

The Soviets direct their deception at many targets. In the Aviation Day demonstrations in July 1955, twenty-nine intercontinental bombers flew by in three flights, when the Soviets actually possessed only ten operational bombers. The purpose of this deception was to lead the West to believe that the Soviets were investing in intercontinental bombers.[38] As a sequel to the bomber deception in 1955, in 1956 when United States General Nathan Twining visited the Soviet Union, the Soviets tried to impress him that Soviet aviation was defensive and peaceful. To accomplish this purpose, they held a flyover in which only seven heavy bombers in a mixed formation were counted. They further gave him a tour of an obsolescent engine facility and transport plant.[39]

One of the classic examples of Soviet deception was the "missile gap" of the early 1960s, a Soviet ploy which actually worked to the detriment of the Soviet Union. After the Soviets successfully launched *sputnik* in October 1957, Khrushchëv boasted that the Soviet Union had all of the rockets it needed, including short range, intermediate range, and long range missiles. Soviet commentators immediately responded to Khrushchëv's boast and claimed that the Soviet Union had the means to deny the United States its previously held strategic advantage.[40]

Concomitantly, Soviet intelligence tried to convince the United States that the Soviet Union could manufacture nuclear weapons. Hence, they sent a double agent, Heinz Felfe, under the control of the KGB, to the CIA with a sample of high grade uranium ore purportedly from mines in Czechoslovakia. This ruse caused the CIA to revise upward its estimate concerning the size of the Soviet nuclear stockpile.[41]

Khrushchëv continued his boasting in November 1958 when he claimed the Soviets were placing ICBMs in production. In February 1959 at the 21st Party Congress he claimed to have begun serial production of ICBMs. Reinforcing Khrushchëv's comments, Marshal Rodion Ya. Malinovskiy, at the same Congress, thanked those who had contributed to equipping the armed forces with missiles. The impression so created was that the Soviet armed forces were equipped with operational missiles. The Soviets claimed an equal capability with that of the United States.[42]

In 1960 Khrushchëv claimed the capability to obliterate from the earth by atomic and hydrogen bombs any country that might attack the Soviet Union. Khrushchëv kept up this braggadocio in January 1960. Both he and Malinovskiy boasted that the Soviets could easily conceal ICBM locations and thus prevent any verification or refutation of Soviet claims. After the U-2 incident in the spring of 1960, Khrushchëv began to withdraw some of his previous claims of superiority in missiles.[43]

In conjunction with Khrushchëv's pronouncements about Soviet strength in intercontinental ballistic missiles, this deceit gave credence to the "missile gap" which John F. Kennedy used successfully in the United States' presidential election of 1960. In addition, the emphasis on the intercontinental threat diverted United States' intelligence agencies from the rapidly expanding Soviet bomber and missile forces deployed against targets in Europe and Asia.[44]

Following the United States' presidential election of 1960, the truth about the missile gap became common knowledge. Although President Eisenhower had known from the U-2 flights over the Soviet Union that there was no missile gap, he could not reveal the truth because of security reasons. By October 1961, however, the new administration had exposed the missile hoax and had begun to reverse the image of Soviet strategic superiority. By 1962, the Soviet boasting had degenerated into defensive statements. Although the Soviets were exposed in their attempted deception, they continued their quest for military superiority.[45]

In 1968 the Soviets organized a special service for the purpose of conducting strategic deception. This new agency, *Glavnoe Upravlenie Stratigicheskoy Maskirovka* (Principal Directorate of Strategic Deception of the General Staff) (GUSM), was formally organized in 1968, and it was the brainchild of Marshal N. V. Ogarkov. Prior to 1967, Ogarkov was the commander of the Volga Military District, historically the terminal assignment for Soviet generals who were considered less than competitive. In 1967, under Ogarkov's supervision, to impress the West with Soviet bridging capabilities, the Soviets constructed a railroad bridge in a few hours under the observation of foreign representatives. The bridge, constructed of substandard material for its light weight, supported the transit of an extremely light locomotive. Although the bridge was actually unserviceable and almost collapsed during the demonstration, the rapid construction and transit of the locomotive so impressed the foreign observers that they did not detect the deception.[46]

Ogarkov's success in this deception not only saved his career and guaranteed his promotion to the highest rank in the Red Army, it brought about the acceptance of his organization, the GUSM, as a permanent part of the Soviet General Staff. From 1968, Ogarkov served as the Chief of the Soviet SALT negotiating team, and in 1971 he was assigned to the staff of the Central Committee. In 1974 he became Deputy Minister of Defense and in 1977 Chief of the Soviet General Staff. With the exception of Mikhail S. Gorbachëv, of the Soviet Marshals and possibly the Soviet politicians, Ogarkov has the reputation for having the most outstanding personality. Although reassigned in 1968, Ogarkov never entirely gave up control of GUSM and has taken a personal interest in its work. From 1974 to 1979, the chief of GUSM was Army General (later Marshal) Sergei F. Akhromeyev.[47]

In recent years there has been a tendency among United States' intelligence services to underestimate Soviet military capabilities. This problem is partly due to self-deception by United States analysts.[48] In considering Soviet deception, however, it is essential to recognize both components of any such operation. For deception to succeed, there must be not only an expert deceiver; there must also be a gullible party who allows himself to be deceived.

Fundamentally, Soviet disarmament and arms reduction schemes derive from Lenin's admonition to disarm the bourgeoisie.[49] The Soviet interest in SALT derived in part from a Soviet need to achieve strategic parity in the public view.[50] The Soviets did not initiate SALT; however, when it became clear that the United States would continue its ABM program the Soviets grasped SALT as a means whereby they could achieve strategic parity and possibly superiority.[51]

The Soviets continued their quest for strategic superiority, and they exploited the opportunities provided by the SALT. Should a SALT agreement be signed, the Soviets could attain an appearance of parity while simultaneously modernizing their armed forces with no fear of a reaction from the United States. The prime purpose behind these Soviet machinations was to discourage the Western, especially the United States', military modernization programs.[52]

The Soviets agreed to participate in SALT four days after the United States decided to deploy an ABM system. Serious SALT began in 1969. Since the United States had unilaterally limited its own offensive weapons, the Soviets were interested initially in a defensive agreement only. There was some incentive for the Soviets to limit offensive weapons since they were spending large sums on their strategic forces.[53] By freezing offensive levels of ICBMs and permitting the increase of Soviet SLBMs, SALT was a guarantee of eventual Soviet strategic superiority when they placed MIRVs on their fourth generation missiles.[54] Although the Soviets signed the SALT agreement, they have been guilty of a number of violations.[55]

In 1974 Brezhnev introduced new concepts and a new vocabulary into the Soviet strategic rhetoric, the nature of which was that military power was secondary to security. The Soviet use of arms control to achieve strategic parity required them to shift their public emphasis away from the need to win a nuclear war. This shift began to appear in the late 1960s,[56] and it was in accord with Lenin's instructions to disarm the bourgeoisie.[57]

Initially when the Soviets promulgated the new rhetoric, there was resistance from many quarters, since the "new thinking" was a drastic departure from past Soviet pronouncements on military superiority and military policy. After Brezhnev made a few public speeches denouncing the Soviet quest for superiority, it became clear to high level Soviet officials that the official rhetoric had changed. Soviet officials now talked about parity instead of strategic superiority.[58] Recent Soviet behavior has been oriented on communicating an image of flexibility and fairness.[59]   The attempt to establish the new Soviet image was evident in the Soviet proposals for reduction of the INF in Europe in 1987.

To seize the strategic initiative, the Soviets planned thoroughly for their conference with the President of the United States at Reykjavik in October 1986. Their stated purpose was to attain an agreement on the elimination of nuclear weapons with equal security for the United States and the Soviet Union throughout the process.[60] Their plan included waiting until the last minute before inviting the United States to participate.   This Soviet manipulation served several purposes.   By waiting until the last minute, the Soviets gave the United States limited time to plan, thus conveying to the world the impression that the United States was ill prepared and unwilling to meet the Soviets. On the other side, it projected an image to the world that Gorbachëv was ready and anxious to work out an agreement on the reduction of nuclear weapons, whereas the United States was not. The lack of preparation time for the United States gave the impression that the United States was fumbling and had no clear position. It also had the effect of making Gorbachëv appear as the dominant personality at the meeting.

*   *   *   *   *   *   *   *   *   *   *   *   *   *   *   *   *   *   *

The Soviets are past masters at deception, and they work at it "scientifically" in theory and application. They plan to achieve their ultimate objective, a single world civilization in which international Communism is the only political, socio-economical, and ideological order permitted, by gaining control of the minds of non-Communists.[61] By capturing the hearts and minds of the masses, they plan to convince the masses that Marxist-Leninist socialism is the solution to the world's problems. Before they can capture the hearts and minds of the masses, the Soviets must disarm and discredit the non-Communist Western governments. The Soviets prefer to accomplish these tasks by peaceful methods, the prime component of which is deception. In their deception campaigns, the Soviets have successfully employed reflexive control with its complex methods of *maskirovka, dezinformatsiya, demonstratsiya,* and *stimulirovniya*. These methods of deception, which include the big lie, are effective since they prey on the apathy and gullibility of the West.

NOTES

1. Alexander L. George, "The 'Operational Code': A Neglected Approach to the Study of Political Leaders and Decision-Making," in *The Conduct of Soviet Foreign Policy*, ed. Erik P. Hoffmann and Frederic J. Fleron, Jr. (Chicago: Aldine Publishing Company, 1971), 181-182. Reprinted with permission of the publisher.

2. Vladimir A. Lefebvre and Victorina D. Lefebvre, *Reflexive Control: The Soviet Concept of Influencing An Adversary's Decision Making Process* (Englewood, Colorado: Science Applications, Inc., 1984), 109.

3. Lefebvre and Lefebvre, *Reflexive Control*, 4.

4. Selden E. Biggs, "Control and Soviet Military Decisionmaking," unpublished research paper, 17-18; V. V. Druzhinin and D. S. Kontorov, *Problemy Sistemologii* (Moscow: Sovetskoye Radio, 1976), 192, 193, 171.

5. Biggs, "Control and Soviet Military Decisionmaking," 20.

6. Ibid.; *Sovetskaya Voyennaya Entsiklopediya* (Moskva: Voyennizdat, 1976-1979).

7. Edward Jay Epstein, "Disinformation: Or, Why the CIA Cannot Verify an Arms-Control Agreement," *Commentary* 74 (July 1982): 21-28.

8. Ibid.

9. John Lenczowski, "Themes of Soviet Strategic Deception and Disinformation," in *Soviet Strategic Deception*, ed. Brian D. Dailey and Patrick J. Parker (Lexington, Massachusetts: D. C. Heath and Company, 1987), 57, 59, 63, 64, 66, 67, 68. Reprinted with permission of the publisher.

10. Biggs, "Control and Soviet Military Decisionmaking," 20-21.

11. Moscow World Service, 11 Nov. 1989, *FBIS Daily Report*, 13 Nov. 1989, 30; *Pravda*, 11 Nov. 1989.

12. Biggs, "Control and Soviet Military Decisionmaking," 21.

13. Lefebvre and Lefebvre, *Reflexive Control*, 33, 144.

14. Ibid., 21-25.

15. Richards J. Heuer, Jr., "Soviet Organization and Doctrine for Strategic Deception," in *Soviet Strategic Deception*, ed. Brian D. Dailey and Patrick J. Parker (Lexington, Massachusetts: D. C. Heath and Company, 1987), 37. Reprinted with permission of the publisher.

16. Ibid.

17. Ibid.

18. John J. Dziak, "Soviet Deception: The Organizational and Operational Tradition," in *Soviet Strategic Deception*, ed. Brian D. Dailey and Patrick J. Parker (Lexington, Massachusetts: D. C. Heath and Company, 1987), 7. Reprinted with permission of the publisher.

19. Natalie Grant, "Deception on a Grand Scale," *International Journal of Intelligence and Counterintelligence*, 1 (1986): 51-77.

20. Ibid.

21. Ibid.

22. Dziak, "Soviet Deception," in *Soviet Strategic Deception*, 1987), 7.

23. Ibid.

24. Epstein, "Disinformation," *Commentary* 74 (July 1982): 21-28.

25. Ibid.

26. Ibid.

27. Dziak, "Soviet Deception," in *Soviet Strategic Deception*, 8.

28. Heuer, "Soviet Organization and Doctrine for Strategic Deception," in *Soviet Strategic Deception*, 37.

29. Dziak, "Soviet Deception," in *Soviet Strategic Deception*, 8; P. A. Goluba, Yu. I. Korableva, M. I. Kuznetsova, eds., *Encyclopedia of The Great October Socialist Revolution* (Moscow: Soviet Encyclopedia Press, 1987), 148.

30. Grant, "Deception on a Grand Scale," *International Journal of Intelligence and Counterintelligence* 1 (1986): 51-77.

31. Dziak, "Soviet Deception," in *Soviet Strategic Deception*, 11.

32. Epstein, "Disinformation," *Commentary* 74 (July 1982): 21-28.

33. Dziak, "Soviet Deception," in *Soviet Strategic Deception*, 11.

34. Epstein, "Disinformation," *Commentary* 74 (July 1982): 21-28.

35. Ibid.

36. Dziak, "Soviet Deception," in *Soviet Strategic Deception*, 12.

37. Ibid., 11-12.

38. Michael Mihalka, "Soviet Strategic Deception, 1955-1981," in *Military Deception and Strategic Surprise*, ed. John Gooch and Amos Perlmutter (London: Frank Cass Company, 1982), 45.

39. Ibid., 46.

40. Ibid.

41. Epstein, "Disinformation," *Commentary* 74 (July 1982): 21-28.

42. Mihalka, "Soviet Strategic Deception, 1955-1981," in *Military Deception and Strategic Surprise*, 47.

43. Ibid., 47-48.

44. Epstein, "Disinformation," *Commentary* 74 (July 1982): 21-28.

45. Mihalka, "Soviet Strategic Deception, 1955-1981," in *Military Deception and Strategic Surprise*, 47-49; Gerard Smith, *Doubletalk: The Story of*

the First Strategic Arms Limitations Talks (Garden City, New York: Doubleday & Company, 1980), 11-12.

46. Viktor Suvorov, "GUSM: The Soviet Service of Strategic Deception," *International Defense Review*, no. 8 (August 1985): 1235-1240.

47. Ibid.; Smith, *Doubletalk*, 46, 48, 49, 181, 182, 283, 445.

48. Epstein, "Disinformation," *Commentary* 74 (July 1982): 21-28.

49. Lenin, *Selected Works* vol. 1, 743, 746.

50. Mihalka, "Soviet Strategic Deception, 1955-1981," in *Military Deception and Strategic Surprise*, 63.

51. Ibid., 65; Smith, *Doubletalk*, 19-20.

52. Mihalka, "Soviet Strategic Deception, 1955-1981," in *Military Deception and Strategic Surprise*, 70.

53. Ibid., 72.

54. Ibid., 80; United States Department of State, *SALT II Agreement*, 18 June 1979.

55. Mihalka, "Soviet Strategic Deception, 1955-1981," in *Military Deception and Strategic Surprise*, 70.

56. Ibid., 86.

57. Lenin, *Selected Works*, vol. 1, 743, 746.

58. Mihalka, "Soviet Strategic Deception, 1955-1981," in *Military Deception and Strategic Surprise*, 88.

59. David S. Yost, "The Soviet Campaign Against INF in West Germany," in *Soviet Strategic Deception*, ed. Brian D. Dailey and Patrick J. Parker (Lexington, Massachusetts: D. C. Heath and Company, 1987), 352-353. Reprinted with permission of the publisher.

60. Gorbachëv, *Perestroika*, 223.

61. Mikhail S. Gorbachëv, "The Socialist Idea and Revolutionary *Perestroika*," *Pravda*, 26 Nov. 1989, 1-3.

VII

SOVIET MILITARY STRATEGY

The Soviet Union, in the same sense that Czarist Russia was an empire, is an empire based on the quest for military security. In each case, the quest for security has required that the government secure its periphery by incorporating the borderlands as buffer areas to prevent the surprise invasion by some external enemy. Eventually, as history records, these buffer states one by one became incorporated into the motherland, an action that required the seizure of additional borderlands a little farther out, and the process continued until the country, Russia or the Soviet Union, encompassed the land mass of Eurasia.

This chronic quest for security has two major effects on the motherland. It requires the maintenance of a huge standing army to be prepared to repel any possible invading force as well as to maintain control of these peripheral areas, some of which have not been willing to serve as a buffer for the motherland. As the second effect of this system, the ever present external threat serves as a device whereby the Communist Party-state can retain control of the entire, diverse Soviet population. The Soviets have exploited the fear from without, whether it is real or imagined, to the maximum degree. Other empires which required the maintenance of a huge army were Rome and the Third Reich. Rome survived for centuries, whereas the Third Reich fell far short of the thousand year life Adolf Hitler predicted. The Soviet empire at present falls between these two. There is always a deficit of military power in an empire, and there is always an external threat merely because the empire exists.

Even today, the Soviets perceive themselves to be surrounded.[1]

Furthermore, the Soviet Union has tremendous military potential in the form of manpower, resources, and determination. The Soviets compare their military power with that of the West in terms of what they call the correlation of forces, which is not quite the same as the Western concept of the balance of power. The Soviets include more than pure military force in their calculation of the correlation of forces, since they consider economic factors and ideology.

The Soviets, like the Czars, claim that their military doctrine is defensive. The defensive argument is one of Gorbachëv's major points in the foreign policy of the "new thinking."[2] In the 1890s the Russian General Staff made a comprehensive study of the history of Russian warfare from the beginning of the Russian state. The editor pointed with pride to the country's military record and admonished the Russians to face the future with confidence. His optimism was based on the findings that between 1700 and 1870 Russia had been at war 106 years fighting thirty-eight military campaigns, thirty-six of which were offensive and two were defensive. This tabulation should dispel the Soviet claim that Russian aggression is a defensive reflex.[3]

Soviet military policy is an instrument of Soviet foreign policy. Czarist Russia and the Soviet Union have had large standing armies based on the perception of their vulnerability due to long borders and the presence of adversaries on those borders. Hence, a large percentage (twenty-five to forty percent) of the Red Army has been displaced forward near the frontier. This deployment has been the pattern from the mid-nineteenth century. The forward Soviet military forces deployed in European Russia and East Europe are in a high state of combat readiness and are highly mobile. The Western perception of the threat from these forward Soviet forces was a major cause of the Cold War. Moreover, since World War II, there has been a steady improvement of the Soviet armed forces in quantity, quality, and mobility. The Soviets justify this increase in military capability on the need for internal security in their non-Russian areas and the necessity to make an invader pay dearly. Their ground force strategy for the European continent has been to engage the enemy as far forward as possible. In so doing, they expect to use their large mass and forward displacement to compensate for a lack of quality. Since the early 1960s the Soviets have carried out a steady modernization of these forces in both conventional and nuclear capabilities.

The Soviets perceive the world balance of power as one of strategic parity between the Soviet Union and the United States. This strategic parity does not imply an equal degree of force on a one-to-one basis when comparing individual weapons and systems. It conveys the meaning of equality and parity between the Soviet Union and the United States in terms of overall power and potential and the military effectiveness of their strategic forces. The Soviets have no intention of renouncing the principle of equality, nor will they tolerate the superiority of the other side.[4] This view has prevailed in the Soviet Union since the Soviets entered the nuclear age.

On the eve of World War II, Soviet nuclear physics was as advanced if not more advanced than nuclear physics in Western countries. The story of Soviet nuclear espionage during World War II has been reported in the open press, and the spies who were apprehended were brought to justice. Even so, the Soviets tried to feign ignorance about United States' nuclear weapons development during World War II. Marshal Georgiy Zhukov wrote in his memoirs an account of the Potsdam meeting in which President Truman informed Stalin that the United States had the bomb. Stalin's apparent disinterest was a façade. As soon as Stalin, Molotov, and Zhukov arrived in their quarters following the meeting, Molotov commented: "They are trying to bid up." Laughing, Stalin replied: "Let them. I'll have to talk it over with Kurchatov today and get him to speed things up."[5] At the time, United States' nuclear experts estimated that it would take the Soviets five to ten years before they had an operational bomb. I. V. Kurchatov, the Soviet physicist in charge of developing the bomb, responded and developed the Soviet bomb, the first explosion of which was reported in September 1949.

In later years, apparently as part of their anti-Western propaganda, several Soviet marshals wrote in their memoirs that the United States' use of the bomb in 1945 against Japan was an attempt to intimidate the Soviet Union and use the bomb as a basis for world domination.[6]

The Soviet victory in the Great Patriotic War (World War II) not only rescued the Soviet Union from the onslaught of Nazism, it gave the

Soviet Union legitimacy. For the first time in its history the Soviet Union could view the sacrifices made by millions of Soviet citizens in the 1930s as having been necessary for the preservation of the motherland of Communism. For the first time, the Soviets felt that they had attained their place in the world. After the war the world recognized them as one of the two superpowers, and they have sought to maintain that status.

Stalin discounted the long-accepted principles of war, which have been acknowledged for centuries as the guiding fundamentals behind military strategy and tactics. Stalin replaced the principles of war in the Soviet military forces by his own ideas which he called the "permanently operating factors." Throughout the Stalin years, Soviet professional officers, although highly educated in the art of war and knowing the role of the principles of war, formulated Soviet strategy on the basis of Stalin's permanently operating factors; they had no choice.

The Soviets detonated their first nuclear weapon in 1949, ahead of the schedule predicted by United States' experts. Since the Soviets fought and won the Great Patriotic War with conventional forces, they continued to maintain a formidable conventional force in the post-war years. Stalin ordered his military to provide him with a nuclear arsenal, but there was some doubt that Stalin fully realized and appreciated the implications and uses of nuclear weapons.[7] Consequently, in the 1950s the Soviets considered nuclear weapons merely as a new, more powerful means of fire support.

Although the Soviets considered nuclear weapons to be nothing other than a more powerful means of fire support, in the late 1940s they began developing missiles. This program began to bear fruit in the mid-1950s, especially after the successful launching of *sputnik* in October 1957. By 1959, the Soviets considered missiles and their delivery of nuclear weapons so important that they created a new, separate branch of the armed forces, the Strategic Rocket Forces, with rank and prestige above the older, traditional services.

The Soviet armed forces comprise five services, four of which are similar to the armed forces of Western nations. The Soviet Ground Forces, the Air Force, and the Navy correspond to conventional military terminology. The Soviets have organized their Air Defense Forces as a separate service similar to the air defense organization of the German *Wehrmacht* in World War II. The Soviets created the Strategic Rocket Forces in December 1959, just at the time when they changed their military strategy from conventional warfare oriented on the European continent to global, nuclear, missile warfare.[8]

The Strategic Rocket Forces are now equipped, trained, and deployed. The troops of this very expensive arm are on permanent alert, with their combat readiness measured in seconds. The Strategic Rocket Forces constitute the main component of Soviet nuclear strategy. Considering the cost of this force and the perceived international threat, the Soviets have no intention of changing it.[9] Even though Gorbachëv has announced the reduction of conventional Soviet military forces in Europe and Asia, the Soviets have no intention of reducing the capability of their Strategic Rocket Forces. On the contrary, during the reduction of other Soviet forces, the missilemen of the Strategic Rocket Forces have increased their vigilance. The Soviets have announced that there will be no change in the combat readiness of these strategic nuclear delivery systems. Moreover, the Soviets have reiterated their "right to retaliatory action" with these forces. The Strategic Rocket Forces remain the primary component of the Soviet strategic nuclear forces, and the Soviets consider any diminution of their role to be impossible.[10] The Strategic Rocket Forces, an offensive arm, constitute the primary Soviet military threat to the United States.

In consequence of the growing importance of nuclear weapons, from 1955 to 1960, the Soviets reduced the size of their armed forces by approximately one-third; however, at the same time they greatly multiplied their firepower by the introduction of new technology.[11] In his speech of 14 January 1960 before the fourth session of the Supreme Soviet, Nikita Khrushchëv made a number of bellicose statements. He declared that in a future war no capital, no large industrial area, and no strategic target would escape attack within a few minutes. He warned that the Soviet Union could survive a surprise attack because it had sufficient weapons dispersed in multiple sites to enable the survival of an initial attack. These Soviet missiles carried both atomic and hydrogen warheads, and should the Soviet Union be attacked, it would "wipe the country or countries attacking us off the face of the earth."[12]

Khrushchëv further said that the Soviet Union would continue to maintain its lead in missiles until there was an agreement on disarmament. The emphasis was now on firepower, not on numbers of men.[13] The fundamental conditions of the country's economic and social system determine the CPSU's international strategy.[14] In the early 1960s the Soviets were experiencing rapid technological success with their missiles and nuclear weapons. With their shift in strategic emphasis to intercontinental nuclear weapons, the Soviets changed their military strategy from an orientation on the European continent to a global orientation. In consonance with the change in Soviet military strategy from a continental, conventional strategy to one of global nuclear warfare, Khrushchëv announced in his speech of 14 January 1960 a massive reduction in conventional Soviet military forces. This announcement met opposition from the Soviet military immediately. Some reductions did follow; however, the first personnel to go were the sick, the old, and the untrustworthy.[15]

With the shift in strategy to global nuclear warfare, the Soviets changed their military emphasis, much of which went to the initial period of war. The Soviets describe the initial period of a war as the interval of time during which the belligerents carry out combat operations of a strategic nature by forces which were deployed prior to first hostilities.[16] They perceive the initial period of the next war as extremely violent and destructive.[17] Being deeply impressed by the success of Hitler's *Blitzkrieg*, the Soviets adapted the *Blitzkrieg* to their own purposes by incorporating the use of nuclear weapons. The idea was to strike an enemy so violently with the initial attack that he would be unable to recover. Soviet writings about the initial phase of a war specify the necessity of achieving complete surprise in wielding the first blow. Knock the opponent completely off his feet, and he will find it very difficult if not impossible to stand and fight. The Soviets perceived the use of nuclear weapons so severe in the initial phase as to wipe small countries completely off the map. The *Blitzkrieg* fits nicely with the Soviet emphasis on the importance of the initial phase of a war.

Beginning in the 1960s, numerous Soviet military authors, writing about *Blitzkrieg* warfare, were explicit about their concept of this technique. The context of these writings is that the Soviet armed forces are equipped with nuclear carrying strategic missiles in such quantities to enable the Soviet Union to attain the strategic goals of war within a short period of time.[18] The *Blitzkrieg* consists of a simultaneous attack against the enemy's industrial base as well as his armed forces with strategic nuclear missiles.[19] Accordingly, the next war is to be short and swift moving and characterized by exceptional violence.[20]

In stressing the importance of the initial period of war, Soviet authors have defined and described in detail the Soviet concept of pre-emption. They have written that the primary task of the Soviet armed forces is to be in constant readiness to repulse a surprise attack and frustrate the strategy of the enemy.[21] The Soviets consider preemption in launching a nuclear missile strike to be the decisive mode for attaining superiority over an enemy and the seizure and retention of the initiative.[22] They define military superiority to be the unilateral capacity to prevent, by a disarming strike, unacceptable damage from an enemy's retaliatory strike.[23] Should the Soviets perceive an enemy planning to launch missiles, they would probably use this perceived intent as a pretext for preemption and launch first. Hence, the determination of enemy intent by the Soviets is highly subjective and dangerous.

Writing in 1962, Marshal Rodion Ya. Malinovskiy said that future wars might begin without the traditional threatening periods as a surprise attack by long range missiles equipped with nuclear warheads.[24] Marshal A. A. Grechko explained that in a future war there will be insufficient time to organize an adequate response. Therefore, surprise in initiating warfare has become especially important.[25]

The Soviets consider disarmament to be a political instrument just as their military policy. This view emanates from Lenin's instructions on disarming the bourgeoisie.[26] In the 1960s the military dictated the Soviet arms control policy; however, this is no longer true. Under Gorbachëv there appears to have been a change in the influence of the Soviet military, and the Soviet military has shown discomfort with *glasnost'*. Soviet military officers have much less influence than previously, but they are involved more in arms control since they determine the specifics. To be sure, the overall military influence is much less than previously, but the Soviet Union needs its military since the Soviet armed forces constitute an important factor in Soviet foreign policy. The Soviets have followed the traditional Russian practice of maintaining armed forces equal to and if possible greater than those of any other nation. Yet, the Soviets are concerned that the present technological race for military hardware will get out of hand and lead to an entirely new arms race at a higher level of technology.[27]

Although the Soviets debated reductions in military forces and in 1989 announced reductions of their conventional forces in East Europe and Asia, there was no evidence of a substantial reduction in Soviet combat capability. Furthermore, despite Soviet pronouncements, as of the fall of 1989, there was no solid evidence of a cut-back in Soviet military spending. They will watch carefully as the Western powers reduce their armed forces.

The Soviet Union maintains its armed forces at a level which makes them reliable in the protection of the Soviet people. Gorbachëv himself has said that "the CPSU Central Committee and the Central Committee Politburo are devoting unremitting attention to the country's defense capability, the combat might of the Soviet Armed forces, and to strengthening military discipline."[28]

Playing the role of peacemaker, Gorbachëv has stressed that world security cannot continue to be based on the fear of revenge - that is, deterrence. Ensuring security requires political action, and the basis must be equal security for all nations. He argues that nuclear war, the arms race, and the quest for military superiority cannot bring political gain. Thus, it is necessary to reduce military confrontation to the lowest level of strategic balance, which excludes nuclear weapons.[29] Again, this view is in consonance with Lenin's instructions to disarm the hated bourgeoisie.[30] The Soviet Union and its allies want to be relieved of the feeling of being under a threat; yet, Gorbachëv reserves the right of the Soviet Union to consider the use of nuclear weapons in retaliation and to plan accordingly so long as there is a threat of nuclear war.[31]

Soviet military doctrine and strategy are enunciated clearly in the Soviet press. In general, Soviet military publications are available in Soviet book stores, and Western visitors may purchase these books at reasonably low prices. Over the years, the Soviets have published numerous books in which the authors clearly describe in detail current Soviet strategy. The Soviets carefully select the authors of these books and they make certain that they are accurate. Publication of official Soviet military strategy usually comes from the Voroshilov General Staff Academy, the Frunze Military Academy, and the Soviet General Staff. There are, however, other Soviet governmental agencies where military thinkers work and write. For example, the Institute of Military History, a General Staff function, has been the source of military writing. Other military academies produce books which reflect official doctrine, strategy, and applications for their particular areas of interest.

Since the early 1960s, the Soviets have published books on military strategy and tactics which describe long term, official Soviet military strategy, tactics, and techniques. The most well-known work on Soviet military strategy is *Military Strategy*, three editions of which appeared in the 1960s. The general editor of *Military Strategy* was Marshal V. D. Sokolovskiy - the same Sokolovskiy who walked out of the Allied Control Commission in Berlin in 1948. The composing editor of *Military Strategy* was Major General Valentin V. Larionov, a well-known, highly competent, informed Soviet officer. The authors of *Military Strategy* were all highly competent, well educated Soviet generals with outstanding combat records.

Military Strategy was the first definitive work on Soviet military affairs to appear since the late 1920s. From time to time, some retired Soviet general will imply that Sokolovskiy's work is out of date;[32] however, to date, there appears to be nothing to replace it. It took the Soviets almost an entire decade to settle their new global nuclear strategy and modify *Military Strategy* to include the refinements. Accordingly, *Military Strategy* appeared in three editions, the first of which was published in 1962. About one year later, in 1963, the second edition was published. The appearance of a second edition of a major book on Soviet military doctrine, policy, or strategy in so short an interval indicates that the Soviets were not certain what their strategy should be. The third edition was published in 1968, at which time the Soviets apparently had worked out the details of their new strategy and incorporated refinements as a result of the "revolution in warfare."

Military Strategy deals with the Soviet intention to employ nuclear weapons in a future war; however, the authors of this volume did not ignore the possibility that conventional wars may still occur. In formulating their strategy for the use of nuclear weapons, the Soviets in this volume signalled that their strategy had undergone a dramatic, fundamental transformation from the continental, conventional strategy of World War II to global nuclear strategy. Henceforth, the Soviet Union would be a world nuclear power concentrating on plans and exercises to deliver nuclear missile strikes against targets anywhere in the world. This transformation to global nuclear strategy in the late 1950s and early 1960s has been the only fundamental change in Soviet strategy since World War II. There have been, however, strategic "refinements."

In accordance with the fundamental change in Soviet strategy to that of global nuclear war, *Military Strategy* explains the Soviet position on the importance of the initial period of a future war and stresses the value and importance of surprise, the *Blitzkrieg*, and preemption.

The third edition of *Military Strategy*, published in 1968, has been considered the definitive work on Soviet military strategy in the nuclear age. Considering the rhetoric by Gorbachëv, his three predecessors, and other high ranking Soviet officials on the renunciation of the first use of nuclear weapons, Western observers have been expecting the Soviets to publish a new document about their "new military strategy." Among some military analysts, the book published by Colonel General Makmut Akhmetovich Gareyev in 1985 under the title *M. V. Frunze: Voyennyy Teoretik (M. V. Frunze: Military Theoretician)* was the expression of the new Soviet military strategy; however, a close reading of this book in consonance with the reading of contemporary Soviet theoreticians reveals that Gareyev did not introduce anything new.

Colonel General M. M. Kir'yan and Colonel General P. A. Zhilin, both recognized Soviet military theoreticians, published books in the 1980s which indicate that Soviet military strategy has not changed. All three of these Soviet military theoreticians, in addition to enunciating the required Communist rhetoric about Marxists being peace-loving people, continue to warn that any attack on the Soviet Union or any other socialist nation will be met immediately with a massive, nuclear retaliatory attack. All three continue to emphasize the importance of the initial period of war and that a world war will be a nuclear war.

The difference is that, whereas all three discuss the importance of nuclear weapons in the initial period of a war, Gareyev and Kir'yan acknowledge the possibility that a world war can begin as a conventional war and then escalate into a world nuclear war.[33]

Following closely the third edition of *Military Strategy* was *The Offensive*, which was published in 1970. This book appears to have stood the test of time and remains an authoritative source of information on Soviet military thought. *The Offensive* was designated as recommended reading on "The Soldier's Bookshelf." *The Offensive* emphasizes surprise, the massing of large forces, and the extensive use of nuclear weapons under all conditions of visibility and weather.[34]

In the military literature of any nation, tactics is an extension of the principles of military strategy at the subordinate levels. Tactics consists of the implementing details of the larger concepts of military strategy, and tactics manuals and documents are written after the approval of major changes in strategy. Tactics follows from strategy and must conform to the strategic principles approved as national policy. This trend of thought applies to the Soviet Union as well as to any nation. *Taktika*, first published in 1966, has appeared in two subsequent editions, the second in 1984 and the third in 1987. *Taktika* has been accepted as one of the "landmark" books in the Soviet "Officer's Library" series. *Taktika* was notably different from previous Soviet books on tactics in that *Taktika* dealt with nuclear missile warfare.[35]

The third edition of *Taktika*, published in 1987, emphasizes the importance of the offensive, discusses the offensive and defensive, and teaches the employment of nuclear weapons as part of the combined arms force. The third edition of *Taktika* continues to emphasize the importance of surprise and in no way diminishes its importance. As an item of interest, Colonel General M. A. Gareyev was the official reviewer of the third edition of *Taktika*.[36]

In the 1970s, the Soviets published numerous articles on the initial period of war. One result of the intensive study of the initial period of war was a book by S. P. Ivanov published in 1974. Ivanov discussed the wars of the nineteenth and twentieth centuries with respect to the manner in which they began. He was especially careful to focus on the military theories of capitalist nations. He also discussed Soviet theories on the importance of the initial period of wars. As examples of the importance and success of armies operating efficiently during the initial period of war, Ivanov related the salient features of the German invasion of the Soviet Union in 1941 and the Soviet campaign in Manchuria against Japan in 1945.[37]

The Soviets were deeply impressed by the dramatic success of the German *Wehrmacht* during the early days of the invasion, so much so that Ivanov concluded that if the strategic initiative is lost in the initial period of a war, it is extremely difficult to regain. Based on the lessons learned from the Germans, the Soviets developed their own *Blitzkrieg* strategy, which they employed successfully against the Japanese in Manchuria in 1945. The Soviet accounts of their success in Manchuria are greatly embellished, primarily for the purpose of using this campaign as a teaching vehicle to instruct the Soviet army in how to carry out *Blitzkrieg* operations. The Soviet Army in Manchuria was facing a vastly depleted Japanese force, and as Ivanov wrote: "A number of the first campaigns showed that a *Blitzkrieg* victory could be achieved in the initial period only over a militarily and economically weak enemy ...."[38]

In the early 1960s, Soviet military writers published many articles emphasizing the importance of beginning a future war with strategic surprise. Some of these authors wrote from a defensive view point in which the Soviet Union had to be vigilant and ready to repel such an attack from the West. Others wrote that the appearance of missiles with nuclear warheads would enable the attainment of decisive goals by Soviet military forces in brief periods of time. More and more, the message came across that the *Blitzkrieg* in which overwhelming force was brought to bear on an unexpecting enemy in a short time was the method by which the Soviet Union could gain an early victory. The objective for nuclear missile strikes had to be the enemy's strategic nuclear weapons, his economic potential, and his military forces. A short, swift war fought with exceptional violence was to be the accepted Soviet method for waging war.[39]

During the 1960s, the Soviets developed their *Blitzkrieg* strategy and incorporated the employment of nuclear weapons in the initial period of war. This strategy was refined in the 1970s, and, although there have been numerous pronouncements by Soviet leaders that they have renounced the first use of nuclear weapons, the military literature at the armed forces level of execution does not reflect any renunciation of surprise, preemption, *Blitzkrieg*, or the first use of nuclear weapons.[40] At the end of October 1989, Marshal S. F. Akhromeyev wrote that the Soviets introduced a new military doctrine in 1987; however Marshal Akhromeyev's association with Soviet deception renders his comment suspect.[41] Furthermore, Akhromeyev's many public statements parrot those of Gorbachëv. In January 1990, Army General M. Moiseyev, Chief of the Soviet General Staff, said that announced Soviet changes in military doctrine have been "reflected" in their field manuals.[42] Yet, Soviet military literature available in the West does not support or reflect a change in military strategy, especially their global nuclear strategy.

Militarily, the Soviets are concerned with their security in three directions. Their major concentration of conventional forces is in East Europe, with an orientation toward the West against NATO. Over the centuries, Russia has been invaded from the west on several occasions, the most recent of which were during World War I and World War II. The devastation wrought on Russian territory was severe, and the Soviets do not want a repetition. In the Far East, the Soviets maintain a large Conventional force of combat ready troops. Soviet experience in the Far East has not been pleasant, and the Soviets remember the Russian defeat at the hands of the Japanese in 1904 and 1905. During the World War II period, the Soviets fought several engagements with the Japanese, in all of which they claimed unquestioned victory. On the Amur in 1937, at Changkufeng in 1938, at Nomonhan in 1939, and in Manchuria in 1945 they claim to have won decisive victories. Their present concentration of forces in the Far East is oriented against the Chinese. In East Europe and in Asia, the Soviets also have a considerable nuclear capability.

The third major direction for Soviet security is global, and the Soviet intercontinental, nuclear, Strategic Rocket Forces are directed against the United States. The Strategic Rocket Forces are armed with the most modern weapons and military equipment,[43] and they constitute the most immediately dangerous military threat to the United States. Soviet nuclear-tipped missiles are aimed at counterforce and counter-value targets in the United States. Countervalue targets are military units and industrial centers where war material is produced. Counter-force targets are United States' strategic missile sites which the Soviets plan to eliminate before the United States can launch missiles. To prevent a nuclear strike on the Soviet Union, the Soviets would of necessity attack these United States' missile sites with a preemptive strike. The attack of countervalue targets could be retaliatory.

Soviet preemptive strategy follows from the nature of the Strategic Rocket Forces. With Gorbachëv's announced reductions in Soviet forces in East Europe and Asia, the Soviets perceived their empire to be under a greater threat. This perception implies that the United States intends to take advantage of their reduced military capability. They have used this view as a pretext for increasing the vigilance of their Strategic Rocket Forces, the missilemen of which are on alert twenty-four hours every day. Furthermore, they express the necessity to increase the combat readiness of these nuclear delivery units. Their announced global strategy is retaliation; however, by increasing the vigilance of their missile crews, they have imposed an increased strain on their servicemen. This strain in conjunction with their retaliatory strategy creates a dangerous situation for world peace.[44] Should a Soviet missileman perceive that the United States is on the verge of launching missiles, he could easily construe this misconception to be an attack. His subsequent action could be to launch Soviet missiles under a condition of peace, thus preempting an enemy missile launch.

The Soviets allege that the existence of the Strategic Rocket Forces and their 1400 deployed strategic nuclear ICBMs convinced the United States to begin arms limitation negotiations. They further claim that the Strategic Rocket Forces possess exceptionally high combat readiness, tenacity, and the ability to implement asymmetric countermeasures in the event of a large scale ABM employment by the United States. In their view, large reductions in strategic offensive armaments would not upset the correlation of forces. The Soviets intend to retain the Strategic Rocket Forces in the leading roll as part of the Soviet strategic nuclear forces even with a fifty percent reduction in strategic weapons.[45]

Soviet military strategy since the early 1960s has been global in scope and nuclear in mode. Although Soviet military strategy is built around the use of nuclear weapons, the huge ground forces in the Far East and in East Europe have a colossal conventional capability and their existence constitutes a threat to the peace and tranquility of the free world. Yet, the Strategic Rocket Forces constitute a greater threat. The existence of these nuclear armed strategic missiles is of itself an offensive gesture.

An integral part of Soviet military strategy is the policy of supporting revolution and opposing counter-revolution anywhere in the world.[46] This policy follows from Marxist-Leninist ideology. Marshal A. A. Grechko wrote in 1971 that the Soviet armed forces are prepared to operate anywhere in the world where the Soviets perceive Party or Soviet interests at stake.[47] There has been no indication that the Soviets have renounced this policy, which propagates the spread of international Communism. Moreover, under Gorbachëv the Soviets have indicated that they will continue to support revolutions and oppose counter-revolution.

The Soviet Union has not surrendered its determination to defend its borderlands, the Soviet socialist republics, by military action should any nation or group of nations attempt to gain their release by force or intimidation. The Soviets operate on the assumption that the existence of formidable Soviet armed forces will discourage any nation or groups of nations from trying to wrest those borderlands from the Soviet Union.[48]

The Soviet Union is the organizer and the prime member of the Warsaw Pact. Under Soviet leadership and logistical support, the Warsaw Pact states have assembled, equipped, and trained the world's most formidable, conventional military force, armed, organized, and under the control of the Soviet Union. In late 1989, when Gorbachëv began making pronouncements about reducing the strength of these conventional forces, he met dissenting views. The Romanian Defense Minister, Colonel General Vasile Milea, writing in *Krasnaya Zvezda*, said that in spite of the progress toward disarmament, the defense capability of the Warsaw Pact had to be consolidated further.[49] Army General V. Lobov, Chief of Staff of the Warsaw Pact forces, pointed to the historical teaching that the Soviets must be prepared to defend the socialist motherland and that the Soviet Union cannot endure under modern military-political conditions without an army.[50] According to the Chief of the Warsaw Pact armed forces, Army General Piötr Lushev, the goal of the military doctrine of the Warsaw Pact is to prevent war.[51] This phrase is a polite way of describing deterrence.

In 1989 Marshal Sergei F. Akhromeyev acknowledged the existing possibility that war can come suddenly, and since history supports this contention, Soviet military policy insures that Soviet interests are protected. Hence, the Soviets still adhere to the policy that they must meet any and all threats from a position of strength.[52]

Gorbachëv is very clear about the combat readiness of Soviet armed forces. The Soviets are doing everything required to insure that their armed forces are up to date, reliable, and in a state of readiness at all times.[53] He has avowed that the Soviets will go to any lengths to provide the Soviet armed forces with everything they need for the defense of the Soviet Union and its allies and to make certain that they are not taken by surprise.[54] In support of this policy, the Red Army has always received a dominant share of the defense budget.

Gorbachëv, speaking at the 27th CPSU Congress, said:

The nature of today's weapons leaves no state any hope of defending itself with military-technical means alone .... Ensuring security is more and more taking the form of a political task, and it can only be solved by political means. Security can not be built forever on a fear of retribution .... Security can only be universal if one considers international relations as a whole .... It is necessary to feel that they [the US and the USSR] are equally secure because the terrors and alarms of the nuclear age give rise to unpredictability in policy and specific actions.[55]

It is possible that these soothing words are part of another Soviet deception campaign, this time on a colossal scale, designed to play on the apathetic mood of the West and destroy Western cohesion. On the other hand, it may be a realization that Lenin's principle of *kto-kogo* - who will prevail over whom - does not work, especially in the nuclear world. He may also have been expressing the realization long recognized in the West that the only logical solution to the nuclear arms race is to maintain equilibrium and work together toward strategic stability.[56] Even so, a defensive Soviet military strategy would not negate the long term Marxist-Leninist goal of a one-world, classless society.

*   *   *   *   *   *   *   *   *   *   *   *   *   *   *   *   *   *   *

In the United States in the 1950s, President Eisenhower adopted the doctrine of sufficiency in response to projections of a strategic "bomber gap."[57] From the initial days of the nuclear age, United States' strategy was based on quantitative and qualitative superiority to ensure a deterrent capability. Superiority was displaced by parity in 1964 as the United States' strategic objective. Inasmuch as the Soviets continued to improve and expand their nuclear missile capability, the United States adopted a sliding scale of comparability and in 1969 discarded parity and adopted the strategy of sufficiency. The strategy of sufficiency lasted only three years, after which it was replaced by essential equivalence.[58] In 1969, early in his first administration, President Nixon accepted the Eisenhower doctrine of sufficiency and made it the key doctrinal basis for SALT.[59] Since Marshal N. V. Ogarkov participated in these talks, the Soviets knew that the United States based SALT on the doctrine of sufficiency. Gorbachëv's "reasonable sufficiency" appears to be a parroting of United States' policy. Apparently, the Soviets believed that the United States wanted to hear the concept of sufficiency from the Soviets.

Although Soviet leaders continue to make attractive statements about peaceful Soviet intentions and their resolve not to initiate nuclear war, Soviet military doctrine continues to advocate the Soviet ability to gain victory in all forms of warfare from limited conventional war to global nuclear war. Moreover, they continue to adhere to the Clausewitz dictum that war is a continuation of politics by other means.[60] Furthermore, they formulate military strategy and tactics in implementation of this military doctrine.

Regardless of the florid rhetoric by Soviet leaders from Leonid Brezhnev to Mikhail Gorbachëv pledging that the Soviet Union will never be the first to use nuclear weapons, the bottom line remains: at the level of execution in the Soviet armed forces, the strategy and tactics of nuclear war, *Blitzkrieg*, preemption, and surprise remain. Since the early 1960s there have been no fundamental changes in Soviet military strategy at the level where the action will occur.

"Tell them what they want to believe."

NOTES

1. Sergei Fedorovich Akhromeyev, Interview, Moscow Television Service, 9 Oct 1989, *FBIS Daily Report*, 13 Oct. 1989, 95-105.

2. Gorbachëv, *CPSU Central Committee Political Report, 25 February 1986*, *FBIS Daily Report*, (Supplement), 26 Feb. 1986, 1-42; *Pravda*, 30 Oct. 1989.

3. Pipes, *Survival is Not Enough*, 38.

4. Gorbachëv, *Perestroika*, 235-237.

5. Georgiy Zhukov, *G. Zhukov: Reminiscences and Reflections*, vol. 2, trans. N. Burova, R. Daglish, P. Garb, G. Kozlov, S. Sossinsky, and M. Sydney (Moscow: Progress Publishers, 1985), 449.

6. Kirill A. Meretskov, *Serving the People*, trans. David Fidlon (Moscow: Progress Publishers, 1971), 366; Sergei M. Shtemenko, *The Soviet General Staff at War, 1941-1945*, 1941-1945, trans. Robert Daglish (Moscow: Progress Publishers, 1981), 435; Zhukov, *G. Zhukov*, vol. 2, 449.

7. Richard Pipes, "Detente: Moscow's View," in *The Conduct of Soviet Foreign Policy*, ed. Erik P. Hoffmann and Frederic J. Fleron, Jr. (New York: Aldine Publishing Company, 1971), 362. Reprinted with permission of the publisher.

8. Akhromeyev, Interview, Moscow Television Service, 9 Oct. 1989, *FBIS Daily Report*, 13 Oct. 1989, 95-105.

9. Ibid.

10. Colonel General Viktor Semenovich Rodin, Chief of the Strategic Rocket Forces Political Directorate, interview, *Sovetskaya Rossiya*, 19 Nov. 1989.

11. Nikita S. Khrushchev, *Disarmament is the Way to Strengthen Peace and Secure Friendship Between Nations* (Moscow: Gospolitizdat, 1960), 35.

12. Nikita S. Khrushchev, "Disarmament for Durable Peace and Friendship," *On Peaceful Coexistence* (Moscow: Foreign Languages Publishing House, 1961), 146.

13. Ibid.

14. Gorbachëv, *CPSU Central Committee Political Report, 25 February 1986, FBIS Daily Report,* (Supplement), 26 Feb. 1986, 1-42.

15. Penkovskiy, *The Penkovskiy Papers,* 232.

16. S. P. Ivanov and M. M. Kir'yan, "The War's Initial Period," *Soviet Military Encyclopedia,* vol. 5 (Moscow: Military Publishing House, 1978), 554-555, 558.

17. I. I. Anureyev, *Weapons for Anti-Rocket and Anti-Space Defense* (Moscow: Military Publishing House, 1971), 3-4.

18. K. Moskalenko, "The Missile Troops Guarding the Security of the Motherland," *Krasnaya Zvezda,* 13 Sept. 1961.

19. Valentin V. Larionov, "New Means of Fighting and Strategy," *Krasnaya Zvezda,* Apr. 1964.

20. Valentin V. Larionov, "New Weapons and the Duration of War," *Krasnaya Zvezda,* Mar. 1965; I. A. Grudinin, "The Time Factor in Modern War," *Kommunist Vooruzhennikh Sil,* Feb. 1966; V. D. Sokolovskiy and I. M. Cherednichenko, "On Contemporary Military Strategy," *Kommunist Vooruzhennikh Sil,* Apr. 1966.

21. G. A. Fedorov, *Marxism-Leninism on War and the Army,* 3d ed. (Moscow: Military Publishing House, 1962), 357; V. D. Sokolovskiy and I. M. Cherednichenko, "On Contemporary Military Strategy," *Kommunist Vooruzhennikh Sil,* Apr. 1966; N. V. Ogarkov, "Guarding the Conquests of Great October," *Agitator* (January 1978): 25.

22. A. A. Sidorenko, *Nostuplenie* [*The Offensive*] (Moscow: Military Publishing House, 1970), 115, 134.

23. G. A. Trofimenko, "Some Aspects of U. S. National Security Strategy," *SShA: Ekonomika, Politika, Ideologika*, no. 10 (October 1970): 15, 17, 23, 26.

24. Rodion Ya. Malinovskiy, *Vigilantly Stand Guard Over the Peace* (Moscow: Military Publishing House, 1962), 24-27.

25. A. A. Grechko, *Armed Forces of the Soviet State* (Moscow: Military Publishing House, 1975), 93.

26. Lenin, *Selected Works*, vol. 1, 743, 746.

27. Paul Kennedy, "What Gorbachëv is Up Against," *The Atlantic Monthly* (June 1987): 29-43; (c) 1987 by Paul Kennedy, as first published in *the Atlantic Monthly*, June 1987.

28. Gorbachëv, *CPSU Central Committee Political Report, 25 February 1986, FBIS Daily Report*, (Supplement), 26 Feb. 1986, 1-42.

29. Ibid.

30. Lenin, *Selected Works*, vol. 1, 743, 746.

31. Gorbachëv, *CPSU Central Committee Political Report, 25 February 1986, FBIS Daily Report*, (Supplement), 26 Feb. 1986, 1-42.

32. Mikhail Mil'shteyn, Interview, *International Herald Tribune*, 28 Aug. 1980.

33. Makhmut Akhmetovich Gareyev, *M. V. Frunze: Voyennyy Teoretik* (Moscow: Voyenizdat, 1985); M. M. Kir'yan, ed. *Voyenno-Technicheskiy Progress i Vooruzhennye Sily* (Moscow: Voyenizdat, 1982); M. M. Kir'yan, *The Element of Surprise in Offensive Operations of the Great Patriotic War* (Moscow: Military Publishing House, 1986); P. A. Zhilin, ed. *Istoriya Voeynnogo Iskusstva* (Moscow: Voyenizdat, 1986).

138 Glasnost'

34. A. A. Sidorenko, *The Offensive*, trans. US Air Force (Moscow: Military Publishing House, 1970), v-viii. The author, Colonel A. A. Sidorenko, holds a Doctor of Military Science degree and was a member of the faculty at the Frunze Military Academy. He is a well known Soviet military writer with numerous publications.

35. A. A. Sidorenko, *The Offensive*, trans. US Air Force (Moscow: Military Publishing House, 1970), vi; V. G. Reznichenko, *Taktika*, 1st ed. (Moskva: Voennoye Izdatel'stvo, 1966); V. G. Reznichenko, *Taktika*, 2d ed. (Moskva: Voennoye Izdatel'stvo, 1984); V. G. Reznichenko, *Taktika*, 3d ed. (Moskva: Voennyoe Izdatel'stvo, 1987), 2. Sidorenko was the composing editor of the 1966 edition of *Taktika* and a contributor to the 1987 edition. *Taktika* was written by a group of officers at the Frunze Military Academy.

36. V. G. Reznichenko, *Taktika*, 3d ed. (Moskva: Voeynnoye Izdatel'stvo, 1987), 11-12, 56-57, 73-74, 16-17, 18, 54.

37. S. P. Ivanov, *The Initial Period of War* (Moscow: Military Publishing House, 1974), 151-187, 245-286.

38. Ibid., 307, 308.

39. M. I. Cherednichenko, "The Initial Period of the Patriotic War," *Krasnaya Zvezda*, 30 Apr. 1961; K. Moskalenko, "The Missile Troops Guarding the Security of the Motherland," *Krasnaya Zvezda*, 13 Sept. 1961; R. Ya. Malinovskiy, *Vigilantly Stand Guard Over the Peace* (Moscow: Military Publishing House, 1962), 2-27; V. V. Larionov, "New Weapons and the Duration of War," *Krasnaya Zvezda*, Apr. 1964; V. V. Larionov, "New Weapons and the Duration of War," *Krasnaya Zvezda*, Mar. 1965; I. A. Grudinin, "The Time Factor in Modern War," *Kommunist vooruzhennikh sil*, Feb. 1966; V. D. Sokolovskiy and M. Cherednichenko, "On Contemporary Military Strategy," *Kommunist vooruzhennikh sil*, Apr. 1966;

40. For indications that the Soviets have not renounced the *Blitzkrieg*,

surprise, and preemption, see the books on military strategy and tactics by Sokolovskiy, Sidorenko, Gareyev, Zhilin, and Kir'yan cited above.

41. *Pravda*, 30 Oct. 1989. Akhromeyev succeeded Ogarkov as chief of GUSM, the deception organization of the Soviet General Staff.

42. "Interview With General M. Moiseyev, Chief of the USSR Armed Forces General Staff," *Pravda*, 21 Jan. 1990.

43. *TASS*, 15 Nov. 1989.

44. Rodin, Chief of the Strategic Rocket Forces Political Directorate, interview, *Sovetskaya Rossiya*, 19 Nov. 1989.

45. *Krasnaya Zvezda*, 17 Dec. 1989.

46. Gorbachëv, *A Time for Peace*, 158.

47. A. A. Grechko, *On Guard Over Peace and the Building of Communism* (Moscow: Military Publishing House, 1971), 90.

48. Akhromeyev, Interview on Moscow Television Service, 9 Oct. 1989, *FBIS Daily Report*, 13 Oct. 1989, 95-105.

49. *Krasnaya Zvezda*, 25 Oct. 1989.

50. *Sovetskaya Rossiya*, 18 Oct. 1989.

51. *TASS*, 28 Nov. 1989.

52. Akhromeyev, Interview on Moscow Television Service, 9 Oct. 1989, *FBIS Daily Report*, 13 Oct. 1989, 95-105.

53. Gorbachëv, *Perestroika*, 205.

54. Gorbachëv, *A Time for Peace*, 83.

55. *Pravda*, 26 February 1986.

56. Michael Mandelbaum and Strobe Talbott, "Reykjavik and Beyond," *Foreign Affairs* 65 (Winter 1986-1987): 215-235.

57. Smith, *Doubletalk*, 23.

58. John M. Collins, *U.S.-Soviet Military Balance: Concepts and Capabilities, 1960-1980* (New York: McGraw-Hill Publications Co., 1980), 128.

59. Smith, *Doubletalk*, 23-24.

60. Department of Defense, *Soviet Military Power*, 10-11.

VIII

DESPERATION

In March 1921, Vladimir I. Lenin, realizing that the new Soviet Union had a serious socio-economic problem which could not be solved under the conditions imposed by War Communism, announced the New Economic Policy (NEP) as a temporary reversion to capitalism for the purpose of rescuing the world's first Communist state from an economic catastrophe.   The NEP succeeded in bringing the new Soviet state through the trying times immediately following the Communist conquest of Russia.   In March 1985, Mikhail S. Gorbachëv inherited a similar socio-economic problem. Mikhail Gorbachëv compared the Soviet socio-economic predicament in 1985 to that in 1921, and he called upon Soviet citizens to renew their belief in Lenin and Leninist methods to revive the Soviet economy in the spirit of the NEP.   One major difference with Gorbachëv's plan was that he intended for his reforms to be permanent and irreversible.   Lenin's plan was temporary.

Lenin had problems other than those with the economy. During his tenure as leader of the new Communist state, corruption, lawlessness, inefficiency, and unrest among the nationalities were rampant. Mikhail S. Gorbachëv's problems in 1985 included many of the same problems Lenin faced in 1917. Lenin's teachings on Communist ideology and his solutions to Soviet socio-economic ills are well documented in his works, and Gorbachëv attributed the spate of Soviet problems in 1985 to a departure from Lenin's teachings.   According to Gorbachëv, the deviation from Lenin's "straight and narrow" course had an adverse effect on all sectors of Soviet society.

A discussion of all Soviet problems is beyond the scope of this work; however, the more pressing problems merit discussion. In 1985 the most evident Soviet problems concerned the Marxist-Leninist economy, which the Communists allege is superior to capitalism. The record, which does not support this superiority, is a matter of concern to the Soviet leaders. According to Gorbachëv, one of the causes of the economic stagnation was the erosion of Marxist-Leninist ideology, from which emanate laziness, a lack of discipline, inefficiency, alcoholism, and a general cultural malaise. The Soviet armed forces, which continue to absorb an inordinate percentage of the national resources, pose a dilemma in that these forces provide the security for the motherland of Communism against the "enemies of the people" - bourgeois capitalist nations. Associated problems, the same which confronted Lenin, pertained to the nationalities, crime, and corruption.

During the civil war, in the power struggle which followed Lenin's death, and from the late 1920s Soviet Communist ideology and practice were oriented to the left, a situation which remained until 1985. During this time the Soviet economy was similar to War Communism with a command method of management. Although this method may have been justified in the 1930s and during the Great Patriotic War (World War II), it prevailed in the post-war period and brought to Soviet society a system which the Soviets now say was alien to socialism. The Soviets allege that these methods constitute one of the reasons for the deplorable state of the Soviet economy.[1]

Recovering from an exceptionally low economic output emanating from the destruction of the Great Patriotic War, Soviet economic development since the war has been average. By 1950, the Soviet Gross National Product (GNP) was about eleven percent of the world wide figure; however, in the 1980s, the GNP remained at about eleven percent.[2] This lack of growth fell short of Communist expectations.

The Soviets and other Marxists boast that the success of the Soviet economic system will prove its superiority over capitalism historically. Ironically, however, in the decade from 1976 to 1985, the Soviets were sorely disappointed because the Soviet national income growth rate exceeded that of the United States by a factor of only 1.3. The Soviets were displeased with this growth rate, since the economic gap between the Soviet Union and the United States increased rather than decreased during that period.[3] The Communist economy did not appear superior to capitalism. Theoretically, the Soviet economic system is supposed to respond immediately to "socialist" corrections, and the Soviets were concerned that their economic system did not meet their expectations.

Almost all of the key indicators of Soviet economic performance declined after 1960. Although there was a short recovery period in the late 1960s, these declining trends indicate that the Soviet economy was degenerating for about thirty years. It appears certain that Soviet growth rates were deteriorating. An economy tends to proceed in cycles, and the upward trend which preceded this downward turn began in the early 1930s after Josef Stalin launched his intense industrialization and collectivization programs. The upward trend of the economic cycle continued after World War II and reached a peak in the late 1950s. After the late 1950s growth rates of key indicators continued to increase; however, for each five-year period the rates of increase decreased. A projection of the trend lines indicated that the Soviet Union would soon face a lengthy economic recession. Thus, in 1985 Gorbachëv had a major challenge if he expected to reverse the downward movement of the trend lines and meet his expectations for the next three Five Year Plans.[4] The problems were so severe that corrections would probably take much longer.

After the early 1960s the deterioration of Soviet productivity was the cause of the downward trend in Soviet economic growth rates. Furthermore, between 1976 and 1985 Soviet factor productivity turned negative, and during that period the Soviet economy was required to use larger amounts of capital, labor, raw materials, and energy to produce the same amount of GNP as formerly. Hence, this drain was the source of Gorbachëv's concern about reviving Soviet factor productivity.[5]

The causes of both the long upward economic trend of the Stalin years and the later sharp decline of the Soviet economy were systemic. In the past, prior to the Gorbachëv era, the Soviets followed what they call an extensive mode of development under which growth depends on the integration of larger amounts of cheap and abundant supplies of energy, capital, labor, and raw materials. A continued pursuit of this policy will have a degenerative effect on the economy, since these natural resources will eventually be used up. Soviet political leaders and economists recognized the necessity to change the Soviet economy to an intensive mode of development whereby growth is a result of reducing the amount of input per unit of output by the introduction of new technology, new labor skills, and new managerial systems. The intensive mode of development incorporates the use of incentives for technological advance and penalties for no advance. Under the intensive system, there is a conservation and some regeneration of resources. Under the extensive mode of development, new technology is penalized for the sake of immediate output.[6]

A long upward trend in an economy takes place when industry uses plentiful low cost resources to produce an ever increasing output. The cycle reaches its peak when the depletion of resources forces the costs to rise. The result is not only an increase of production costs, but a reduction of output in some sectors. Eventually the continued accelerated use of resources will lead to a long economic recession. The correction of the downward trend requires a reduction in the amount of input required per unit of output or the acquisition of plentiful new supplies of adequate resources.[7]

Stalin's economic system exacerbated the negative aspects of the extensive mode of development. Under Stalin's system, the Soviets made three major changes in the traditional Russian economy: 1. an extensive organization of their resources to achieve maximum output immediately; 2. a diversion of resources from agriculture and consumer goods to heavy industry; 3. centralized planning and management to supervise the diversion of resources through forced collectivization, to create higher levels of labor productivity at low levels of personal consumption, and to ensure efficiency and meet assigned goals by purging corrupt or inefficient managers. The result was, indeed, a short term increase in the output of the Soviet economy; however, the Soviets achieved the increase at the expense of accelerating the decline of long-term growth.[8]

The Soviet economic system has not permitted those features of capitalism which serve as self-regulating mechanisms and devices for purging the system of inefficiency. Such capitalist features include stopping production during changeover periods for modernization, bankruptcy, forced unemployment during slack periods, and domestic and foreign competition. On the other hand, central planning and administration insulated the Soviet economy from the pressures for efficiency and quality that are characteristic of a free market economy.[9]

Under the extensive mode of development, the attainment of maximum short-term output requires a more rapid consumption of raw materials, energy, capital, and labor. Since the Soviets restricted the modernization of their industry, they did not compensate by improved efficiency for the rate of resource depletion. The ensuing effect was a marked rise in the costs of resources per unit of output. Concomitantly, the failure to make technological improvements created a Soviet work force characterized by underemployment, lack of skills, lack of incentive, and an inordinate degree of manual labor in lieu of mechanization.[10]

The Stalinist economic system also created a long term negative pressure on economic performance. Stalin's forced collectivization of agriculture in the 1930s had a demoralizing effect on labor, which caused low productivity among agricultural workers and a slow technological improvement in the agricultural sector. By the mid-1950s poor agricultural performance served as a major impediment to the entire Soviet economy. Even though Soviet leaders took emergency measures in the form of huge resource allocations and the retention of more workers in agriculture, Soviet agriculture experienced repeated recessions and a failure to increase production beyond its historical plateau.[11] To complicate matters more, between 1962 and 1987, there was gross mismanagement in the use of agricultural land.[12]

The continued diversion of resources from consumer goods to heavy industry caused an increasing demoralization of the workers, which became worse in the 1970s with increasing alcoholism, absenteeism, abortions, infant mortality, and a general decline in public health. The paucity of consumer goods forced the collection of large personal savings which tended to reduce the efficacy of monetary awards and added fuel to the growing black market.[13] In 1989 the Soviets were concerned about the large accumulation of savings, since it offset the value of the ruble as a medium of exchange and reduced further the effect of monetary incentives for improved efficiency.

In time, Soviet resources became scarce and more expensive. Managers sought solutions to the problem by increasing the manpower in the production process and paying bonuses for extra effort. When these measures did not succeed, managers resorted to falsification of reports. These questionable practices had a deleterious effect on labor, management, and consumers. The reluctance to discard the extensive mode of economic development created a situation which was leading rapidly to economic disaster.[14]

Rather than modernize their industry by converting to an intensive mode of production using new equipment and high technology, the Soviets replaced worn out, obsolete equipment with new obsolete equipment. Funds for this replacement came from increased sales of oil, gas, and raw materials on the world market. Since these funds did not go into the modernization of Soviet industry, the situation remained the same except that more capital was being squandered on a deteriorating economy. The economic stagnation, poor attitudes, and declining growth rates had a negative effect on the Soviet people, who became more inefficient and continued to produce goods of poor quality.[15]

In the 1970s difficulties in the Soviet economy began to increase, and the rates of economic growth diminished markedly. Tasks for developing the economy set forth in the CPSU Program were not fulfilled, even the lower targets of the Ninth and Tenth Five-Year Plans. Furthermore, it was impossible to fulfill the Soviet social program for those years. Backwardness was permitted in science and education, health care, culture, and everyday public services. The Soviets did not make a timely evaluation of the negative change in the economic situation nor did they recognize the urgency for the transfer of the economy from extensive methods to intensive methods of development and the application of new scientific-technological methods to the national economy. Because of inertia, the economy continued to develop on an extensive basis to a significant degree and became oriented toward bringing additional labor and material resources into production. Consequently, the rates of growth of labor productivity and some efficiency indicators fell seriously. Attempts to correct the situation by new construction exacerbated the problem.[16]

Soviet managers permitted a decline in machine building, in the petroleum and coal industries, in electronics, ferrous metallurgy, and chemicals, as well as in capital construction. These negative processes emerged in the 1970s and continued in the early 1980s. The conversion from an extensive to an intensive mode of development would not be simple for the Soviet economy, but would require a great deal of effort, time, and dedication by workers and managers.[17]

The large growth in industrial output between 1950 and the mid-1970s was due to an increase in the labor force, not an increase in efficiency. After the early 1970s the Soviet Union imported millions of tons of grain each year for food, and the standard of living began to fall following several years of improvement. Agriculture used almost thirty percent of the state investment and employed twenty percent of the labor force. This means that the Soviets allocated about $78 billion annually to agriculture to maintain their standard of living. Furthermore, they allocated an additional $50 billion for food subsidies to keep the people happy. In the Soviet Union there were increasing labor and energy shortages and an excess of bureaucratic planning. The cost of extracting oil increased seventy percent in the period from 1976 to 1985. In industry, high technology is essential if the Soviets expect to compete on the international market, much less increase their industrial output with a corresponding reduction in the amount of input.[18]

Complicating the need to modernize their industry, the Soviets have a problem with their currency. The Soviets claim that shortly after the revolution, they made the ruble hard currency. During the NEP, however, they introduced a convertible currency which drove the older money out of circulation within a three year period. Some seventy years later, the Soviet Union had not achieved a currency which could be used as a medium of exchange on the international market. Soviet domestic prices showed no correlation with world prices. Another associated problem was the Soviet policy of paying subsidies in hard currency to *kolkhozes* and *sovkhozes* for grain when they exceeded their quotas. The Soviets recognized that they could not buy high technology from Western countries unless they could pay for these products in hard rubles.[19] Accordingly, they needed hard currency for foreign trade, not to pay internal subsidies.

The first step in solving any problem, no matter how great or small, is the identification of the problem. The Soviets recognized their problem, probably from its inception in the early 1960s. The basic problem with the Soviet economy was the extensive mode of economic development inaugurated during the Stalinist years. Under Gorbachëv's leadership, the Soviets are planning for and seeking the means for transforming the Soviet economy to one of intensive development, and they hope to make progress on this project in the Thirteenth Five Year Plan.[20] As recently, however, as February 1990 the Soviets considered their economy to be in a critical condition.[21]

When Gorbachëv became General Secretary in March 1985, the Soviet economy was in such dire straits that the Soviets could not easily reverse the situation. The Soviets believed that an acceleration of socio-economic development would solve the economic problems and make a marked contribution to strengthening world socialism. Accordingly, in 1985 under Gorbachëv's leadership the Soviets attempted to accelerate their socio-economic development. Gorbachëv's target date for doubling the Soviet GNP was the year 2000.[22] Gorbachëv at once began an intensive psychological program to change the mind set of Soviet citizens and thereby motivate them to make a massive effort to reverse the declining trend in the national economy. The attempt to change Soviet attitudes was a colossal undertaking and slow to be effective.[23] The Soviet socio-economic situation was so bad that even four and one-half years into Gorbachëv's tenure the economy continued to deteriorate. Gorbachëv attributed the problem to a decline in labor and managerial discipline, inter-ethnic conflict, and strikes, some of the very ailments which he was trying desperately to heal.[24]

Historically, the Soviet Union maintains the largest conventional armed force in the world. Although the Soviets have incorporated the use of nuclear weapons in their continental military strategy and have relied on nuclear weapons one hundred percent for their global strategy, the cost of their conventional forces is much higher than the cost of nuclear forces. Nuclear weapons are comparatively cheap weapons. Hence, for the economically desperate Soviet Union a major reduction of conventional forces, especially in East Europe among the Warsaw Pact forces, would constitute a major economic savings.[25] Yet at the same time, these forces are so large that a sizeable reduction in strength would not reduce the combat capabilities of Warsaw Pact forces or the Red Army and would be invaluable politically as well.

The Soviet Union created its defense potential over a period of several decades with no regard for cost and expense. In supporting this massive armed force, the Soviet people denied themselves many necessities and made numerous personal sacrifices.[26] Hence, a drastic reduction of this military capability will not be easy.

In the Soviet Union the armed forces have excellent, modern, sophisticated equipment. The heavy industry devoted to the fabrication of military supplies, hardware, and equipment is by far superior to the heavy industry which supports the remainder of the Soviet economy. The favored position enjoyed by the Soviet armed forces constitutes one of the major drains for Soviet resources. The military siphons off the best resources in terms of raw materials and scientific manpower, and the technology supporting the modernization and maintenance of Soviet weapons is as good as that in any Western country. Gorbachëv and his cohorts recognized that military favoritism was ruining Soviet morale and dragging the entire Soviet Union to the brink of economic ruin. According to Marshal Sergei F. Akhromeyev, the Soviet economic concentration on their armed forces brought the nation to an economic impasse in which military expenditures choked the economy. The expenditures on the maintenance of their armed forces became an insupportable burden for the Soviet economy. In 1989 the nine percent [which the Soviets admit] of the Soviet GNP devoted to the armed forces exceeded that of any developed country in the world.[27]

Under Gorbachëv's leadership, the anticipated acceleration of Soviet economy development and the accompanying accelerated social development dictated that the Soviets had to bring military spending and productive spending into balance.[28] There appears, however, to be a problem associated with reducing the size of the armed forces and the defense budget. Marshal Akhromeyev, in a interview with a *TASS* correspondent regarding the Soviet budget for 1990, said that the reduction of the defense budget would have to be resisted. He acknowledged that a reduction in military expenditures would help resolve the problems with the production of consumer goods. Akhromeyev pointed to the numerous problems and shortcomings in the armed forces but admitted that there were even more serious problems with the Soviet national economy.[29] This is the same Marshal Sergei F. Akhromeyev who in

1985 proclaimed the evils of nuclear warfare.[30] Nevertheless, the Soviets did not want to reduce their military spending, especially that part of the defense budget that pays for research and development. The Supreme Soviet, however, has the final word on budget allocations.[31]

Following his peace-loving rhetoric, in 1989 Gorbachëv announced the reduction in force of the Soviet armed forces in certain areas; however, the size of the Soviet armed forces was so great that drastic reductions in numbers would not have a deleterious effect on the combat operational capability of the Red Army. Accompanying these announcements the Soviets talked about improving the quality of training and combat efficiency. This "better for less" program would ensure the continuing combat capability of Soviet forces. This quest for improvement means that the West can expect no decrease in Soviet strategic combat capability as a result of any Soviet force reduction. Furthermore, there is an uneasiness in the Soviet Union over what the Soviets consider to be an excessive reduction of their armed forces.[32]

The socio-economic disorder that has plagued the Soviet Union created personnel problems in the Soviet armed forces. The Soviet press, in the spirit of *glasnost'*, published numerous stories about the difficulties experienced by Soviet military personnel. These difficulties appear to have affected servicemen transferring to the reserves as well as veterans of the war in Afghanistan.[33] In the reduction of military forces announced by Gorbachëv, these problems with former servicemen will probably increase.

Although Gorbachëv has referred to Communists as Bolsheviks, there are no more Old Bolsheviks such as those who brought Lenin to power in 1917. To some Party members, Marxist-Leninist ideology lost its luster during the period of stagnation, and among many Party members there appears to be a growing disbelief in Communism. This growing disbelief is logical considering the failing Soviet economy and the number of times the Soviets have rewritten the history of the Communist Party.[34]

In the sphere of ideology, Gorbachëv had good reason to be concerned. In public, Soviet authorities praised the Party and Communism, but in their private lives they displayed a degree of corruption and moral degeneration that was deplorable. They would lie, deceive, scheme against each other, intrigue, inform, and in general do their utmost to further their own ambitions. There was a feeling among some Soviets that the ideals for which their ancestors fought were nothing more than bluff and deceit.[35] The Communist "ideals" constitute one device Marxists have traditionally used to instill Party discipline and control the masses. The absence of morality, especially among high ranking army officers, was one of the evils which Gorbachëv tried to fight by a renewal of Marxist-Leninist ideology.

One of the problems associated with the overall stagnation of Soviet society was a laxness by Party members in teaching Marxist-Leninist ideology. This laxness can be attributed in part to an ignorance on the part of Party secretaries, committees, and bureaus of proper educational methods. In 1985 they did not know how to organize the education of the people in Marxist-Leninist ideology.[36] Gorbachëv acknowledged that the Leninist approach and the Leninist understanding had not been followed closely during the years since Lenin.[37] This lapse was important because, in the final analysis, the problem of ideology is a struggle for the hearts and minds of the Soviet people as well as the hearts and minds of all people subjected to Communist influence.[38]

Gorbachëv faced ideological problems in the military sphere. For example, in the Moscow Military District in 1989, there was a growing pacifist sentiment among young men of draft age, many of whom said they would not like to serve in the Soviet armed forces.[39] This discontent appeared to be another area in which the development of the new Soviet man had not succeeded.

Associated with the stagnation of Soviet society, and especially the stagnation of the economy, were a plethora of social problems, among which were weak law enforcement and corruption in office.[40] Other problems included a high infant mortality rate[41] and a rising crime rate.[42] In 1989, the Soviet news services continued to report a problem with organized crime.[43] *TASS* reported in October 1989 that eighty percent of KGB personnel in all operational units were engaged in fighting organized crime in the Soviet Union.[44] There was also a major problem with unorganized crime, much of which was related to alcohol or drug abuse.[45] The Soviet Minister of the Interior, Vasiliy Trushin, reported to the Supreme Soviet on 27 October 1989, four and one-half years into Gorbachëv's *glasnost'*, that the rate of growth of crime in the Soviet Union was not being reduced. One of the reasons for this increase in crime, according to Trushin, was the lack of sufficient law enforcement personnel and equipment.[46]

To cope with many of the social problems and to deal with the difficulties arising from the increase in crime, the Ministry of Internal Affairs (MVD) announced in October 1989 that it would increase the size of its troop strength. The appropriations for these troops were to increase from one hundred to two hundred percent.[47]

In the Soviet Union alcoholism increased at an alarming rate beginning in the 1960s. The problem became so serious that Gorbachëv expressed concern that it threatened the future of the Soviet Union. Efforts to restrict the sale of alcoholic beverages were met with an increase in the manufacture of illicit alcohol[48] and a concomitant increase in the import of sugar, adding to the problem with international trade.[49]

In spite of the Marxist-Leninist belief in atheism and the Soviet attempt to discourage religion in the Soviet Union, in 1989 there were about seven million Soviet citizens who professed faith in Jesus Christ.[50] In the past the Soviets have paid lip service to religious freedom but at the same time discouraged religion by giving it labels such as a belief in superstition and myth and attributing religious faith to ignorance. Nevertheless, from time to time Soviet citizens become disillusioned with the Soviet system and come to the realization that there is more to life than a materialistic explanation for the universe, man, and physical phenomena.[51] In addition to the millions of Christians in the Soviet Union, the atheistic Soviets are confronted with millions of Muslims whose religious beliefs are as strong as those of Christians.

Gorbachëv continued to emphasize the international character of the Soviet Union in which many different nationalities are alleged to be united in one country where nationalist narrow mindedness and chauvinism, parochialism, Zionism, and anti-Semitism have no place. He boasted that in the Russian language his multi-ethnic country has a common means of communication. He tried to project an image of the Soviet Union as a country in which many nations belong to one big international family, a union and fraternity of free nations in a free country.[52] Although the Bolsheviks placed the label "republic" on the first Communist state, it did not fit the Western understanding of that term.

Indeed, the openness signified by *glasnost'* has exposed problems with the concept that the Soviet Union is a large international family in which everyone communicates in the Russian language. In 1989 daily news releases were filled with stories of unrest and a desire for change, and there was a plethora of problems related to the nationalities. There was concern in the Soviet Union over the internal migration of certain minorities, many of whom were educated specialists.[53] In 1989, the Soviets continued to have problems in Armenia and Azerbaijan.[54] In early 1990 unrest in these two areas of the Caucasus broke out into open warfare. To restore order and stop the killing of Soviet citizens, Gorbachëv declared a state of emergency and ordered Red Army troops into these areas on 20 January 1990.[55] There were reports from the Soviet Union that Latvia wanted to secede from the Soviet Union,[56] and the people in Latvia introduced legislation in the Latvian Supreme Soviet to guarantee the sovereignty of their republic.[57] Exacerbating the problem, reports from the Soviet Baltic republics showed that attacks on the Soviet armed forces were becoming more intense.[58]

In the Ukraine, some of the people were reported to be nostalgic about former times under a different system and a different ideology. The Soviets tried to pass these reports off as the ravings of a few disgruntled people who were ignorant of history.[59] In the Ukraine, there was opposition to Russian being the state language and a desire to adopt the Ukrainian language as the official state tongue.[60] *Glasnost'* encouraged widespread criticism of Soviet institutions, a condition which the Soviets did not like. The Soviets tried to counter this criticism by carefully written articles in which they labeled their critics as irresponsible, ignorant, under foreign influence, or by some other negative label. The official effort was to smear the critics with "anti-Soviet paint."[61]

In 1989, the list of nationality problems grew daily. In Moldavia, the people continued to clamor for recognition as an ethnic group. They objected to the Soviet decision to eliminate the space for nationality from passports, and they objected to the elimination of the Moldavian language from public life.[62]   In Uzbekistan, there was a movement to make the Uzbek language the state language.[63]   In Byelorussia the people wanted the free development of a national language.[64]

The Soviets perceived the growing wave of inter-ethnic conflict as a legacy from the period of stagnation.[65]   The problem was partially due to the forced redistribution of ethnic groups from one geographical area to another under Stalin.[66]   The nationality problems which the Soviets experienced represent a great disappointment in the failure of Marxist internationalism, especially within the Soviet Union itself.   Accordingly, one of Gorbachëv's goals was to harmonize inter-ethnic relations.[67]

Gorbachëv received great international publicity for his reforms, but *glasnost'* could get out of control if the Soviets relax too much.   For example, a report from Belgrade in October 1989 announced that the Constitutional Democratic Party (Cadets), which Lenin outlawed in 1921, was being reformed in Moscow.   The report stated that ten delegates attended the Founders Congress.[68]   This small number of delegates indicates an innocuous element of dissent; however, it was an open expression of disagreement with the Soviet one-party system.   In November 1989 Gorbachëv said that the "difficult tasks of *perestroika* dictate the expediency of retaining the one party system" in the Soviet Union.[69]   Yet, on 5 February 1990 Gorbachëv proposed political pluralism.[70]

In October 1989 the Soviets released their socio-economic figures for the first nine months of 1989.[71]   In January 1990, they released the economic data for the entire year.[72]   These statistics indicate that the corrective measures employed under *perestroika* did not take effect to the degree that the Soviets anticipated.   This deterioration underlined Gorbachëv's contention that the Brezhnev era was indeed a period of stagnation which the Soviets could not easily overcome.   The Soviet economic ills were too severe to permit an early, short term correction. The problems appear to be identical with those identified by Gorbachëv in the early days of his tenure as Party General Secretary.   Gorbachëv continued to attribute the problems to strikes, ethnic conflicts, a reduction in discipline, and poor management.   The difficulty was that the corrective measures were not effective.[73]

* * * * * * * * * * * * * * * * * * *

The failure of the Soviet economy has been a major source of embarrassment to the Soviets. To compound the problem, the low quality of their products did not attract the international markets which are essential to the establishment of a favorable balance of trade and the commensurate convertible currency and foreign credits with which to purchase much needed technological industrial equipment.

On 11 March 1985 when Mikhail S. Gorbachëv became General Secretary of the CPSU, he was in the unenviable position of being the front man for a major reconstruction of the Soviet socio-economic system, including a rededication to Marxist-Leninist ideology. According to the Soviets, their problems were due to the departure from Marxist-Leninist ideology after Lenin's death. The totalitarian rule of Josef Stalin has received credit for much of this departure from Lenin's "straight and narrow" path; however, Nikita S. Khrushchëv and Leonid I. Brezhnev have received their share of the blame for the numerous problems which plague the Soviet Union. Although Gorbachëv would not admit that the situation in 1985 was "desperate," in 1989 he repeatedly admitted the "critical" state of the Soviet socio-economic system.[74]

"Tell them what they want to believe."

NOTES

1. *Pravda*, 9 Oct. 1989.

2. Zbigniew Brzezinski, "The Soviet Union: World Power of a New Type," in *The Soviet Union in the 1980s*, ed. Erik P. Hoffmann (New York: The Academy of Political Science, 1984), 148-159. Reprinted with permission of the publisher.

3. Ye. Primakov, "New Philosophy of Foreign Policy," *Pravda*, 9 Jul. 1987.

4. Reprinted with permission from Crane Russak, Richard Cohen and Peter A. Wilson, "Superpowers in Decline? Economic Performance and National Security," *Comparative Strategy*, 7 (1988): 99-132.

5. Ibid.

6. Ibid.

7. Ibid.

8. Ibid.

9. Ibid.

10. Ibid.

11. Ibid.

12. Nikolay Ivanovich Ryzhkov, speech, Moscow Domestic Service, 2 Oct. 1989, *FBIS Daily Report*, 3 Oct. 1989, 48-51.

13. Cohen and Wilson, "Superpowers in Decline?," *Comparative Strategy*, 7 (1988): 99-132.

14. Gorbachëv, *Perestroika*, 6.

15. Ibid., 6-7.

16. Gorbachëv, *CPSU Central Committee Political Report, 25 February 1986, FBIS Daily Report*, (Supplement), 26 Feb. 1986, 1-42.

17. Ibid.

18. Kennedy, "What Gorbachëv Is Up Against," *The Atlantic Monthly* (June 1987): 29-43.

19. N. Petrakov, "To Restore the Erstwhile Glory of the Ruble," Iterview by N. Zhelnorova, *Argumenty I Fakty*, no. 39 (30 September - 6 October 1989): 5-6.

20. Gorbachëv, *Perestroika*, 262; Mikhail S. Gorbachëv, "Concluding Remarks," *Pravda*, 6 Nov. 1989; Mikhail S. Gorbachëv, Moscow Television Service, 12 Dec. 1989, *FBIS Daily Report*, 13 Dec. 1989, 51-55.

21. *Krasnaya Zvezda*, 27 Oct. 1989; Gorbachëv, "Report at the CPSU Central Committee Plenum 5 February 1990," *Pravda*, 6 Feb. 1990.

22. Gorbachëv, *CPSU Central Committee Political Report, 25 February 1986, FBIS Daily Report*, (Supplement), 26 Feb. 1986, 1-42.

23. *TASS*, 28 Oct. 1989.

24. Ibid.

25. Akhromeyev, Interview, Moscow Television Service, 9 Oct. 1989, *FBIS Daily Report*, 13 Oct. 1989, 95-105.

26. *Pravda*, 12 Oct. 1989.

27. Akhromeyev, Interview, Moscow Television Service, 9 Oct. 1989, *FBIS Daily Report*, 13 Oct. 1989, 95-105.

28. Ye. Primakov, "New Philosophy of Foreign Policy," *Pravda*, 9 Jul. 1987.

29. "Interview with Marshal Sergei F. Akhromeyev," *Krasnaya Zvezda*, 6 Jul. 1987.

30.   Sergei F. Akhromeyev, "The Great Victory and Its Lessons," *Izvestiya*, 7 May 1985.

31.   "Interview with Marshal Sergei F. Akhromeyev," *Krasnaya Zvezda*, 6 Oct. 1989.

32.   *Krasnaya Zvezda*, 27 Oct. 1989.

33.   *Izvestiya*, 25 Oct. 1989.

34.   Penkovskiy, *The Penkovskiy Papers*, 203, 204; *Pravda*, 4 Nov. 1989.

35.   Ibid., 55, 56.

36.   *Krasnaya Zvezda*, 7 Oct. 1989.

37.   *Pravda*, 30 Oct. 1989.

38.   *Pravda*, 24 Oct. 1989.

39.   *Krasnaya Zvezda*, 30 Sept. 1989.

40.   Gorbachëv, *Perestroika*, 93.

41.   Moscow Television Service, 14 Oct. 1989, *FBIS Daily Report*, 16 Oct. 1989, 71.

42.   Moscow Television Service, 10 Oct. 1989, *FBIS Daily Report*, 16 Oct. 1989, 71-72.

43.   *Krasnaya Zvezda*, 4 Oct. 1989; *Pravda*, 24 Sept. 1989.

44.   *TASS*, 30 Oct. 1989.

45.   L. G. Sizov, Interview, Moscow Television Service, 18 Sept. 1989, *FBIS Daily Report*, 2 Oct. 1989, 92-93; *Izvestiya*, 11 Oct. 1989.

46.   Moscow Domestic Service, 27 Oct. 1989, *FBIS Daily Report*, 30 Oct. 1989, 58-59; *TASS*, 27 Oct. 1989.

47.   *Izvestiya*, Oct. 1989.

48. Gorbachëv, *Perestroika*, 88.

49. *Die Welt*, 31 Oct. 1989; *Argumenty I Fakty*, 21-27 Oct. 1989, 1-3.

50. News cast, WVTF, FM 89, Roanoke, Virginia, 30 Nov. 1989.

51. Penkovskiy, *Penkovskiy Papers*, 172, 355-358.

52. Gorbachëv, *Perestroika*, 106-107; Mikhail S. Gorbachëv, "The Socialist Idea and Revolutionary *Perestroika*," *Pravda*, 26 Nov. 1989, 1-3.

53. *Sovetskaya Rossiya*, 22 Sept. 1989.

54. *TASS*, 10 Oct. 1989.

55. *Trud*, 27 Jan. 1990.

56. *TASS*, 9 Oct. 1989; *TASS*, 12 Oct. 1989.

57. *Izvestiya*, 23 Oct. 1989.

58. *Krasnaya Zvezda*, 17 Oct. 1989; *Krasnaya Zvezda*, 19 Sept. 1989.

59. *Pravda*, 10 Oct. 1989.

60. *Literaturna Ukraina*, 12 Oct. 1989.

61. *Pravda*, 7 Oct. 1989.

62. *Izvestiya*, 6 Oct. 1989.

63. Moscow Television Service, 20 Oct. 1989, *FBIS Daily Report*, 23 Oct. 1989, 74-75; *TASS*, 21 Oct. 1989; *Krasnaya Zvezda*, 22 Oct. 1989.

64. *TASS*, 20 Oct. 1989.

65. *Pravda*, 27 Sept. 1989.

66. Ibid.

67. Gorbachëv, "Holiday Reception in the Kremlin," *Pravda*, 8 Nov. 1989.

68. *Tanjug*, 26 Oct. 1989.

69. Gorbachëv, "The Socialist Idea and Revolutionary *Perestroika*," *Pravda*, 26 Nov. 1989, 1-3.

70. Gorbachëv, "Report at the CPSU Central Committee Plenum 5 February 1990," *Pravda*, 6 Feb. 1990.

71. "Jan-Sep 1989 Socio-Economic Figures Released," *Izvestiya*, 29 Oct. 1989, 1-3.

72. *Pravda*, 28 Jan. 1990.

73. "Jan-Sep 1989 Socio-Economic Figures Released," *Izvestiya*, 29 Oct. 1989, 1-3; *Pravda*, 28 Jan. 1990; Gorbachëv, "Report at the CPSU Central Committee Plenum 5 February 1990," *Pravda*, 6 Feb. 1990.

74. Gorbachëv, "Holiday Reception in the Kremlin," *Pravda*, 8 Nov. 1989.

IX

THE NEW THINKING

The Soviets began developing what Gorbachëv calls the "new thinking" as early as the 1960s and possibly sooner, but the development of a new rhetoric was not without obstacles. This course of action was necessary to enable the Soviets to find a solution to some of the problems they were suffering. A reformulation of the Soviet rhetoric required a major departure from tradition, and it met resistance. During the decade of the 1960s, it became apparent to the Soviets that they needed to change their approach to the West, especially to the United States, since the historic Soviet *modus operandi* was not succeeding. By the mid-1960s, it had become apparent that the Soviet economy needed a major overhaul. The Stalinist economic system was no longer working, and it was having a deleterious effect on the entire country. By the 1960s, the Soviet military machine had acquired a sufficient degree of modernization to be a challenge to the West, and with the publication of the third edition of *Military Strategy* in 1968, the Soviets believed that they had finally formulated a workable military strategy that would maintain their position in the world as a major power.

To solve their problems, the Soviets needed to establish better relations with the West, the purpose of which was to provide a "breathing space" whereby the Soviets could correct their many problems. A major objective of the breathing space was a reduction of Western armed forces, the accomplishment of which would permit the Soviet Union to allocate more of its resources to areas of the economy other than the military. Besides, the disarmament of the bourgeois, capitalist West would be in accord with the teachings of V. I. Lenin.[1]

The Soviets had major foreign policy problems in several other areas. The problems in Hungary in 1956 left a lingering distrust of anything Soviet in East Europe. The Soviets suffered a setback in the failure of Khrushchëv's Cuban missile deployment in 1962. There was a major breach with China in 1962 and 1963. The year 1963 witnessed a Franco-German treaty, a major foreign policy set-back for the Soviets, who had tried to break apart the Western cohesion associated with the rearmament of West Germany. The Soviet invasion of Czechoslovakia in August 1968 did more damage to Soviet international prestige.

In developing the "new thinking," certain Soviet intellectuals, probably members of the Central Committee, had to convince their colleagues of the necessity for such a long range project and then formulate and carry out a detailed plan for achieving their objectives. The main effort of the early Soviet "new thinkers" was to determine what the West, in particular the United States, wanted to hear from Soviet sources. Then, they had to convince the majority of the Central Committee and the Politburo of the feasibility of such a plan.[2]

The "new thinkers" began their project by studying the United States and by having a few Soviet authors introduce bits and pieces of this "new thinking" to test its reception at home and abroad. To learn about the United States, the Soviets reactivated and organized special institutes, what the West calls think tanks, specifically for that purpose. To test the waters, they published books and articles with samples of the "new thinking." They also selected a few individuals to pave the way for a new approach to the West. After successful testing, the Soviet leaders were convinced that their plan would succeed and they brought forth their carefully trained and groomed salesman, Mikhail S. Gorbachëv.

The Soviets began "testing the waters" of a new rhetoric as early as 1959 when Ye. I. Rybkin wrote a book in which he renounced the policy of preemption and declared that the Soviet Union would never start a war.[3] In 1963, Major General Valentin V. Larionov was the co-author of an article in which he declared that the Soviet Union would not be the first to use nuclear weapons.[4]

In 1964, a minor official in the Foreign Ministry, N. M. Nikol'skiy, wrote a book in which he challenged Lenin's endorsement of the Clausewitz dictum that war is a continuation of politics by other means. In so doing, he called upon Hegel's third law of the dialectic to demonstrate the idea that nuclear war had negated itself.[5] The law of the negation of the negation was echoed in 1965 by Major General N. Talentsky.[6] Nikol'skiy wrote books in 1970 and 1978 with the same theme as his book on negation in 1964.[7] With the publication of the second book, there appeared a series of vehement articles countering Nikol'skiy's arguments.[8] In the 1970s, however, the law of the negation of the negation began to appear in the speeches and articles of other Soviet writers and some leaders.[9] These arguments for and against the law of the negation of the negation were published before Mikhail S. Gorbachëv became General Secretary of the CPSU.

There were, however, Soviet authors and officials who did not agree that nuclear war has negated itself. Some even appeared to contradict themselves on this issue. For example, in 1985, Colonel General Dmitriy A. Volkogonov, while arguing that the issue was annihilation or existence, maintained that Lenin's interpretation of Clausewitz's dictum remains valid today.[10]

Beginning in the 1960s, there was a detectable change in the Soviet approach to the West. Adam Ulam noted in one of his more popular textbooks that in 1968 Soviet foreign policy had begun to change.[11] There were several individuals in the Soviet Union who perceived the necessity to change Soviet rhetoric, retreat a bit, and find and prepare an individual with the personality necessary to sell the new rhetoric to the West. The Soviets, however, had not yet mastered the essential rhetoric and public relations techniques necessary to convince the West that they had changed their *modus operandi* nor had they prepared and brought forward an individual who could approach the West, project a new image, and convince anyone that the Soviets had changed. The individual equipped with this new image would become the "new" Soviet leader. All of this remained in the future. There was a long road ahead for these reformers, but they made a beginning in the 1960s.

The Soviets initiated several major, long-range projects the purpose of which was to discover what the West wanted to hear from the Soviets. The Soviets also had to learn the proper language in which to

phrase these ideas and find the right person to sell the program. For
the Soviets, this was not an easy task. They knew about the Rand
Corporation, the Institute for Defense Analysis, the George Kennan
Institute at the Smithsonian, and other so-called think tanks in the
United States, the purpose of which was to study and learn about the
Soviet Union.[12] Accordingly, the Soviets set out to establish their own
think tanks to study the West, in particular to study the United States.

At the beginning of the 1960s, the Soviets had at least two
organizations which could possibly become think tanks for studying the
United States. The first organization was the Institute of World
Economy and International Relations of the Soviet Academy of Sciences
(*Institut Mirovoy Ekonomiki i Mezhdunarodnykh Otnosheniy*)(IMEMO),
which was originally organized in 1925 as the Institute of World
Economics and Politics. Organized in 1930 was the Pacific Studies
Institute, renamed the Oriental Studies Institute in 1950. Under the
Stalin regime, the study of international relations suffered a reverse
because Stalin looked down upon international relations as a bourgeois
science. Consequently, these two organizations became dormant until
after Stalin's death. In the late 1950s those institutes, closed under
Stalin, were reopened and new institutes established. The Africa
Institute was organized in 1959, and the Latin American Institute in
1961.[13]

At the 20th Party Congress in 1956, Anastas Mikoyan complained
about the demise of IMEMO, since the Soviet Union was deficient in
the study of capitalism.[14] Officially, the Soviets reopened IMEMO in
April 1956 with Anushavan A. Arzumanyan as the director. Employing
more than 1000 people, it is today one of the Soviet Union's leading
research centers for international studies, working on a broad range of
topics including international economics, problems of theory, and area
studies. Arzumanyan, a member of the pre-revolution intelligentsia who
accepted Bolshevism, remained the director until his death in 1965, upon
which he was succeeded by Nikolay Inozemtsev.[15]

The reopening of IMEMO aroused suspicion among the other
Soviet research institutes, and in 1960 there was a serious challenge
from the new Africa Institute, the founding of which IMEMO had tried
to block. IMEMO also opposed the opening of the Latin America

Institute in 1961, primarily because of its regional approach. IMEMO wanted the Soviet government to continue its global approach to foreign policy; whereas, the establishment of the regional institutes might lead the government to follow a regional foreign policy. Nevertheless, the Soviet government did establish a number of institutes devoted to regional studies. To fend off the trend toward regionalism, IMEMO conducted studies on several regional questions, such as the United States' policy toward Cuba and the 1962 missile crisis.[16]

The increasing complexity of international relations in the 1960s fostered the establishment of a number of new academic institutes. The Soviets organized the Institute of the Far East to monitor the Sino-Soviet conflict. Organized in 1967, the Institute of the International Workers' Movement had the purpose of studying problems of the international Communist movement.[17]

With the proximity of detente, there appeared to be a need for an institute to study the United States and take advantage of improved relations. Under the direction of the Central Committee, CPSU, the Soviets organized the Institute of the United States and Canada (IUSAC) in 1968. Initially, it concentrated only on the United States, but in 1974 the institute was renamed to reflect the inclusion of Canada. Georgiy A. Arbatov, who had been a section chief in the Central Committee, was the organizer and first director of IUSAC. Prior to the establishment of IUSAC, there was no Soviet research institute the sole purpose of which was to study and analyze United States' political and economic developments. Previously, IMEMO would study specific aspects of the United States, and the Institute of International Workers' Movement would study a special aspect of United States' labor. Special periods in United States' history were the objects of study from time to time by scholars at the Institute of World History and at Moscow State University. Yet, there was no one agency which could concentrate its entire effort on the United States and answer the myriad questions about the United States which Soviet officials might have for the late 1960s and 1970s.[18]

The staffing of IUSAC was one of Arbatov's first problems. He recruited low ranking diplomats and journalists who had served abroad, as well as several well-known retired military officers. In 1969, IUSAC was removed from the Central Committee and assigned to the Soviet Academy of Sciences, a move which improved the academic image and facilitated contact with think tanks and other intellectual organizations in the United States. In the early 1970s the competition for employment with IUSAC became tough, and the popularity of IUSAC made it easier for Arbatov to recruit top quality scholars. Many highly competent young people joined IUSAC for access to foreign literature, contact with United States' scholars, and travel to the United States and other Western countries.[19]

One of the early, successful projects carried out by IUSAC was a study of United States' management techniques, which IUSAC sent to the Central Committee for eventual implementation in the Kama River Truck Plant. During the early years of IUSAC, research specialists spent much time studying current United States' publications. The total immersion in United States' literature soon provided these researchers with an American exterior and gave the impression to United States' visitors that the IUSAC staff spoke a common language and shared similar views on foreign affairs. This American exterior was authorized by the Central Committee for the purpose of carrying out the IUSAC propaganda mission.[20]

Among the retired military officers assigned to IUSAC, three in particular share an excellent reputation in the West, especially among some Soviet experts. All three, Major General Valentin V. Larionov, General Mikhail Mil'shteyn, and Colonel Lev S. Semeyko, have travelled to the United States on several occasions. American visitors to Moscow have frequently had the opportunity to carry on extended conversations with these officers, and they have been highly effective propagandists for the Soviet Union. For example, General Larionov was on the program for the Second International Security Conference in Norfolk, Virginia, on 25 May 1989.

Within IUSAC, the Department of Ideology studies trends in American ideology, public opinion, and the mass media. Members of this department have written on religion, advertising, and consumerism in the United States.[21] The Soviets are concerned about the Soviet citizens who have departed from Marxist-Leninist ideology and profess their belief in Jesus Christ.[22] In studying religion in the United States where there is freedom of religion, the Department of Ideology undoubtedly observed that an increasing number of Americans are not attracted to Christianity, but are pursuing other beliefs such as humanism, atheism, the new age movement, and cults. In contrast, in the Soviet Union where freedom of religion has been restricted, Christianity is growing. If the Soviet Union permitted freedom of religion, it is possible that Christianity would soon lose its attraction. Thus, one way the Soviets might stop the movement toward Christianity would be the granting of freedom of religion.

A major activity of the Department of Ideology in IUSAC has been the study of United States' public relations techniques. Members of IUSAC have visited public relations firms in the United States to study the tactics and techniques which American businesses have found successful in selling their products to American customers. As part of this program they have also visited American agencies specializing in the creation of the correct public image for aspiring American politicians; they learned how to give a politician the "Madison Avenue" treatment. In their visits to the United States, they have learned what Americans like to hear and how to use those words which sell commercial products and which influence Americans to vote for a particular politician. Gorbachëv became an expert in the "Madison Avenue" approach, and he has displayed great facility in the use of words, phrases, and ideas which help sell his "new thinking" to the West.

Following what they have learned from United States' public relations techniques, the Soviets conduct numerous public opinion polls and place great emphasis on the results. Gorbachëv has shown strong public support in polls of Soviet citizens as well as in polls conducted in Western Europe and the United States.[23] The Soviets are depending heavily on world public opinion to gain support for Gorbachëv's restructuring program, and they appear to have enjoyed considerable success in the United States and Western Europe. As a result of polls, the Soviets claim unprecedented international popularity among the masses and the intelligentsia.[24]

IUSAC Director Georgiy Arbatov attracted considerable attention in the Western press and in academic circles. He and Genrikh A. Trofimenko, as well as other IUSAC officials, enjoy an excellent reputation in the West as individuals who have an influence on decision makers; however, they enjoy no such prestige in the Soviet Union. Neither IUSAC as an organization nor Arbatov appeared to have a share in Soviet decision making. IUSAC and Arbatov provide large volumes of information to the Central Committee, the Foreign Ministry, and the KGB. Arbatov has had access to the top Soviet decision makers such as Brezhnev and Gorbachëv, a relationship which has been important primarily because of the influence he has on their public relations tactics and strategy. He has also served as an important purveyor of Soviet propaganda to the West.[25] Arbatov's views on detente and IUSAC work on special topics such as Sino-American relations and American management techniques appeared to coincide with the interests and views of Soviet leaders. He probably served as an advisor on American attitudes and reactions.[26]

Arbatov became the leading actor in the IUSAC propaganda effort. What Arbatov said is not as important as how he said it. His appearances on American television were notable for their "disarming" effect. His apparent sincerity and outspoken manner seem to belie American views of Soviet severity and censorship, while his remarks on the Soviet Union or on Soviet-United States relations were obvious distortions. To the Soviets it is important to have a person who speaks intelligently and can express Soviet views in intelligent language. Although it is refreshing to see an intelligent face in the Soviet Union, such is very deceptive, since the news and views so presented are distortions.[27]

Georgiy Arbatov and Genrikh Trofimenko, especially Arbatov, served as the "guinea pigs" for projecting the "new thinking" Westward. Arbatov's numerous appearances on television, his press interviews, and his contacts with Westerners were designed to test the new image which IUSAC developed for some future Soviet leader. Arbatov selected the new rhetoric from IUSAC research and study on American public opinion, the American media, American public relations techniques, and the language and phrases which Soviet officials observed at arms control, disarmament, and SALT meetings.[28] Arbatov adopted and assumed what he considered to be the most effective image to project to the West. Western reactions were closely observed, and those words, those phrases, and those ideas which received a negative reaction were culled. For example, in an interview with journalist William Ottman, Arbatov quoted from the Bible extensively. This ploy did two things: it showed that the Soviets, atheists they may be, have read the Bible and are familiar with it; it also revealed that the West did not respond positively to a Marxist throwing scripture at them. In particular, Arbatov used the parable which Jesus Christ gave about "the mote in thy brother's eye" in an effort to show that the West was hypocritical. He also quoted from Ecclesiastes 9: 18 to promote the Soviet disarmament and anti-war initiatives.[29] It appears that Gorbachëv does not quote directly from the Bible as freely as Arbatov. Gorbachëv's references to God are usually in the context of what some Western leader has said.[30] Gorbachëv does, however, from time to time quote passages from the Bible which he erroneously attributes to the Soviet people.[31]

IUSAC reports are usually short and attempt to present American views on topics of political and economic interest. They are concerned with American public opinion on these topics. One of the tasks at IUSAC is to determine which trends in the United States are stronger at a particular moment. IUSAC analysts concentrate on American views as presented in the American press and publications.[32]

IUSAC has the responsibility for recommending means and goals by which the Soviets can influence American public opinion.[33] At times, IUSAC will adopt United States views and methodology.[34] One reason for the Americanization of IUSAC researchers is to enable them to communicate better with American scholars, and they all use an American approach and vocabulary.[35] The IUSAC staff have contact with foreigners, primarily United States' citizens, in three ways: as delegates to international conferences, as escorts for visitors to IUSAC, and by foreign travel. A few institute members, for example, Arbatov, Trofimenko, and Boris N. Zanegin, appear to be better known to the American academic community than to their own countrymen. As observed in the American media, certain IUSAC personalities appear more frequently as spokesmen for the official Soviet view; they constitute sort of a public relations team or press office. The Soviets carefully control almost all contact between IUSAC personnel and Westerners. Moreover, there has been an increase in the aggressive nature of this relationship by IUSAC to influence American contacts for the dissemination of more propaganda.[36]   In the 1980s Arbatov and Trofimenko were seen more and more on American television and in the American press, usually defending some Soviet position or propounding the positive features of the Soviet system.[37]

Of the approximately 400 members of IUSAC, each year about six or seven are assigned to posts in the United States, such as the Soviet Embassy in Washington, the Soviet Consulate in New York, or the UN. The appointments, which Arbatov arranges through the Foreign Ministry, last from six months to one year.   The most frequent visitors to the United States are department heads and section chiefs, who usually go for brief periods to attend academic conferences, or in some cases as IUSAC representatives to special sessions of the UN.   There is a permanent IUSAC representative at the Soviet Embassy in Washington, the main purpose of whom is to obtain publications for research.[38]

For example, Sergei Rogov, at the time a staff member of IUSAC, was in the United States in the winter of 1979 during which time he visited the campus of Texas Christian University where he sat in a political science class and answered student questions.   His escort was a liberal professor who was overheard telling Rogov about his own liberal views.[39]

The nature of IUSAC contacts with Americans changed over the years as such meetings became more frequent.   While initially these encounters appeared to be a true academic exchange, they developed into attempts by IUSAC to obtain more biographical and political information as well as an attempt to disseminate propaganda favorable to the Soviet Union.   Arbatov and Trofimenko in their more frequent appearances on American television were simultaneously trying to create the illusion of free speech in the Soviet Union.[40]

Other institutes were also studying the United States.   In the mid-1970s IMEMO disagreed with the Institute of the World Workers' Movement (IWWM) on detente and United States-Soviet relations. IMEMO strongly supported detente.   The director of IWWM, Timur Timofeyev, wrote a study arguing that detente was largely the result of the efforts of the Soviet Union and its allies, specifically, a result of the Soviet "Program for Peace" adopted in 1971 by the 24th Party Congress.

Timofeyev argued further that this program led to the first SALT agreement, the opening of West Germany, and greater economic cooperation with the West. Oleg Bykov argued the IMEMO position that detente came about as a result of contributions from both East and West. Another point of contention between IMEMO and IWWM concerned the relative importance of ideology on detente. Timofeyev argued that sustained and uncompromising ideological confrontation with the West was essential to detente; whereas, Bykov, not rejecting the validity of ideological competition between the superpowers, argued that East and West could cooperate on many issues despite their ideological differences. Bykov specifically called for a "humanitarian approach" to many global problems.[41]

While director of IMEMO, Inozemtsev maintained close relations with the directors of the Far East Institute, Sladkovskiy, and IUSAC. The three institutes cooperated closely in many projects dealing with peace and disarmament. Their studies revealed similar positions on the subjects of detente, United States-Soviet relations, and Soviet-Japanese relations. This close cooperation can be attributed partly to similar political convictions of the three directors. IMEMO also maintained good relations with IUSAC, again because of the personal friendship between Arbatov and Inozemtsev.[42]

IMEMO researchers frequently work temporarily for government agencies, such as the State Committee on Foreign Economic Relations, which hires junior researchers to work abroad. The contracts last several years, but upon their return the employees are guaranteed their previous jobs with IMEMO. The Soviet Council of Ministers also provides the IMEMO staff opportunities to travel abroad.[43]

Within IMEMO, the Department of Socio-Political Problems of Developed Capitalist Countries specializes in domestic problems in the West, especially current social problems. One of the objects of research is social stratification, which the Soviets call "class struggle under modern conditions." In the Department of International Organizations, headed by Grigoriy Morozov, researchers specialize in the study of peace and war, and they spend considerable time on the topics of conflict and conflict resolution and arms control and disarmament.[44]

The International Department, headed by Vladimir Yakubovskiy, organizes IMEMO's relations with foreign scholars and research bodies. It not only arranges for foreign visitors to IMEMO, it sends IMEMO staff members abroad.[45] Since IMEMO is one of the Soviet Union's leading institutes for international studies, it attracts high quality university graduates, many of whom have lived abroad for extended periods of time. Similar to IUSAC, the competition for positions with IMEMO is competitive; however, nepotism prevents the selection of the best and brightest for all positions.[46]

Major research projects at IMEMO examine a variety of topics, some of which include United States-Soviet detente, problems of the superpower relationship, and the impact of regional conflicts on the world-wide correlation of forces. Other topics of interest are arms negotiations, talks on nuclear and conventional arms control issues, and the positive Western response to past Soviet arms control initiatives. IMEMO also looks for Western pronouncements indicating a similarity of views between the West and the Soviet Union on these topics.[47]

The Soviet institutes may have more influence now than in the past since the Soviet leaders appear to listen to them more. The institutes do not, however, participate directly in policy formulation. IMEMO, as well as Georgiy Arbatov in IUSAC, seems to be influential. It appears that the influence of Arbatov and IUSAC diminished in the 1980s, whereas in the 1970s they had more influence.

Soviet leaders at the highest level were among the first to enunciate the rhetoric of the "new thinking." Among major Soviet political leaders, Leonid I. Brezhnev was one of the last to make a public statement concerning the overwhelming Soviet military power. In a speech on the fiftieth anniversary of the Bolshevik revolution in 1967, he stated that the Soviet armed forces could win a victory worthy of the Soviet people.[48] Soon after this speech, Leonid I. Brezhnev's rhetoric and the rhetoric of other Soviet leaders and officials began to change to a milder tone and an anti-war theme.

As Arbatov's *modus operandi* became the accepted guide for Soviet behavior toward the West, other high ranking Soviet leaders began to fall in line with the "new thinking" and its associated rhetoric. Utterances by Defense Ministers, former Defense Ministers, Chiefs of the General Staff, former Chiefs of the General Staff, foreign policy officials, and especially the General Secretaries of the Communist Party have a tendency to persuade many Westerners that the Soviets have changed. This effect is, of course, exactly what the "new thinking" is designed to accomplish. For example, as early as 1968 Marshall V. D. Sokolovskiy wrote of the unacceptability of nuclear war and the necessity to prevent it.[49] In 1978 Marshal D. F. Ustinov referred to nuclear war as "the most terrible danger for all of mankind."[50] *Pravda* quoted KGB chief Yuri V. Andropov that nuclear war would bring victory to no one.[51] In contradicting Lenin's adoption of Clausewitz's dictum, Konstantin U. Chernenko said in 1981 that it is criminal to consider nuclear war as a rational, legitimate continuation of politics.[52] Andrei Gromyko frequently uttered anti-nuclear statements.[53] Marshal Sergei Sokolov predicted the extinction of civilization in the event of a world nuclear war.[54] Marshal N. V. Ogarkov's numerous statements against nuclear war are well known and are especially interesting since he had expressed an exact opposite view in 1979.[55] Ogarkov was joined by his successor, Marshal S. F. Akhromeyev, in pronouncing incalculable disaster for all peoples should the world be engulfed in nuclear war.[56] Much ado has been made about Ogarkov and Akhromeyev supporting the anti-nuclear position; however, this is not unexpected since both have been chief of the GUSM, the deception arm of the Soviet General Staff.

Since the Soviet Defense Minister, Army General Dmitriy T. Yazov, was appointed by Gorbachëv, it is no surprise that Yazov has from the beginning mouthed the phrases of Gorbachëv's "new thinking." He joined the throng of other high ranking Soviet military men to declare that the Soviet Union will never initiate combat operations and will not be the first to use nuclear weapons.[57] This statement obviously does not preclude the Soviet use of nuclear weapons should an aggressor be the first to employ them.

The event which caused many United States' analysts to believe that the Soviets had changed their military strategy was Leonid I. Brezhnev's speech at Tula, 18 January 1977. At Tula, Brezhnev denied that the Soviet Union was trying to gain superiority in armaments for a first strike capability. He announced that Soviet goals were to prevent the development of events as far as a first or second strike. In addition to renouncing superiority, Brezhnev also renounced the Soviet use of preemption and nuclear war.[58] Brezhnev had made speeches with the same theme on several previous occasions, and he continued to make such statements frequently after the Tula Speech.[59]

There was an opinion among some Western analysts that Brezhnev's Tula speech was a reaction to a CIA report published in the *New York Times*, 26 December 1976. This report, dubbed the "Team B Report" to distinguish it from a report by a group of analysts with a more optimistic outlook, was a ten year projection of Soviet intentions. According to the "Team B Report," the Soviets were seeking strategic superiority over United States' military forces.[60] A short term analysis of Soviet utterances by high level leaders might lead an analyst to conclude that Brezhnev was announcing a change of course; however, an analysis of these events in the context of the Soviet "new Thinking" rhetoric indicates that the "Team B Report" merely provided an opportunity for Brezhnev to enunciate this key statement as a step in the long-range "new thinking" campaign.

"New thinking" is the practical application of Soviet research on what and how the West wants to hear. Mikhail S. Gorbachëv is the most intelligent Soviet leader since Vladimir I. Lenin. Moreover, Gorbachëv has a personality that no Soviet leader to date has equalled. Yet, the West knows Gorbachëv primarily through the medium of Soviet propaganda, and the Soviet propensity for creating and modifying official records should serve as a signal for caution in accepting Gorbachëv at face value. His experience as an expert on agriculture raises the question about where he obtained his polish, his personality, his persuasive manner, and the qualifications to be the Soviet leader. He and his wife display social graces which appear to be out of character for Soviet leaders and their families. Gorbachëv's heritage - the Stalin years - does not support the development of the personality, the compassion, or the international *savoir faire* which he so adeptly projects. Perhaps Gorbachëv is the real, new Soviet man.

Gorbachëv's domestic policies are one of the tools he has used to persuade the West that he is genuine. His new approach to foreign policy has promoted changes which the West has sought for decades. Yet, none of his changes could be accomplished by one man acting alone, as it has appeared. The Soviets would have the West believe that Gorbachëv came to power with a slim majority in the Politburo. The Soviets prepared him well for his role, and he is the star player in the "new thinking" drama.

Upon his accession to the post of Party General Secretary, Mikhail S. Gorbachëv became the Soviets' most vocal enthusiast for the "new thinking." Having a pleasant personality, a friendly smile, and a "disarming" manner, he continued the themes of his predecessors in this matter and carried them further. As the "reform" minded head of state, Gorbachëv is very convincing in what he says. All of his arguments are pat, and his enunciation of the new Soviet position is clear and convincing. He uses "logic" to argue against the use of nuclear weapons, and his arguments for a nuclear free Europe are most attractive. He has continued the "peace-loving Communist" line propagated by Lenin and all Marxist-Leninist literature. In so doing, he stresses the Soviet claim about concern for Soviet security and that the Soviet armed forces are purely defensive. This argument supports the Marxist-Leninist international objective to disarm the bourgeoisie. Since the Soviets and their Warsaw Pact allies have the largest concentration of conventional weapons in the world poised in Eastern Europe ready to "defend" the Pact states from Western aggression, Gorbachëv proposes to reduce the size of conventional forces. This proposal is reasonable, since the United States and its Western allies have found it necessary to maintain nuclear weapons in Western Europe as a deterrent to the Soviet use of those forces.[61] Yet, the primary threat to the United States is from the Strategic Rocket Forces, the capabilities of which the Soviets do not intend to reduce.[62]

Gorbachëv, like Lenin, repeatedly insisted that Marxists told the people the truth.[63] Yet, Foreign Minister Eduard Shevardnadze announced in October 1989 that the Soviets had been lying about the Krasnoyarsk radar station since construction began. He admitted that the Soviets built this radar station in violation of the ABM Treaty.[64] Although the intent of this confession appears to reflect the "new thinking," it served to reinforce the universal suspicion that the Soviets frequently lie about many matters of international importance. If the Soviets lied about the radar site at Krasnoyarsk, perhaps they are lying about *perestroika*, *glasnost'*, democracy, and all other reforms which Gorbachëv has so vocally publicized.

*   *   *   *   *   *   *   *   *   *   *   *   *   *   *   *   *   *   *

The Soviets are highly confident that their "new thinking" is achieving the desired results. For example, in October 1989 the NATO Commander, General John Galvin, spoke out in favor of an increase in the NATO nuclear arsenals to compensate for the advantage in conventional forces enjoyed by the Warsaw Pact. The Soviets countered this plea by alleging that General Galvin's words are not in keeping with the spirit of the times, that they constitute a reversion to militaristic thinking, and that the "new thinking" is winning more authority and recognition. The Soviet argument was an attempt to allay the fear of a "threat from the East."[65]

The "new thinking" fits the Soviet pattern for global deception. "New thinking" serves all of the Marxist-Leninist requisites for eventual world conquest, especially by peaceful means, and it is a clever, long term scheme to persuade the West to disarm. Soviet study of the West, especially the United States, by the research institutes has provided the Soviets with sufficient information to permit the application of reflexive control methods. The "new thinking" and actions in consonance with *glasnost'*, *perestroika*, and "democracy" appear almost irreversible, but in effect they are the components of a massive disinformation campaign.

"Tell them what they want to believe."

NOTES

1. Lenin, *Selected Works*, vol. 1, 743, 746.

2. Mikhail S. Gorbachëv, Moscow Television Service, 16 Nov. 1989, *FBIS Daily Report*, 20 Nov. 1989, 67-79.

3. Ye. I. Rybkin, *War and Politics* (Moscow: Military Publishing House, 1959).

4. Valentin V. Larionov and I. Glagolev, "Peaceful Coexistence and the USSR's Defense Might," *International Life*, no. 11 (November 1963): 43, 46.

5. N. M. Nikol'skiy, *The Primary Contemporary Question: The Problem of Annihilation* (Moscow: Gospolitizdat, 1964), 356-381.

6. N. Talentsky, "Thoughts on Past Wars," *International Affairs*, no. 5 (April 1965): 23.

7. N. M. Nikol'skiy, *Nauchno-technicheskoye revolyutsiya: Mirovaya ekonomika, politika, naselenie* (Moskva: Gospolitizdat, 1970), 158-163; N. M. Nikol'skiy and A. V. Grishin, *Nauchno-technichheskiy progress i mezhdunarodnye otnosheniya* (Moskva: Gospolitizdat, 1978), 248-255.

8. A. A. Shirman, "The Social Activism of the Masses and the Defense of Socialism," *Filosofskoe nasledie V. I. Lenina i Problemy sovremennoy voyny*, eds. A. S. Milovidov and V. G. Kozlov (Moskva: Gospolitizdat, 1972), 171-174; I. Sidel'nikov "Mirovoye sosushchestvovaniye i bezopasnost' norodov," *Krasnaya Zvezda*, 14 Aug. 1973; N. Prokp'ev, "Problems of War and Peace in the Modern Era," *International Life*, no. 12 (1967) 82-83; V. M. Bondarenko, *Contemporary Science and the Development of Military Affairs* (Moscow: Military Publishing House, 1976), 131-132; P. A. Zhilin, "Past Lessons and Future Concerns," *Kommunist*, no. 7 (1981): 71.

9. Fedor M. Burlatskiy and A. A. Galkin, *Sotsilogiya, Politika, Mezhdunarodnye otnosheniya* (Moskva: Gospolitizdat, 1974), 284, 287; L.

I. Brezhnev, *Pravda*, 9 May 1975; S. F. Akhromeyev, "Military Detente: The Demand of the Times," *Krasnaya Zvezda*, 2 Dec. 1980; Fedor M. Burlatskiy, "A New Strategy? No! Nuclear Madness," *Literaturnaya gazeta*, 2 Dec. 1981, 14; K. U. Chernenko, "The Soviet Peace Program for the 1980s," *Pravda*, 23 Apr. 1981; Yu. V. Andropov, "Leninism: The Inexhaustible Source of the Revolutionary Energy and Creativity of the Masses," *Pravda*, 23 Apr. 1982; N. V. Ogarkov, *Vsegda v gotovnosti k zachite otchestva* (Moscow: Military Publishing House, 1982), 26; D. F. Ustinov, "Averting the Threat of a Nuclear War," *Pravda*, 12 Jul. 1983; V. G. Kulikov, "Curbing the Arms Race," *Krasnaya Zvezda*, 21 Feb. 1984; D. A. Volkogonov, "A Strategy of Adventurism," *Zarubezhnoye voyennoye obozreniye*, no. 5 (May 1984).

10. D. A. Volkogonov, "War and Peace in the Nuclear Age," *Krasnaya Zvezda*, 30 Aug. 1985.

11. Adam B. Ulam, *Expansion and Coexistence: Soviet Foreign Policy, 1917-73*, 2d ed. (New York: Praeger Publishers, 1974), v.

12. Georgiy A. Arbatov and William Ottman, *The Soviet Viewpoint* (New York: Dodd, Mead and Co., 1983), 21-22.

13. Yury Polsky, *Soviet Research Institutes and the Formulation of Foreign Policy* (Falls Church, Virginia: Delphic Associates, Incorporated, 1987), 1. Reprinted with permission of the publisher.

14. Ibid., 5.

15. Ibid., 4, 6, 7.

16. Ibid., 9, 10, 11.

17. Barbara L. Dash, *A Defector Reports: The Institute of the USA and Canada* (Falls Church, Virginia: Delphic Associates Incorporated, 1982), 4. Reprinted with permission of the publisher.

18. Ibid., 4-5.

19. Ibid., 5-6, 7.

20. Ibid., 10.

21. Ibid., 20.

22. News cast, WVTF, FM 89, Roanoke, Virginia, 30 Nov. 1989.

23. *TASS*, 21 Oct. 1989.

24. Ye. Primakov, "New Philosophy of Foreign Policy," *Pravda*, 9 Jul. 1987.

25. Dash, *A Defector Reports*, 21-22.

26. Ibid., 211.

27. Ibid., 214.

28. *Izvestiya*, 16 Nov. 1989.

29. Arbatov and Ottman, *The Soviet Viewpoint*, 4, 120. "Wisdom is better than weapons of war: but one sinner destroyeth much good." Ecclesiastes 9: 18.

30. Gorbachëv, *Perestroika*, 192.

31. Gorbachëv, *A Time for Peace*, 135. In this instance, Gorbachëv wrote: "Our people have a simple but wise saying: 'As you sow, so shall you reap.'" This quotation comes from Galatians 6: 7: "Be not deceived; God is not mocked: for whatsoever a man soweth, that shall he also reap."

32. Dash, *A Defector Reports*, 35-37, 61.

33. Ibid., 62.

34. Ibid., 64.

35. Ibid., 70, 85.

36. Ibid., 148.

37. Ibid., 172.

38. Ibid., 171-172.

39. The author was present in the classroom where he sat next to Rogov.

40. Dash, *A Defector Reports*, 175-176.

41. Polsky, *Soviet Research Institutes*, 19-21.

42. Ibid., 22-24.

43. Ibid., 27-28.

44. Ibid., 32-34.

45. Ibid., 38.

46. Ibid., 43-44.

47. Ibid., 57-61.

48. Leonid I. Brezhnev, "Speech at the Celebration of the 50th Anniversary of the October Revolution," *Pravda*, 3 Nov. 1967.

49. V. D. Sokolovskiy, *Military Strategy*, 3d ed. (Moscow: Voyenizdat, 1968), 239.

50. D. F. Ustinov, "Six Heroic Decades," *Kommunist*, no. 2 (1978): 26.

51. Yu. V. Andropov, "Leninism - The Inexhaustible Source of the Revolutionary Energy and Creativity of the Masses," *Pravda*, 23 Apr. 1982.

52. K. U. Chernenko, "The Soviet Peace Program for the 1980s," *Pravda*, 23 Apr. 1981.

53. A. A. Gromyko, "A. A. Gromyko's Address," *Pravda*, 28 Sept. 1984.

54. S. L. Sokolov, "The Great Victory," *Kommunist*, no. 6 (1985): 65.

55. N. V. Ogarkov, "Military Strategy," *Soviet Military Encyclopedia*, vol. 7 (Moscow: Military Publishing House, 1979), 564; N. V. Ogarkov, "A Reliable Defense to Peace," *Krasnaya Zvezda*, 23 Sept. 1983; N. V. Ogarkov, "The Unfading Glory of Soviet Weapons," *Kommunist Vooruzhennikh Sil*, no. 21 (1984): 25.

56. S. F. Akhromeyev, "The Great Victory and Its Lessons," *Izvestiya*, 7 May 1985.

57. *TASS*, 22 Oct. 1989.

58. Leonid I. Brezhnev, "Tula Speech," *Pravda*, 19 Jan. 1977.

59. *Pravda*, 22 Jul. 1974; *Pravda*, 14 Jun. 1975; *Pravda*, 25 Nov. 1976; *Pravda*, 3 Nov. 1977. Brezhnev made similar speeches on 29 June 1976 and 21 June 1977.

60. *New York Times*, 26 Dec. 1976, sec. 1, 1.

61. Gorbachëv, *Perestroika*, 188-190, 213, 220.

62. Colonel General Viktor Semenovich Rodin, Chief of the Strategic Rocket Forces Political Directorate, interview, *Sovetskaya Rossiya*, 19 Nov. 1989.

63. Gorbachëv, *CPSU Central Committee Political Report, 25 February 1986*, *FBIS Daily Report* (Supplement), 26 Feb. 1986, 1-42.

64. *TASS*, 25 Oct. 1989.

65. *Selskaya Zhizn*, 4 Oct. 1989.

X

THE GORBACHËV ERA

In the Soviet Union, the 1960s began with a mood of optimism. This decade was the golden age of strategic parity, detente, security, internal dynamism, and enormous power. By the end of the Brezhnev era in 1982, however, the mood had changed. Stagnation had set in and the country had taken a turn for the worse. There were numerous problems, pessimism ruled, the correlation of forces appeared to have turned against the Soviet Union, and the economy witnessed a decline in growth rates.

On the eve of the seventieth anniversary of the Bolshevik revolution, a majority of Soviet leaders decided that they could no longer wait to formulate and implement new policies to reverse the deleterious trends that plagued the Soviet Union at home and abroad.[1] By 1985, the Soviets had developed their "new thinking" and formulated other corrective measures to the point that they believed they could implement them effectively.[2] Their carefully groomed and trained salesman, Mikhail S. Gorbachëv, was already in Moscow and was a member of the Politburo. The remaining act was to elect him General Secretary of the Communist Party of the Soviet Union. The death of Konstantin U. Chernenko in late 1984 gave them the opportunity.

In Moscow Gorbachëv had close political ties with Chernenko, Andropov, and the Party ideologue, Mikhail Suslov. Moreover, he was personal secretary to Andropov and Chernenko.[3] Mikhail S. Gorbachëv appeared to be the man picked by the Central Committee to solve the problems of stagnation, restore the ideology to that of true Marxism-Leninism, and advance the "ideals" of Marxist-Leninist socialism throughout the world. The cure for the numerous Soviet problems was the "new thinking." If Gorbachëv could change Soviet attitudes and motivate the Soviet people to think as socialists, the Soviet Union could heal the sick economy, reduce the size of its armed forces, and correct the numerous problems such as crime, alcoholism, and poor discipline. Gorbachëv's political objectives included introducing democracy into the system, even though there was to be only one political party, the Communist Party. Above all, the "new thinking" was designed to restore Soviet dedication to Marxist-Leninist ideology. Once the ideological corrections were made, the other Soviet problems were supposed to be self-correcting.

Accordingly, the 27th Party Congress adopted a number of tasks: transformation of the Soviet economy from an extensive mode of development to an intensive mode with the reconstruction of production, the introduction of efficient organization and management, improvement of the well-being of the people, and a strengthening of Soviet defense capabilities.[4]

Gorbachëv and the current generation of Soviet leaders were born in the 1920s and the 1930s, the period of Stalinist terror, forced collectivization, the great purges, and the achievement of a heavy industrial base which enabled the Soviets to build a military force that gave them great power status following their victory over the Nazis in World War II. Therefore their "moral" heritage is one of deceit, murder, and lies which goes back to the days of Lenin, the Bolsheviks, and Stalin. These people are now of age and are in control of the Soviet Union. Mikhail S. Gorbachëv, born 2 March 1931, is an heir to this Leninist-Stalinist legacy.

Although there are several biographies of Mikhail S. Gorbachëv, the West knows little about him other than the controlled propaganda released by the Soviets. Among the émigrés and defectors who knew Gorbachëv, Lev Yudovich, Zdenek Mlynar, and Fridrikh Neznanzky have provided limited and inconclusive data.[5] Mikhail S. Gorbachëv was born to a peasant family in *Privol'noye* village, *Krasnogvardeyskiy rayon, Stavropol kray*. Having spent World War II in his village, in 1946 he worked at a Machine Tractor Station as a combine operator's helper. In high school, he was an active *Komsomol* member where his work resulted in the award of a medal and priority consideration for acceptance at law school.[6] A Kuban Cossack, Gorbachëv went to Moscow as a socially crude young man trying to rid himself of his provincial background.[7]

Entering Moscow State University in 1950, Gorbachëv was a devoted Communist who would resort to any means to maintain the integrity and authority of the Party organization and to advance himself. For example, in 1951, he encouraged the *Komsorg* (*Komsomol* Organizer) to drink until he passed out, reported the *Komsorg* for his behavior, manipulated the *Komsorg's* demotion, and took his place. Throughout this period until Stalin's death, Gorbachëv enthusiastically supported Stalin and the Party line.[8] Gorbachëv was an ardent, orthodox Stalinist more active and doctrinaire than other *Komsorgs*, and therefore he was accepted into the Communist Party in 1952 at a time when students were not usually accepted as Party members. An opportunist, he was ruthless in politics. Following Stalin's death in 1953 he made a radical change in his *modus operandi*.[9] When Khrushchëv rose to power, Gorbachëv supported Khrushchëv.[10]

Prior to Stalin's death, Gorbachëv kept to himself and never engaged in political discussion; however, after Stalin's death he changed completely. In his political conversations, he referred to two Stalins: one good, the other bad. Stalin's leadership in the Soviet victory over the Nazis was good, but his domestic policy was marked by mistakes. Nevertheless, Vladimir I. Lenin remained Gorbachëv's political idol.[11]

In 1954 Gorbachëv experienced a political defeat when he lost his bid for the full-time position as Secretary of the newly merged *Komsomol* organizations at the Moscow Law Institute and the Moscow University Law School. Returning home to the Kuban after this defeat, he became a leading *Komsomol* and Party functionary in Stavropol where he disassociated himself with his former friends and selected new friends from high ranking Party officials, the most important of whom was Fedor Kulakov.[12]

Fedor Kulakov became Gorbachëv's patron and introduced him to Mikhail Suslov, Andropov, and other high ranking Party members. Kulakov and Suslov, later members of the Politburo, probably

recognized Gorbachëv's potential as a front man for the national
leadership as early as the late 1950s.[13] Moreover, Gorbachëv was a
good Party member who carried out faithfully all Party instructions.[14]

Having earned a law degree in Moscow in the early 1950s,
Gorbachëv later earned a degree in agriculture. In 1970 he became the
first secretary of the Stravropol *Kray* Party Committee, and in 1971 he
was elected to be a full member of the Central Committee, CPSU.
Gorbachëv was appointed the Central Committee secretary for
agriculture in 1978.

When Mikhail S. Gorbachëv moved to Moscow in November 1978
as the Party Secretariat's agricultural expert, he kept a low profile.[15]
When he became a full member of the Politburo in 1980, he began
meeting informally with Abel G. Aganbegyan and other "forward
looking" Soviet economists and increased the frequency of the meetings
after becoming Andropov's lieutenant.[16]

The first Soviet leader to have a complete education, Gorbachëv
became General Secretary of the CPSU on 11 March 1985. He is a
lawyer and graduate of Moscow State University. Lenin, also, was a
lawyer, but Lenin did not complete his formal education. Furthermore,
in early 1985 Gorbachëv appeared to have no constituency and little
experience.

In Moscow in 1985, Gorbachëv built his power base with the
people from the Central Committee whom he knew from his association
as a Central Committee official. Thus, the Central Committee became
one of Gorbachëv's main constituencies.[17] In addition to the Central
Committee, with Gorbachëv the KGB is a highly influential group, the
core of which Andropov set up. Andropov promoted Gorbachëv,
Chebrikov, Aliyev, and Shevardnadze. Of the four key people whom
Gorbachëv relied upon from the beginning, Ryzhkov, Aliyev, Chebrikov,
and Shevardnadze, three were KGB generals.[18]

Beginning with the demise of Stalin, Party leaders have insisted
on a return to collective leadership. Thus, the Party General Secretaries
in the Soviet Union must have the support of the collective leadership
to attain that position; this means at least the support of the Politburo
and the Central Committee. Furthermore, they must maintain the
support of this Party leadership to remain in office and to gain approval

for new programs, especially programs which differ markedly from those of the immediate past. Many analysts have surmised that Gorbachëv's majority in the Politburo was rather close when he became General Secretary. By late 1989 it became clear that he had methodically consolidated his position by eliminating his opponents or weaker supporters one by one. Considering the number of Politburo members that Gorbachëv removed and replaced by late 1989, one can conclude that his Politburo majority was indeed slim on 11 March 1985.

In the past, Soviet leaders catered to the elites in the large bureaucracies.[19] The cultural, scientific, and educational bureaucracies are the largest, but they have the weakest elites. Gorbachëv, however, broke with the past and apparently declared war on most of the elites. Many Brezhnev office holders did not want to let go, and there was much opposition to Gorbachëv's actions. Nevertheless, Gorbachëv wanted to replace many of these people, a goal which he achieved early in his tenure. Gorbachëv is Russian and is in practice insensitive to non-Russians. Hence, the Politburo became more Russian under Gorbachëv than anytime before, and the Secretariat became almost all Russian. In many cases, Gorbachëv replaced the leaders in the Soviet republics with ethnic Russians, and he targeted most of the non-Great Russian *nomenclatura* (one to one and one-half million top level bureaucrats) for removal. In 1985 when Gorbachëv declared war on the *nomenklatura*, he continued the replacement of the old guard which Andropov had begun. Andropov replaced about one-third of the first secretaries of the *obkoms*; Gorbachëv replaced the remaining two-thirds.[20] Although the most enthusiastic supporters of Gorbachëv were the educational and scientific elites, he alienated the Soviet military leaders by threatening to reduce their funds.

Mikhail S. Gorbachëv is the most audacious Soviet leader since Vladimir I. Lenin. He recognizes the relationship between the economic and political systems and that both need reform. He knows that the economic process must rest on a better political system, which he says will emanate from *glasnost'* and democratization.[21]

In 1917 the Bolsheviks, as non-elected usurpers, had no legitimate claim to power, and the same is true today of the Communist leaders in the Soviet Union. Consequently, one of the primary concerns of the

Soviet Union has been the quest for legitimacy and acceptance in the international arena as a major world power. World War II left the Soviet Union in a position of military ascendancy; however, economically, the Soviets have always lagged behind the West. An integral part of the Soviet quest for legitimacy is fulfillment of their claim that socialism will bring to the Soviet Union, and all other Communist states, an economy far superior to that of capitalism. Yet, to date the Soviets have not realized the Communist economic supremacy of which they boast.

Perhaps to establish the basis for political legitimacy, in March 1989 the Soviets under Gorbachëv permitted the first elections in which the people could choose from more than one candidate for each office. The result of this exercise in "democracy" was an unexpected defeat for many Communist leaders who had assumed their positions to be secure.

In the late 1970s it became obvious that something was wrong with Soviet society when the Soviet Union began to lose momentum, economic failures increased, and other difficulties became apparent. Gorbachëv described the condition as stagnation, which acted as a brake on social and economic development.[22] As Party General Secretary, both Yuri V. Andropov and Konstantin U. Chernenko spoke of improving the economic system.[23] Andropov, while General Secretary, initiated drives against corruption, alcohol, and malingering. Furthermore, Andropov appointed Nikolay I. Ryzhkov to head the Economic Department of the Secretariat and charged him with the study of economic restructuring. In 1984 the Politburo under the leadership of Konstantin U. Chernenko formed a commission to study economic improvement.[24] In 1985 an investigation revealed that within the preceding fifteen years economic growth rates had fallen by over one-half, causing the economy to approach the point of stagnation by the 1980s. The Soviet leaders "discovered" that the Soviet Union was falling behind in technology, production efficiency, and product quality.[25]

The most prominent characteristics of the Soviet economy over the past thirty years have been a decline in the GNP, a growth of productivity, and a minute contribution to growth rates from factor productivity. Indeed, the Soviet Union has made many astounding economic gains over the past seventy years. Yet, living standards in the Soviet Union have remained below those of the capitalist West.[26]

In 1985 the major problem was that the Soviet economy had been operating under the old Stalinist economic system of an extensive mode of development wherein the emphasis was on maximum output. This condition was especially prevalent in heavy industry and capital construction. Managers emphasized the selling of their products at higher prices by increasing the amount of raw materials, labor, and time put into the production process. The consequence was not only an excessive consumption of raw materials, energy, and other resources, but a shortage of output. The immediate stop-gap measure for increasing output was to increase the input even more; however, this solution was counter-productive.[27]

Amid this maze of economic frustrations, the propaganda of success blared forth, telling the Soviet people that things were improving and that they lived in a trouble-free society. This attempt to brainwash the people backfired, since it merely exacerbated the situation. The people knew the truth; things were terrible and were getting worse. There was a general deterioration in society; drug addiction, crime, alcoholism, and laziness were growing. The Party leadership also began to suffer in the world of feigned prosperity.[28]

The deterioration in the Soviet economy can be partially attributed to rising costs and the reduced effectiveness of the mechanisms the Soviets applied to maintain social rest.[29] Furthermore, in the Soviet Union production is regulated not by the capitalist law of supply and demand, but by rules and regulations. To make matters even worse, international trade has been stifled because the ruble has no exchange rate on the international market.[30]

When Gorbachëv became General Secretary, growth rates of the national income for the last three Five Year Plans had fallen by more than one-half. Most planned targets had not been met since the early 1970s, and the quality of output was substandard. Alcohol abuse, crime, and drug abuse were indicators of the deterioration of social values. There was a general disregard for law, and report-padding, bribery, and toadyism had a degenerative moral effect. An attitude of permissiveness was rampant.[31] There were too many accidents, all of which reduced efficiency.[32] Gorbachëv's challenge was clear. After becoming General Secretary of the CPSU in 1985, Gorbachëv concentrated first on improving the Soviet economy. Closely associated with improving the economy was his objective of changing the moral and psychological mind set of the Soviet people.[33] Gorbachëv perceived the solution to be a reinstatement of the Leninist principles of democratic centralism, socialist self-government, greater openness, and the use of cost benefit methods. These techniques had to be integrated with modern management methods and quality control. The target date for the program to become effective was the year 2000.[34]

Gorbachëv and his cohorts perceived in the Soviet economic situation a major paradox. Since the beginning of the Five Year Plans under Stalin in 1928, the Soviet Union had made enormous strides in industrial production. It was the largest producer of steel, fuel and energy, and raw materials in the world; yet, there were shortages in each of these products due to waste and inefficiency. There were other symptoms of a sick economy. One of the world's major grain producers, the Soviet Union had to import large quantities of grain for food. Other similar problems pointed to an urgent need to revamp the entire Soviet socio-economic system. This process would not be easy, since a by-product of the stagnation was an erosion of Marxist-Leninist ideology among the Soviet people. The Soviets had to do something to reverse these downward trends.[35]

Since the loss of momentum, the numerous difficulties and problems, and the stagnation were supposedly alien to socialism, Gorbachëv perceived the main cause of Soviet problems to be that the Central Committee and the leadership had failed to recognize the need for change and formulate a viable solution. He observed that the theoretical concepts of socialism remained at the 1930s and 1940s level, and the dialectics of socialism's motivating forces and the contradictions of reality had not been subject to scientific research.[36] For certain, there was no progressive outcome of this dialectic process.

To achieve economic renewal, it was essential for the Soviets to introduce modern technology such as the use of industrial robots, especially in machine building. Tasks included reducing production, improving efficiency and productivity of labor, and providing incentives in agricultural. Following Lenin's example, Gorbachëv emphasized the necessity to learn from the lessons of the past.[37]

According to Gorbachëv, a revolutionary movement requires a revolutionary theory, and since *perestroika* is a revolution, it requires the application of Marxist-Leninist revolutionary theory.[38] Gorbachëv's *modus operandi* was to "revive the living spirit of Leninism" in politics and ideology.[39] The new program included the election of managers, multiple candidates for election to soviets in some districts, joint ventures with foreign firms, removal of restrictions on farms producing food, wider cooperative enterprises, encouragement of individual enterprise in small scale production and trade, an efficient functioning of research, and educational activities.[40]

Modelling his revolution on Lenin's NEP, Gorbachëv prescribed a transformation of management from one of "administrative" methods to one of "economic" methods, a procedure which required "extensive democratization" of management. This effort would entail a marked reorganization of the Soviet centralized management to a democratic one based on the hybrid of democratic centralism and self-management.[41]

In his report to the Central Committee plenum on 27 January 1987, Gorbachëv said that democratization was essential to guarantee that reforms would be irreversible.[42] In his speech of 25 June 1987, Gorbachëv acknowledged that Soviet economic problems had their origins in the Stalinist economic system, and he introduced an economic reform program which included a time table for economic reform and the need to incorporate market relations into the operations of a planned economy.[43]

In Gorbachëv's view, the Soviets had to restore the Leninist principles of openness, public control, criticism and self criticism, and sincerity of words and deeds. Success and irreversibility of revolutionary transformations could be ensured by a deepening of socialist democracy, creativity of the Soviet people, and the vanguard role of all Communists. In January 1987 Gorbachëv asserted that history demonstrates that the Soviet socialist system has ensured political and socio-economic rights, personal freedom, and the advantages of Soviet democracy. The "new thinking" promotes the Soviet concept of free labor and free thought in a free country in which advancement in production, science and technology, literature, culture, and the arts is possible only through an environment which promotes democracy and self-government.[44] Indeed, these "new thinking" concepts were alien to the era of stagnation.

Within or without the context of the "new thinking" the Soviets have had no intention of adopting another socio-economic or political system. Gorbachëv said there will "... certainly not [be] any break up of our political system."[45] In the Soviet Union the introduction of self-administration in production was of paramount significance, and the development of democracy in production was the most important trend in deepening and broadening socialist democracy. The Soviets wanted to incorporate cost accounting and responsibility into the industrial management of an economic system in which profits would depend on quality and quantity of products and services.[46]

Gorbachëv's plans were all encompassing. *Perestroika* means a sharp turn to production intensification and an increase of quality and efficiency. The Soviets must transfer attention from quantitative to qualitative indicators, from interim goals to end goals, from consumption of resources to their renewal, from a build-up of raw materials to the improvement of their use, and an acceleration in the development of the scientific sectors of the industrial and social system. The success of these goals depends on machine building, the foundation of conservation technology. Gorbachëv enunciated the task for machine building to raise the technical and economic levels and the quality of machinery, equipment, and instruments by the end of the Twelfth Five Year Plan. There was to be mass assimilation of computer technology and the radical reconstruction of the fuel and energy complex. There was to be a more efficient use of scientific potential and higher education and the introduction of new managerial methods. Above all, the Party was to change the social and economic situation in the country and create the conditions for deeper intensification and guaranteed production.[47]

Gorbachëv declared that the restructuring of the economy had to rely on science. He called for a reexamination of theoretical ideas and concepts, such as the interaction between productive forces and production relations, socialist property and economic forms of implementation, relations between goals and money, and centralism and independent economic organization. The production relations and management techniques employed under the extensive mode of development were obsolete. Since it was necessary to increase the rate of growth immediately, the Communist Party drew up plans for intensive economic reforms and began implementing them. The Twelfth Five Year Plan was to concentrate on refurbishing the national economy on a scientific and technical basis. Altogether, the Soviet economy needed a better use of production potential, more efficient labor, better discipline, better management, and a better attitude.[48]

In the Soviet Union there was no shortage of labor. There was, however, a low level of productivity and insufficient incentives. In 1985 millions of products were returned for poor quality. Raw materials were squandered, rendering worthless the labor of thousands of workers. The excessive number of jobs led to underemployment, whereas more automation and mechanization would reduce the number of people in industry and improve the quality of output. Exacerbating the transition to labor saving methods were the high prices the Soviets were paying for the extraction and delivery of ore, oil, coal.[49]

In formulating the Thirteenth Five Year Plan, the Soviets oriented on the quality of economic growth through an all-around intensification of production, the introduction and practice of resource conservation, acceleration of scientific and technological progress, and modernization.[50]

Gorbachëv proclaimed that the key to agro-industrial renewal lies in a wide use of intensive technology. In the agro-industrial area, the Soviets must employ new management methods, significantly extend the independence of collective and state farms, and make creative use of Lenin's idea of the tax in kind. Farmers can sell their excess to the state, at collective farm markets, or at cooperatives, or they may retain it for personal use.[51]

In 1985 Gorbachëv's long term plans were ambitious, especially for the forthcoming fifteen year period. They included the doubling of resources directed toward improving living conditions and constructing more dwellings. There was to be a struggle against drunkenness, an improvement of family relations, a reduction of industrial injuries, and a reduction of waste. To encourage efficiency, Gorbachëv resolved to enforce the socialist principle: from each according to his abilities, to each according to his labor.[52] To accomplish their economic goals, the Soviets were prepared to enter joint business ventures with Western businessmen.[53]

In Gorbachëv's proposal for elections to the Central Committee by secret ballot, members of the Party committee would have the right to enter any number of candidates on the voting list so long as they were all Communist Party members. With the importance of Party control "from above," it was important in the democratization of Soviet society to raise the level of control "from below." Repeatedly Gorbachëv told the Soviet people that the important thing was to create and strengthen all instruments and forms of real control by the workers. The idea was to have the control of local organizations in the hands of the people so that complaints to higher organizations would disappear; solving problems at the local level would take the pressure off the upper level leadership.[54]

During the period of stagnation, the Soviets suffered a lapse in their dedication to Marxist-Leninist ideology.[55] Thus, in a sense, Gorbachëv appeared to be trying to resurrect the Soviet man and form a true "Communist personality." He asserted that there was no other realistic way to form a personality, to mold a young person's civic position, than involvement in public affairs. Work on the ideological front had to be launched in earnest in many directions, and the Central Committee was to orient all Party organizations to draw all Party members, all Communists, into ideological work.[56]

Gorbachëv has not renounced Marxist-Leninist ideology. Indeed, he reasserted its value as the correct course for all mankind. Gorbachëv spoke of Marxism-Leninism as the true scientific theory of social development and quoted Lenin that Marxism discovered the laws and logic of change in capitalist economies and the historic development of those laws.[57] To him, social progress is expressed in the development of the international Communist and working class movement and in the growth of the new democratic movement of the times, including the anti-war and anti-nuclear movements.[58] Soviet internationalism continues to include developing nations. "The course of social progress is closely tied to anti-colonial revolutions, national liberation movements, ..."[59]

Gorbachëv reinforced the Marxian dialectic by saying that the first and foremost group of contradictions concerns the relations between countries of the two systems, capitalism and Communism. Marxist socialism does not renounce any of its principles or ideals since capitalism negates itself as it develops. Following Lenin's teachings, he observed that the policy of military confrontation has no future, and in the years ahead, the main struggle will center on the policy that can maintain peace. He predicted that among the first symptoms to grow acute are the contradictions between labor and capital, then will come the commercial and economic struggle on the world market. The United States, Western Europe, and Japan abound in visible and concealed contradictions. The Soviets perceive that the contradictions in capitalism are growing sharper, and that the solutions to world problems must be radical.[60]

In agreement with the Marxian dialectic, Gorbachëv expressed confidence in continued progress. He repeatedly reiterated, as did Lenin, that Communists are realists:

> The realistic dialectics of present-day development consists in a combination of competition and confrontation between the two systems and in a growing tendency towards interdependence of the countries of the world community. This is precisely the way the struggle of opposites, ..., is taking shape.[61]

Under Gorbachëv's program, there was a relaxation in the official policy on religion. This policy was in agreement with Lenin's decision not to aggravate religious elements which might react by revolt. The relaxation may also be the result of the "new thinking" whereby the Soviets learned from the West that freedom of religion encourages beliefs other than Christianity. Implementing religious freedom, on 4 October 1989, the Soviets permitted the reopening of a theological seminary in Kiev, which the "republican" government returned to the Russian Orthodox Church in 1988.[62] In Lithuania, All Saints Day and Christmas were reinstated as holidays.[63] In late 1989, the Soviets made other religious concessions.

In substance, Gorbachëv's program differed little from those of previous Soviet leaders. For example, Gorbachëv initially appeared to engage in a power struggle similar to that of Khrushchëv. Whereas Khrushchëv was concerned with de-Stalinization, Gorbachëv was engaged in de-Brezhnevization. Khrushchëv and Gorbachëv were concerned with rationalizing the Soviet situation with that in East Europe. Both recognized the need to improve relations with the West, and both expressed a readiness to pursue third world objectives.

Gorbachëv introduced dramatic changes in the Soviet Union. Under Brezhnev, the leadership was old, and when he died, there was a passing of the older generation. Gorbachëv infused new blood into the leading Party organizations. After Gorbachëv restructured the bureaucracy, there were few Soviet political generalists; most were well educated with technical training and experience in their field. Gorbachëv was committed to far-reaching reforms and placed great emphasis on the human factor with an effort to change the psychology of the Soviet people. This goal was difficult when applied to a passive, cynical population, but it brought memories of the earlier attempt to create the ideal Soviet man.

Gorbachëv tried to overcome a failure of developed socialism; however, the context in 1985 was different than in 1921 when Lenin introduced the NEP. Like that of his predecessors, Gorbachëv's initial program was self-serving in that it was designed to eliminate his opponents. In analogy with an earlier period, Stalin's purges in the 1930s opened the way for younger people, and Gorbachëv's program appeared to do the same.[64]

To renew the Soviet knowledge of Marxist-Leninist principles, the Soviets under Gorbachëv began a serious educational program to refresh the devotion to Communism and the humanist ideals of socialism. This renewal was intended to put the CPSU back in its position as the vanguard of the proletariat.[65]

The Communist Party of the Soviet Union never relaxes its efforts to bolster the country's defense capability. According to Gorbachëv in 1987, Communists and all army and navy personnel would continue to act with the greatest responsibility to upgrade their skills and increase the combat readiness of all arms and services. The Soviet people and the Party would do everything to strengthen the armed forces, and they expect no aggressive forces to catch the Soviet Union unawares.[66]

Speaking at the French Military Academy on 5 July 1989, the Chief of the Soviet General Staff, Army General Mikhail A. Moiseyev, told the audience that the Warsaw Pact and the Soviet Union are pledged not to take military action against a state or alliance unless they are exposed to aggression. He added that the Warsaw Pact and the Soviet Union must have sufficient armed forces of the correct composition and structure to guarantee a reliable defense of the state and the alliance. He did not explain, however, the meaning of "exposure to aggression." Moiseyev explained that the Soviet Union will repel aggression using defensive action only. It appears that the Soviets have renounced all offensive military, ground maneuvers, which is a most unrealistic policy.[67]

The Soviet regime inherited the Russian monarchial obsession with national security and the consequent investment of large sums in the armed forces. The Soviets follow the traditional Russian practice of maintaining armed forces equal to or greater than those of any other nation. Annually, the Soviet armed forces absorb large amounts of trained manpower, competent scientists, excellent machinery, and capital investment. Accordingly, the Soviets are concerned that the present technological race for military hardware will get out of hand and lead to a new arms race at a higher level of technology.[68] At the rate of increase in defense spending in 1987, the Soviet Union could be spending as much as seventeen percent of its GNP by the year 2000, the target date for the completion of Gorbachëv's restructuring. Such spending would divert even more resources from the civilian sector and deplete the capital so seriously needed for investment.[69] In 1989, Gorbachëv talked about reducing the budget allocations for the armed forces, but the realization of those reductions has not been observed. If there is any reduction of military spending, the Soviets intend to improve the quality of military hardware and military science to prevent the degradation of their military capability.[70]

Gorbachëv's open press policy does not mean that the Soviets have abandoned their control of the press; it does, however, indicate that they have changed their techniques for controlling the media. The Soviets consider it essential to "regulate the information flow which has swept into our country."[71] In October 1989 Gorbachëv appeared before an assembly of *Pravda* editors where he emphasized that *Pravda*, as the official Party organ, has the responsibility to support *perestroika* and all Party positions. Therefore, *Pravda* must set the tone for public opinion on *perestroika*, and *Pravda* must endorse *perestroika* as a continuation of the October revolution of 1917. Since the Central Committee has been uncomfortable with the opinions and views expressed by people under the new freedom, editors must understand that they have a responsibility to support Gorbachëv's program. There was a lack of understanding about what is expected, and Gorbachëv admonished *Pravda* to set the tone for all mass media. He said that the media must overcome the negative things that have appeared recently in the press, and the press should not create "confusion" since the press, as a public servant, must serve Soviet society.[72] Under *glasnost'*, the Soviets do not control the press by censorship, they control it by intimidation.

A few days after Gorbachëv gave his speech on Soviet media responsibility, *Pravda* published an editorial supporting the General Secretary. According to *Pravda*, the mass media must accept guidance from the Party in ensuring the revolutionary transformation of Soviet society. The Soviet people need accurate political and moral guidelines, and the leading integrating force in Soviet society is the Communist Party.[73] Thus, the media must support and promulgate the Party view. There is evidence that, even under *glasnost'*, the Soviets have removed an editor who did not support the Party view.[74]

Gorbachëv, like Lenin, talks about truth, but some of his statements and arguments are of questionable veracity.[75] In this matter, Gorbachëv has not broken the tradition set by earlier Soviet leaders; he continues to lie. His lies and half-truths are as flagrant as those of his predecessors. Gorbachëv wrote in *Perestroika* that the Soviet Union imports grain for the purpose of maintaining international trade.[76] Gorbachëv claims that the Soviets "took part in the establishment of the state of Israel."[77] Examples of his mendacious verbiage are numerous, and, in practice, Gorbachëv's *glasnost'* equates to necessary truth, or fewer unnecessary lies.

Under Gorbachëv, the Soviets have acknowledged that they assumed the responsibility for harnessing the potential of third world countries "for the benefit of world progress."[78] Thus, the Soviets have not renounced their support of revolution; for example, they have emphasized their intention to continue support of Nicaragua in spite of public announcements of the suspension of arms shipments to that country.[79] This policy emanates from the basic tenets of Marxism.

*   *   *   *   *   *   *   *   *   *   *   *   *   *   *   *   *   *   *

After Stalin died, conditions changed dramatically in the Soviet Union. Within four months the Korean War ended. In May 1955, the Austrian State Treaty neutralized Austria. There was a reconciliation with Tito in Yugoslavia, and at the Twentieth Party Congress, the Soviets acknowledged different paths to Communism. Gorbachëv tried to effect changes equally or more dramatic than the post-Stalin leaders.

Yet, with Gorbachëv, the Soviet economy has not experienced a sudden recovery. In mid-1989 negative tendencies were still apparent in a lack of discipline, inter-ethnic conflict, and strikes. Absenteeism continued to be a problem which caused a loss of productivity.[80] The net result was a slowdown in the economy.[81] The economic data released by the State Committee for Statistics for the entire year, shows that even though the GNP experienced a three percent increase, the economic situation in the Soviet Union remained complex. There was increased tension in the market place, and the country's economic dynamism had diminished. Indications are that many of the plans for economic and social development were not fulfilled in 1989.[82]

Under Gorbachëv there was a reenactment of an old pattern with two theses. First, reform under Gorbachëv spelled a softening. Means were diverted to home use and the ends were altered. There was a trend toward a less militant socialism since the Soviet empire and militant socialism are too expensive. Second, the Soviets continue to lie, since cultural motives, security, commitments, Soviet foreign policy, and Marxist-Leninist ideology, will remain unchanged. This pattern in the "new thinking" appears to be deception.

Gorbachëv's antics have been more tactics than substance. The major question before the world is how much can Gorbachëv change and how far are the Soviets willing to go to convince the West of their sincerity? Domestically, there are strict limits to *glasnost'*, *perestroika*, democracy, and other changes. Gorbachëv has, however, announced dramatic changes in the governmental structure, the election of officials, and religious freedom. Indeed, the implementation of these reforms will be an indication of Soviet sincerity. Superimposed on all of his domestic reforms, Gorbachëv said that he wanted no challenge to the Communist Party. Yet, during the meeting of the Central Committee, CPSU, from 5 to 7 February 1990, Gorbachëv proposed the introduction of a pluralistic political system which in effect would remove the constitutional guarantee of Communist Party domination of the Soviet Union.[83] In theory this introduction of "democracy" would permit the formation of political parties other than the Communist Party. This move is in reality Marxist since it speeds the process of giving the political control to the dictatorship of the proletariat. Gorbachëv and the "new thinkers" were quite clever in planning this reform. The major problem is that events may have moved a little faster than the "new thinking" plan prescribed.

Gorbachëv's domestic reforms are designed to reinforce and give credibility to the "new thinking" in foreign policy. When addressing Western Europe, he talks about "we Europeans." Gorbachëv's foreign policy was to focus on a different policy for different countries depending on the target country. This ploy is no change from the past, but the Gorbachëv effect is new. Gorbachëv, a superb public relations man, has an appeal based on his more innovative domestic policies. Internationally, he intended no fundamental change. Furthermore, his tactics changed from intimidation to a quest for peace, and he projects the image of readiness to compromise. He abandoned threats and used inducements, which may be a Soviet attempt at reflexive control. His *modus operandi* included incremental retreats like Lenin, but the West did not easily adjust to these new tactics. In public the Soviets allege that their foreign policy is not directed against the United States, but in reality this is exactly what they are doing. The Soviets have merely changed their *modus operandi* from the direct to an indirect approach.

Gorbachëv's most popular "buzz words" are *perestroika*, democracy, and *glasnost'*. *Glasnost'* could be compared with the "thaw" characteristic of the de-Stalinization period of the 1950s and 1960s. While Khrushchëv's thaw did not go as far as Gorbachëv's *glasnost'* appears to be leading, the openness of *glasnost'* has been a welcome breath of fresh air to many Westerners who want to see a convergence of cultures between East and West. This openness means that many negative aspects of the Soviet system will be reported by the press. Heretofore, airplane crashes, earthquakes, prostitution, crime, infant mortality rates, alcoholism and other social problems and disasters were classified since they tended to reveal imperfections in the Soviet system. The openness of press releases tends to lull the West into believing that now the Soviets are "just like us," since they have the same problems we have, and they are admitting it.

Regardless of where he came from or who he is, Mikhail S. Gorbachëv has made a revolutionary impact on Soviet domestic policies, the East European satellites, and Western civilization. The rapidity with which he has pronounced changes to traditional Soviet policy has placed the Western world in a state of amazement. Although many Westerners accept Gorbachëv's reforms at face value, there remains a large segment in the West which advises caution. Gorbachëv has displayed some impatience with the reluctance of the West to accept blindly his reforms. He wonders aloud why the West does not believe him, and he wants the West to forget the past and accept the peaceful rhetoric of his "new thinking."

"Tell them what they want to believe."

NOTES

1. Department of Defense, *Soviet Military Power*, 9.

2. Mikhail S. Gorbachëv, "The Cause of *Perestroika* Needs the Energy of the Young," *Pravda*, 16 Nov. 1989.

3. Jerry F. Hough, "Gorbachëv Consolidating Power," *Problems of Communism* 36 (July-August 1987): 21-43.

4. Gorbachëv, *A Time for Peace*, 165.

5. Michta, *An Emigre Reports*, v.

6. Ibid., 1.

7. Ibid., 13, 20.

8. Ibid., 3.

9. Ibid., 34-36.

10. Ibid., 8.

11. Ibid., 5-6.

12. Ibid., 6-8.

13. Ibid., 40-42.

14. Ibid., 45.

15. Timothy J. Colton, "Approaches to the Politics of Systemic Economic Reform in the Soviet Union," *Soviet Economy* 3 (April-June 1987): 145-170. Reprinted with permission of the publisher.

16. *New York Times*, 10 Jul. 1987, sec. 4, 1; Colton, "Approaches to the Politics of Systemic Economic Reform in the Soviet Union," *Soviet Economy* 3 (April-June 1987), 151.

17. Michta, *An Emigre Reports*, 50.

18. Ibid., 63.

19. The big bureaucracies are the Party apparatus, the state bureaucracy, the economic bureaucracy, the armed forces, and the police.

20. Michta, *An Emigre Reports*, 52.

21. Mikhail S. Gorbachëv, "The Socialist Idea and Revolutionary *Perestroika*," *Pravda*, 26 Nov. 1989, 1-3.

22. Gorbachëv, *Perestroika*, 4-5.

23. Colton, "Approaches to the Politics of Systemic Economic Reform in the Soviet Union," *Soviet Economy* 3 (April-June 1987): 145-170.

24. Ibid.

25. Gorbachëv, *Perestroika*, 4-5.

26. Peter Hauslohner, "Gorbachëv's Social Contract," *Soviet Economy*, 3 (January-March 1987): 54-89. Reprinted with permission of the publisher.

27. Gorbachëv, *Perestroika*, 5-6.

28. Ibid., 7-9.

29. Hauslohner, "Gorbachëv's Social Contract," *Soviet Economy*, 3 (January-March 1987): 54-89.

30. John R. Galvin, Interview, *Armed Forces Journal International* 126 (March 1988): 50-52.

31. Mikhail S. Gorbachëv, *Report to the CPSU Central Committee Plenum, 27 January 1987*, *TASS*, 27 Jan. 1987.

32. Ibid.

33. Gorbachëv, *Perestroika*, 13, 14.

34. Gorbachëv, *Report to the CPSU Central Committee Plenum, 27 January 1987, TASS*, 27 Jan. 1987.

35. Gorbachëv, *Perestroika*, 6-7.

36. Gorbachëv, *Report to the CPSU Central Committee Plenum, 27 January 1987, TASS*, 27 Jan. 1987.

37. Ibid.

38. Gorbachëv, *Perestroika*, 35-36.

39. Ibid., 52.

40. Ibid.

41. Ibid., 19-20.

42. *TASS*, 27 Jan. 1987.

43. *Pravda*, 27 Jun. 1987.

44. Gorbachëv, *Report to the CPSU Central Committee Plenum, 27 January 1987, TASS*, 27 Jan. 1987.

45. Ibid.

46. Ibid.

47. Gorbachëv, *CPSU Central Committee Political Report, 25 February 1986, FBIS Daily Report* (Supplement), 26 Feb. 1986, 1-42.

48. Ibid.

49. Ibid.

50. Gorbachëv, *Perestroika*, 261; Mikhail S. Gorbachëv, *Pravda*, 6 Nov. 1989; Moscow Television Service, 12 Dec. 1989, *FBIS Daily Report*, 13 Dec. 1989, 51-55.

51. Gorbachëv, *CPSU Central Committee Political Report, 25 February 1986*, *FBIS Daily Report* (Supplement), 26 Feb. 1986, 1-42.

52. Ibid.

53. Gorbachëv, *Perestroika*, 153.

54. Gorbachëv, *Report to CPSU Central Committee Plenum, 27 January 1987*, *TASS*, 27 Jan. 1987.

55. Gorbachëv, "The Socialist Idea and Revolutionary *Perestroika*," *Pravda*, 26 Nov. 1989, 1-3.

56. Gorbachëv, *Report to the CPSU Central Committee Plenum, 27 September 1987*, *TASS*, 27 Jan. 1987.

57. Gorbachëv, *CPSU Central Committee Political Report, 25 February 1986*, *FBIS Daily Report* (Supplement), 26 Feb. 1989, 1-42.

58. Ibid.

59. Ibid.

60. Ibid.

61. Ibid.

62. *TASS*, 4 Oct. 1989.

63. Moscow Domestic Service, 22 Oct. 1989, *FBIS Daily Report*, 24 Oct. 1989, 64.

64. Gorbachëv's emphasis on younger members on the Politburo is apparent from his appointments.

Member	Age at Appointment	Date
Viktor Petrovich Nikonov	58	April 1985
Nikolay Nikitovich Slyun'kov	58	January 1987
Aleksandr Nikolayevich Yakolev	64	March 1986
Lev Nikolayevich Zaykov	64	July 1985
Nikolay Ivanovich Ryzhkov	58	September 1985

V. A. Ivashko   September 1989
Andrei Andreyevich Gromyko (age 78), appointed in July 1985, has
been "promoted" off the Politburo.

65. *Pravda*, 15 Sept. 1989; *Pravda*, 30 Sept. 1989.

66. Gorbachëv, *Report to the CPSU Central Committee Plenum, 27 January 1987*, TASS, 27 Jan. 1987.

67. *Defense Nationale* (October 1989): 57-71.

68. Kennedy, "What Gorbachëv is Up Against," *The Atlantic Monthly* (June 1987): 29-43.

69. Ibid.

70. *Krasnaya Zvezda*, 28 Nov. 1989.

71. *Pravda*, 4 Nov. 1989.

72. Moscow Television Service, 24 Oct. 1989, *FBIS Daily Report*, 25 Oct. 1989, 60-65; *Pravda*, 25 Oct. 1989.

73. *Pravda*, 31 Oct. 1989.

74. *Argumenty I Fakty*, no. 46 (18-24 November 1989): 2.

75. Gorbachëv, *Report to the CPSU Central Committee Plenum, 27 January 1987*, TASS, 27 Jan. 1987.

76. Gorbachëv, *Perestroika*, 209.

77. Gorbachëv, *A Time for Peace*, 293.

78. Gorbachëv, *Perestroika*, 157.

79. *Pravda*, 22 Oct. 1989; *TASS*, 24 Nov. 1989.

80. *TASS*, 20 Oct. 1989; *Pravda*, 28 Jan. 1990; Gorbachëv, "Report at the CPSU Central Committee Plenum 5 February 1990," *Pravda*, 6 Feb. 1990.

81. *Pravda*, 21 Oct. 1989.

82. *Pravda*, 28 Jan. 1990.

83. Gorbachëv, "Report to the CPSU Central Committee Plenum 5 February 1990," *Pravda* 6 Feb. 1990.

XI

DIALECTICS

According to Mikhail S. Gorbachëv, the dialectic is still very much alive, and to solve Soviet problems, he turned to the works of Lenin as the "inexhaustible source of dialectical creative thought."[1] In the Marxian dialectic there is an inevitability of economic, political, and ideological competition between the capitalist and socialist systems. Gorbachëv reiterates that in the dialectical unity of opposites the competition between capitalism and socialism will lead to a new philosophy of peace, peaceful coexistence of the two systems. This new thesis will struggle peacefully with its antithesis and in the final analysis history will be the judge.[2] At the 27th Party Congress in 1987, the Soviets corroborated the dialectical unity and struggle of opposites, specifically the struggle between the socialist and capitalist systems.[3] Although Gorbachëv's "new thinking" appears to abandon the historical Marxist class warfare, a close reading of his speeches reveals that the ultimate Soviet goal has not changed. Gorbachëv, as a proponent of Marxism-Leninism, perceives the ultimate victory of socialism in a one-world, social, political, and economic order.[4]

To be sure, neither Gorbachëv nor any other Soviet leader has any intention of abandoning the fundamental principles on which the Bolsheviks founded the Soviet Union.[5] Marxist-Leninist in principle, *perestroika* began on the initiative of the Communist Party and, in contrast to Gorbachëv's remarks on the matter, might be considered a "revolution from above." *Perestroika* itself is an exercise of the dialectic, in that as a contradictory process it incorporates the struggle between the old and the new. The outcome, a new thesis, is expected to be a major change, an improvement, in Soviet economic, political, cultural, and social development.[6]

Gorbachëv bases *perestroika* on democracy, which requires mass initiative, socialist self-government, improved discipline, *glasnost'*, and criticism. Furthermore, he says that *perestroika* is the development of the principles of democratic centralism: more socialism and more democracy.[7] In contrast to Lenin's teachings that socialism must at times "take two steps back" for every step forward, Gorbachëv perceives his revolution as a jump forward in socialist development.[8] Lenin's frequent, unexpected "changes in tactics," which in many instances were duplicity, are the kind of dialectics in political thinking which Gorbachëv is trying to instill in the Soviet people. He perceives the necessity for a renewal of the dialectic because the socialist political economy has lost touch with the dialectics of reality which Lenin taught.[9]

Gorbachëv views his reform program as an exercise in the dialectic, and the Soviets observe the struggle at work everywhere. The Soviet economy is the most obvious struggle between opposites. The dialectic appears in the East-West military and political confrontation. The dialectic is the fundamental struggle between Marxist-Leninist ideology and Christianity, democracy and dictatorship, strength and security, internal reforms and external security, nationalism and internationalism, military strength and disarmament, and lies and the truth. These and other conflicts constitute the components of the dialectic between Communism and capitalism.

Veracity has never been a Soviet trait. Gorbachëv wrote in *Perestroika*: "History shows that we can keep the word we gave and that we honor the obligations assumed."[10] In this regard, the General Secretary has taken liberty with history. While the Soviets honored to the letter the Nazi-Soviet Non-Aggression Pact of 23 August 1939, the same cannot be said of most other treaties they have signed. Recent Soviet violations of international agreements and treaties are legion, and they are well documented and publicized.[11] The conflict between truth and lies may be dialectic, but a positive outcome is questionable.

One of the targets for Gorbachëv's book *Perestroika* is the people of the United States. In the foreword "To the Reader," he wrote that

Perestroika was not necessitated by the disastrous state of the Soviet economy. Yet, in Chapter One he methodically spells out the disastrous ills of the Soviet economy with the view to making revolutionary changes in the entire Soviet society.[12]   The rapid, drastic changes which he initiated in late 1989 and early 1990 indicate that the Soviet Union was indeed on the brink of disaster.

In the area of military strategy, one can observe Soviet duplicity. For several years, the Soviets have been disseminating two lines of thought, directed at two distinct groups. The first line, disseminated by the Party elite, is the florid rhetoric renouncing nuclear warfare, surprise, preemption, and the quest for military superiority. This line, an integral part of the "new thinking" rhetoric, has been directed toward the West, specifically the United States, where people in general want to hear messages of peace and tranquility. This line is nothing more than disinformation - deception.

The second line of military thought consists of the instructions and guidelines for the Soviet armed forces. This line is found in official Soviet writings on military subjects and is directed toward the Soviet military officers who are responsible for developing military strategy and tactics and implementing Soviet war plans. The two lines are different and contradictory, even though they emanate from the same Soviet government. The working of the dialectic between these two lines has not yet yielded a new, more progressive thesis.

Gorbachëv's use of half-truths is impressive. In his attempt to lure Western Europe into the Soviet camp, he repeatedly talks about the common heritage of Western Europe and the Soviet Union. His rhetoric, however, is a poorly concealed effort to rewrite history. In *Perestroika* Gorbachëv wrote: "Europe 'from the Atlantic to the Urals' is a cultural historical entity united by the common heritage of the Renaissance and the Enlightenment, of the great philosophical and social teachings of the nineteenth and twentieth centuries."[13]   A study of history reveals that Russia did not experience the European Enlightenment, Protestantism, or individual capitalism. The only Russians who experienced the Enlightenment were the nobility who were abroad and those who surrounded the monarch. The limited Renaissance influence in Russia entered the empire via the Byzantine Empire and was not

West European. Christianity entered Russia through Constantinople.

The Soviets consider the large number of socialist countries to be part of the international socialist community, and they expect the world socialist community to participate in the dialectic between capitalism and Communism. Although they do not agree on the everyday problems of economics, Party control, international affairs, and social welfare, the socialist countries, in the Soviet view, are indeed members of this international fraternity of socialism. Even though the socialist countries do not operate under central control, the Soviets perceive all to be united in the common belief in Marxism-Leninism.[14] They all have one common characteristic: they oppose capitalism and are dedicated to obliterate it. The Soviets expect the number of socialist countries to grow, and in this process, they perceive the operation of the dialectic. In a multi-colored, multi-dimensional world, the Soviets perceive differences of interests among states. Yet, in this dialectical milieu, they perceive progress in the emergence of an interconnected, integral international community - one world.[15] In this interdependent, integral new world, the Soviets intend to retain their socio-economic system and their ideology.[16] The parties comprising the Communist movement "pursue a common ultimate goal: peace and socialism," the unifying force of the international working class movements.[17]

Gorbachëv and his cohorts are concerned about cooperation and international solidarity among the socialist states. The Soviets intend to take advantage of the success socialism enjoyed in the post-World War II years in its growth and role in international politics. Many of the new socialist states looked to the Soviet Union as their example, which helped foster the development of socialism. In their turn they now support the Soviet Union, and Gorbachëv perceives the unfolding of current events in the Soviet Union as a result of joint activity and concerted effort by all Communist countries. While Communist countries will remain independent, they are assured of success only if they develop common interests and project a united effort in the interests of world socialism. Collaboration of the ruling Communist parties is essential to this cooperation, one objective of which is a common and coordinated foreign policy of all Communist states.[18]

The Soviets perceive the dialectic at work in the realm of strength and security. The dialectic follows from their approach to nuclear warfare which they developed in the early 1960s. Their present rhetoric on the use of nuclear weapons is to reject Clausewitz's dictum that war is a continuation of politics by other means, employ the third law of the dialectic, which is the negation of the negation, and conclude that the nuclear solution to international disputes is impossible. The new thesis which emanates progressively from this struggle is a phased reduction of armaments until there are no military forces in the world. The Soviets describe the new thesis as military sufficiency at successively lower levels until all armed forces have been eliminated.[19] The disarmed bourgeoisie is a long term Leninist goal.[20]

The Soviets use war scare propaganda in an attempt to intimidate the West. For example, in the early 1980s the Soviets launched a campaign to convince the West that the danger of nuclear war was increasing. Although the campaign reached a peak when Yuri V. Andropov was General Secretary of the CPSU, Gorbachëv still propagates this theme repeatedly to advance his disarmament schemes.[21]

In the field of military strategy, the Soviets perceive the working of the dialectic. They claim that their military doctrine is directed toward preventing a war of annihilation; yet, their military strategy is directed toward repelling anyone who encroaches on the sovereignty of any country of the "socialist community."[22] Thus it appears that the Soviet Union would wage a war of annihilation - retaliation - to prevent a war of annihilation should the socialist community be threatened. In this event, the Marxian dialectic would be self-defeating.

The Soviet armed forces are international and serve to defend the entire socialist community and the worldwide "historical victories" of Communism. Furthermore, the Soviet Armed Forces are not limited to the defense of the Soviet Union and the socialist countries; they may operate in any part of the world where Communist Party or Soviet interests are in question.[23] Moreover, the Soviets do not hesitate to use their armed forces against their own citizens in the peripheral regions of the Soviet Union to prevent their empire from disintegrating.[24] This policy is not surprising, since the Soviet Union, as a sovereign state, has the responsibility for maintaining law and order in its national territory.

In the military arena the Soviets make decisions about the ratio of conventional versus nuclear forces, continental versus global strategy, support of revolution, reduction of forces, and other strategic questions. These decisions are made by a collegial body, the Politburo, with participation by government officials, the Chief of the Soviet General Staff, the Foreign Minister, the Soviet Defense Minister, and specialists.

The dialectic plays an integral part in the Soviet military decision making process and will lead a Soviet military officer to a conclusion different from the one deduced by a Western officer. The difference is inherent in the thought processes of the two cultures. The Soviet thought process is entirely different from that of a Westerner because the Soviet uses the Marxian dialectic. There are also different moral laws which govern the thinking of the two cultures.[25] Whereas the Soviet thought process is based on Marxist-Leninist morality, the Western thought process is conditioned by the Judeo-Christian ethic.

Former Chiefs of the Soviet General Staff, such as Ogarkov, Kulikov, and Akhromeyev, frequently make statements supporting Politburo decisions. Chiefs of the Soviet General Staff serve no set term, and in many instances a retiring Chief of the Soviet General Staff is assigned to another important post, such as Commander of the Warsaw Pact Forces.[26] An assignment of this nature is not a state of disgrace.[27] Similarly, a change in the Defense Minister does not imply banishment of the incumbent.[28] When they parrot the Party line, these reassigned officers give credence to Gorbachëv's *glasnost'*. Moreover, as loyal Soviet military officers these men are expected to support the official Party-state position. This support should surprise no one.

Current Soviet writings on the importance of conventional warfare do not indicate that the Soviets have relegated nuclear warfare to a secondary position. Since the early 1960s, Soviet military authors have been writing about conventional war and the possibility that a major war could be conventional.[29] Hence, the Soviet rhetoric on conventional arms is merely a continuation of an old theme and is not dialectic.

A major element of Gorbachëv's peace program is the reduction of military forces. Around 1960, United States' military leaders considered preemptive or preventive nuclear strikes as a possible solution to United States' security problems.[30] Following closely behind the United States, the Soviets adopted preemption in the early 1960s, since this concept satisfied their security requirements.   Conditions changed, and essential equivalence (parity) became a United States' SALT policy written into the Joint Resolution on the Interim Agreement.[31]   Yet, the Soviet concept of parity differs from that of the United States.   The Soviets would consider less than sufficient a force level which the West considers excessive.[32]   Therefore, there will be difficulty in discussing force reductions between East and West.

Gorbachёv's proposed reductions in Soviet military forces have received great international publicity and praise.   Yet, previous Soviet force reductions have attracted little international comment.   During the NEP, Lenin reduced the size of the Red Army by a factor of nine.   At the end of the civil war, the Red Army had a strength of five million; by 1923, however, the strength had been reduced to 550,000.[33]   Stalin reduced the size of the Red Army in 1937 through his purges and again in the immediate post-World War II years.   Nikita S. Khrushchёv implemented a force reduction in the Soviet armed forces in the early 1960s.   These Soviet force reductions were unilateral and were carried out with no attempt at a "trade off" in similar reductions by the West.   Regardless of force reductions, the Soviets will probably maintain military forces of sufficient size and quality to repel any threat which they perceive to their security.

Soviet reductions in military force can be deceptive, since those troops relieved from active duty go immediately to reserve status from which they can be recalled with no delay.   The Soviets maintain a large pool of trained reserves which they continually infuse with newly discharged soldiers.[34]   According to Marshal Sergei F. Akhromeyev, the Soviet Union does not want a professional army.   The "persisting military danger" to the Soviet Union dictates that the Red Army be based on universal, compulsory military service.   An army based on universal, compulsory military service guarantees the possession of well trained, mobilized reserves ready for employment.   Moreover, a conscript army requires less money and material resources than a large, active-duty, regular military force.[35]

Speaking on Moscow television, 31 October 1989, Deputy Defense Minister Shabanov argued that the security of the Soviet Union cannot be attained in the foreseeable future by political means alone; therefore, the Soviets must maintain an armed force that will ensure the nation's defense. The size of this force, according to Shabanov, must be based on the principle of "sensible sufficiency."[36] In January 1990, the Soviets talked of "defense sufficiency."[37] Apparently the dialectic between no reductions and reasonable sufficiency is still at work.

In 1989 most of the rhetoric about a reduction in military forces pertained to Soviet and Warsaw Pact conventional forces; but, the primary military threat from the Soviet Union is the existence of their Strategic Rocket Forces, which are in a high alert status continuously. Nuclear armed intercontinental missiles are programmed to strike targets in the United States within about thirty minutes from launch. Targets in the United States are both countervalue and counterforce targets with the counterforce targets, United States intercontinental missile systems, being the primary targets. The Soviets have no plans for reducing the size or effectiveness of the Strategic Rocket Forces and have instituted a program to improve their capabilities.[38]

The Soviet socio-economic system is a factor in the determination of the CPSU's international strategy. The Soviet ideal is a world without weapons and coercion, a world in which every country may choose its path of development and its way of life freely.[39] Yet, this situation will obtain only when the bourgeoisie (the West) is disarmed.[40] In proposing and implementing military force reductions, the Soviets exercise the dialectic between reform and security. Force reduction is necessary for the release of resources to the civilian economy and for the "new thinking" rhetoric whereby the Soviets intend to motivate the reduction of Western military forces. Domestically, however, a reduction in Soviet military forces could lead to a loss of internal control, a situation which the Soviets can ill afford.

The Russian people are among the most religious in the world. Their spirituality can be traced to an awe of the mysteries of nature and the fairy tales and superstitions which have come down through the ages, primarily by word of mouth. This heritage of pagan superstition may be the reason the Soviets refer to Christianity as a belief of the ignorant, the superstitious, and the mythological. Christianity came to Russia through Constantinople, the "second Rome." On the Russian pagan beliefs Prince Vladimir superimposed Christianity in 988 when he became a Christian and extended the faith to his subjects. The result was a strange mixture which became Russian Orthodoxy. This heritage caused the Russian version of Christianity to be more emotional and meditative than Christianity in the West. Although the Communists are avowed atheists, they do not hesitate to call on the religious faith of the Russian people in a national emergency. For example, after the German invasion in 1941, Stalin, speaking on the radio using liturgical speech, made an emotional appeal to the people, asked them to remember their great Russian past, and called on the Russian Orthodox Church for cooperation. In 1985 Mikhail S. Gorbachëv was handed a situation which approached the status of an emergency. Subsequent events indicate that Soviet problems were worse than the Kremlin leaders perceived. Past practices indicate that the newly granted religious freedom in the Soviet Union may be a temporary call for help.

Lenin was familiar with the Bible, and he did not hesitate to quote the scriptures or mention the name of God when it suited his purpose. At times, he would modify passages from the Bible to apply to a specific situation.[41] Gorbachëv, too, quotes the Bible; however, at times he attempts to attribute the quotation to Marxists. For example, in his report to the CPSU Central Committee on 25 February 1986, he said: "But, as we say, 'man does not live by bread alone.'"[42]

Under Gorbachëv there has been a relaxation of restrictions on religious activity; however, this new policy is deceptive since the Soviets intend to use religion to help achieve Gorbachëv's objectives. For example, in Kazakhstan a meeting of religious leaders and the first secretary of the Kazakh Communist Party found the Party secretary admonishing the church leaders to assist the Supreme Soviet in improving inter-ethnic relations and furnishing food and consumer goods. He noted that many religious organizations assist in the struggle for peace and humanism. He further admonished the clergy to teach and observe the moral and human principles of charity, philanthropy, mother and child protection, and help for the elderly and invalids. He delivered these admonitions in the guise of restoring "Leninist principles relating to religion."[43]

Furthermore, the Soviets have permitted Orthodox and Lutheran priests to hold memorial services for victims of Stalin's purges.[44] The

Soviets have also restored certain religious holidays in Lithuania.[45]   In a meeting 17 October 1989 with the synod of the Russian Orthodox Church and other high ranking church officials, Foreign Minister Shevardnadze reaffirmed the "mutual respect" between the state and the church. He pointed out that the Soviet Government "values highly" the moral and ethical values taught by the Russian Orthodox Church and other religions.[46] Gorbachëv hints that more religious freedom is nigh.

Communism runs counter to the fundamentals on which Western civilization rests.   Communism is antithetical to the entire Judeo-Christian ethic, which played an important role in the foundation of Western civilization. The Soviet system embodies atheism and actively pursues programs to convince Christian believers of the great "myths and falsifications" by which they have been "deluded."   While paying lip service to religious toleration, the Soviets make life unbearable for believers who try to live their Christian faith.   To the Soviets, the Communist Party is supreme, and God is merely a figment of the imagination of mystics, superstitious people, charlatans, and the ignorant. Class struggle, the foundation of Marxism, has no place in Christianity. Therefore, the Soviets are resolved to eradicate the "God myth." To them, the answer is "scientific" socialism. The dialectic between Christianity and Marxism cannot lead to a new, more progressive thesis.

Atheistic education is an integral component of Gorbachëv's restructuring program, and the Soviets expect to use the full force of Marxist-Leninist ideology to accomplish this purpose. The dialectic is very much alive in the Soviet anti-religion campaign.   "The struggle against religious ideology requires all conscious working people and Communists, above all, to be drawn into the ranks of champions of atheist education."[47]

Gorbachëv's meeting with Pope John Paul II on 1 December 1989 conveniently fits the "new thinking" strategy. To convince the West that he is a genuine reformer, he must deliver on all of his promises. If he falters even once, his entire program of *perestroika* will be doomed. He will not only lose the confidence of the Soviet people, the West will see him for what he is.   Thus, he must carry his reforms to the limits expected by the West. Indeed, his statement upon leaving the session with the pope reveals the true purpose of his visit. Gorbachëv said that

Moscow was addressing church issues "in a spirit of democracy and humanism and within the framework of *perestroika*."[48]

Gorbachëv projects the image of a reformer; however, he is not the first reformer in the Soviet Union. Both Vladimir I. Lenin and Nikita S. Khrushchëv were reformers. Lenin's NEP was a reform of War Communism, which did not work. Khrushchëv's reform was an attempt to correct some of the flaws in the Stalinist system. Neither of these reform periods lasted ten years. On the other hand, the periods following these reformers lasted much longer. The Stalinist era, from Lenin to Khrushchëv, was twenty-five years; the Brezhnev era lasted eighteen. Gorbachëv's permanent reforms may sound impressive, but past Soviet practices indicate that genuine reforms will be limited and short lived. "History" will depict the degree of permanence.

The situation in 1921 was so bad in Russia that Lenin had to do something quickly and drastically or he would lose what he had won by intimidation, treachery, and subversion. Consequently, Lenin displayed a degree of flexibility which has not been observed among Soviet leaders until the entrée of Gorbachëv. The NEP was Lenin's retreat to a more defensible position, a retreat to which Gorbachëv attributes the survival of the Bolshevik revolution.[49]

The NEP did solve the immediate problems for the Bolsheviks, but the NEP did not endure. After Lenin died in 1924, the ensuing power struggle ended with Josef Stalin in control. Having attained total control by 1928, Stalin ended the NEP and inaugurated the first of a series of Five Year Plans for the Soviet economy. Although Stalin's methods succeeded in marked economic advances, they were fundamentally defective and led to the stagnation of the Soviet socio-economic system. Accordingly, Stalin's successors condemned his methods and sought better solutions to Soviet problems. The Soviets know that the West is anticipating an answer to the question of how long and how far the Kremlin leaders will permit the "new thinking" to proceed. The answer lies in the degree to which the Soviets are dedicated to the strategy of the indirect approach.

In seeking better solutions to their problems, the Soviets looked back to Lenin for the correct Marxist methods. Therefore, Gorbachëv, as have other Soviet leaders, repeatedly invoked the name of Lenin and

Lenin's deeds as the authority for reform. Lenin, however, said and did many things that do not conform to what Gorbachëv claims he wants to do. The democracy, the justice, the equality, the renewal, and the openness which Gorbachëv advocates had an ominous meaning under Lenin.

Gorbachëv's domestic program is not entirely new. Khrushchëv adopted the philosophy of Libermanism, which was a partial reversion to capitalism, and Brezhnev implemented it. In 1961, the 22nd Party Congress passed a law limiting the tenure of top level officials to fifteen years.[50] In 1965, after the fall of Khrushchëv, Alexei N. Kosygin, Chairman of the Council of Minsters, submitted an economic reform program whereby management would be decentralized, central planning would be simplified, and there would be an increase in efficiency and productivity. Incentives for these reforms were profits, bonuses, loans, and credits.[51]

Four and one-half years into Gorbachëv's tenure, there appeared to be concern that the measures taken to improve the Soviet economy were not working and were not producing tangible results.[52] The Soviet GNP was not rising as rapidly as desired, and there was a decrease in the growth rate of industrial production. Shortages, including a shortage in food production, were increasing. On 20 October 1989, in a discussion of these problems, the Soviet Council of Ministers partially attributed these problems to strikes and a deterioration of labor discipline.[53] The Soviet economic statistics for the entire year of 1989 were disappointing and indicated that the economy had not reached the peak of "crisis development" and had not turned around.[54]

Within the Soviet Union the dialectic may be operating between Western democracy and Soviet democracy. The components of Soviet democracy are democratic centralism and the dictatorship of the proletariat. Although democratic centralism and the dictatorship of the proletariat are integral to Marxism-Leninism, the operation of *glasnost'* may be giving the Soviet people a glimpse of Western democracy that will compete with the Marxist-Leninist concept of democracy. Indeed, the wringing of a new thesis from this struggle will be an ordeal.

Vladimir I. Lenin and Mikhail S. Gorbachëv emphasized the democratic nature of Marxist socialism. Gorbachëv cites Lenin in calling upon Soviet citizens to deepen the democratization of the socialist order, and he asserts that democracy is the essence of socialism.[55] The Western understanding of democracy is different from the meaning which Gorbachëv and other Soviets use. In the Soviet mind, democracy does not imply a government from people of different political parties who elect public officials in free, open elections. On the contrary, Marxist-Leninist democracy has meant a consensus according to which the people, the masses, approve the decisions and actions taken unilaterally by the Communist Party.

Under Marxist democracy the people are expected to conform to Party teachings. Although the people are supposed to rise up in indignation when an official is engaged in non-Marxist practices, their indignation is to be conditioned by a sound indoctrination with Marxist-Leninist ideology. The inculcation of Marxist responsibility is the reason Lenin, Gorbachëv, and other Marxists have continually emphasized the necessity to indoctrinate the people in Marxist-Leninist ideology. The true Communist - the ideal Soviet man - is so imbued with socialist principles and so dedicated to Marxists beliefs that he responds correctly and automatically to any irregularity in the system. "The [Communist] Party acts as the guiding force and the main guarantor for the development of socialist self-government."[56] In spite of the rhetoric, there has been no Communist party, no Communist program, and no Communist movement that has led to the winning of a parliamentary majority in a democratic system.[57] The dictatorship of the proletariat does not conform to Western democracy.

Lenin wrote that frequently it would be necessary for Communists to take "two steps back" for each step forward. In contrast to Lenin's "two steps back," in *Perestroika*, Gorbachëv wrote that his program for renewal and reform was a jump forward.[58] He further stated that the dire state of the Soviet socio-economic system demanded that the renewal and reform process be undertaken with speed since there was insufficient time to wait for the "natural" processes.[59] In the ideological, social, and economic areas, Gorbachëv inaugurated reforms early in his tenure as Party General Secretary; however, his political reforms lagged behind in the "new thinking." Marxism-Leninism teaches that when pure Communism becomes a reality, the state will wither away and society will be under the political control of the dictatorship of the proletariat. Until that time, the Communist Party was to wield absolute control of the state as the vanguard of the proletariat since the proletariat were not sufficiently educated and informed to know what was best.

Marx, Engels, and Lenin formulated the theory of the Communist state, but they did not spell out the path whereby the proletariat would assume political control of the state from the Communist Party. The Soviet leaders recognized this deficiency in Marxism-Leninism, and Gorbachëv assumed the responsibility for guiding the proletariat to their rightful role in the political system.[60] In developing the "new thinking" program, the Soviet leaders decided to speed things up and give the Soviet people the experience requisite to assuming their role as the dictatorship of the proletariat. In the plenary meeting of the Central Committee of the Communist Party on 5 February 1990, Mikhail S. Gorbachëv proposed the inauguration of political pluralism (democracy), which meant that the Communist Party would relinquish its monopoly on the authority to control the Soviet government. In theory, this proposal means that it is possible that political parties other than the Communist Party can form and participate in the Soviet democratic process.

Gorbachëv's proposal, although viewed in the West as an indication of the impending collapse of the Soviet Union, is Marxist-Leninist in form, content, and intent. It is not Stalinist or Communist in the sense of traditional Communist practices. Yet, the successful implementation of a multi-party system under which the Communist Party endures as the dominant political force would strengthen the Marxist-Leninist objectives and the Communist hold on the Soviet Union. A successful, democratic Communist Party would hasten the dictatorship of the proletariat and the withering away of the state. In the Soviet Union a Communist government emplaced by the people, the proletariat, through free elections would facilitate the realization of the ultimate Marxist-Leninist objective of one world in which the enemies of the people, the bourgeoisie, have been eliminated.

The implementation of the political phase of the "new thinking" is the most risky component of this grandiose plan. The key to the success of this "new thinking" move is control. The Communist Party, and especially Gorbachëv, must exercise the utmost care in this process of inaugurating popular democracy to insure that there is no loss of control over Soviet society. Excess haste in this fundamental process could culminate in a loss of political control with anarchy as the consequence.

Glasnost' has intensified the working of the dialectic and has caused internal problems, especially with Soviet writers. Initially it appeared that some Soviet writers believed the propaganda of the "new thinking" and were writing in support of pacifist ideas. In 1987 during a plenary session of the Board of the Soviet Writers' Union, the Chief of the Main Political Administration of the Army and Navy, Colonel General Dmitriy A. Volkogonov, admonished Soviet writers for misinterpreting the "new thinking" as reflecting a pacifist policy and for raising doubt about the morality of Soviet nuclear deterrence. Volkogonov told the Soviet writers that they must understand reality and that until a reliable mechanism is found to avert the danger of war, it will be necessary to rely on military means. A pacifist attitude casting doubt on the morality of nuclear retaliation would be a most serious mistake. Other Soviet officials also admonished Soviet writers for propagating a pacifist attitude.[61]

Another product of Gorbachëv's *glasnost'* is a spirit of pacifism among draft age young men in the Moscow area. The negative attitude toward military service has become the target of more intense concentration on "military patriotic" education and Marxist-Leninist ideology.[62] Furthermore, the Soviets have experienced protests against conscription by draft age men in other geographical areas.[63]

In East-West relations, the dialectic was evident in the meeting between the United States President, Ronald Reagan, and General Secretary Mikhail S. Gorbachëv at Reykjavik. Gorbachëv observed the Soviet objective to be nearer and more perceptible in a situation that was becoming more complex and contradictory. On the one hand he observed agreement within reach, but on the other hand enormous barriers. Gorbachëv concluded that the Soviets can wait for the dialectic to produce the new thesis.[64] In the dialectic process, the outcome should have been an agreement favorable to the Soviet Union, representing progress, a new set of conditions, and a new thesis.

The working of the dialectic is evident daily in the Soviet press reports of continuous unrest among the ethnic minorities where the nationality problem is a continuous irritation to the CPSU. Typical complaints from the peripheral regions include the suppression of religious freedom, lack of national identity, absence of independence, and the requirement to use the Russian language. Complaints by the Soviets include crime, strikes, and disrespect for Soviet soldiers. In the formation of the Soviet empire, the quest for security motivated the Soviets to incorporate these borderlands as buffer areas to prevent a surprise attack. In most cases, this annexation was accomplished against the popular will and was enforced by the Red Army. Furthermore, as the Soviets extended their quest for security after World War II, they gained control of East Europe.

The Soviet empire, as is the case of any empire based on the quest for security, depends on its armed forces to control these outlying areas. Once an empire loses its capability for control, the peripheral areas will break away. Should the Soviets reduce the size of the Red Army below the capability to control these areas, the centrifugal forces in these peripheral areas will cause a rapid disintegration of the Soviet empire. Gorbachëv and his cohorts in late 1989 permitted a relaxation in East Europe. Almost immediately, the people in several of these peripheral areas installed non-Communist governments.[65] If Gorbachëv wants to retain credibility for his "new thinking," he has no choice other than to accede to these changes. If the Soviets say "no" even once, the entire "new thinking" program will be destroyed. In late 1989 relaxation in East Europe was having an effect in peripheral areas which were part of the RSFSR. Specifically, the Baltic "republics" began clamoring for independence. The Soviets are in a dialectical dilemma: they must decide whether to continue the "new thinking" with its accompanying relaxation and loss of control, or to retain control and lose their new image.

The problems in the Soviet Union among the various nationalities continue to worry the Soviets. Gorbachëv blames this nationalism on the Soviet departure from Lenin's policies on the nationalities. He describes the Soviet state as the embodiment of the revolutionary will and aspirations of a multi-national family of equal peoples. He refers to the international unity of the working peoples of all Soviet nations and nationalities and the right to self determination.[66]

Gorbachëv proclaims that the most important principle in the multi-national Soviet state is the free and equal use by all Soviet citizens of their mother tongue. He adds to this freedom the learning of the Russian language, "voluntarily" adopted by the people as a means of communication between nations.[67]

In his praise of the Soviet attitude and policies towards the ethnic groups and nationalities, Gorbachëv perceived the working of the dialectic. "The dialectics look like this: the growth of educational and cultural standards, alongside modernization of the economy, leads to the emergence of an intelligentsia in every nation; the growth of national self-consciousness and the growth of a nation's natural interest in its historical roots."[68] The complaints from Soviet ethnic groups do not support Gorbachëv's healthy growth rhetoric. Gorbachëv's depiction of the nationalities as members of one big happy Soviet family is nothing more than an exercise in the big lie - disinformation.

The dialectic is at work even within the Politburo, where Gorbachëv appears to have detractors. In an interview on 26 September 1989 criticizing *perestroika*, Ye. K. Ligachev argued that capitalism cannot improve socialism. He asserted the impossibility of modernizing socialism and correcting the deficiencies in the Soviet economy by the methods of capitalist management. He perceived in *perestroika* many contradictory policies. The Soviets are fighting alcoholism but have at the same time increased the production of alcohol. The Soviet economy will not produce sufficient food until the peasants have a satisfactory life and the proper technical equipment. Although small private farms are the most efficient, the Soviet Union should rely primarily on the large collective farms. He asserted that conditions in the Soviet Union are not the same as during the NEP. Ligachev, whose father-in-law was executed in the purges of 1937, saw contradictions everywhere he looked.[69]

* * * * * * * * * * * * * * * * * * *

Perestroika is an exercise of the dialectic. It consists of a continuous struggle between those methods and techniques which the Soviets have tried and have failed and those which the Soviets have tried and have succeeded. Gorbachëv's insistence that *perestroika* consists of learning by experience describes his concept of the present-day struggle for something that will work. Those things that do not work are to be discarded and something new is to be tried. Gorbachëv has continually emphasized the necessity to follow Lenin's example in this matter. The "new thinking" includes the concept that Communists learn by experience. They are frequently wrong in their decisions, but they learn by their mistakes.

In the working of the dialectic, Gorbachëv observes numerous instances in which decisions of the past were incorrect and had a long term deleterious effect. The daily press releases from the Soviet Union contain a plethora of examples in which the dialectic is at work. All learning by experience is accomplished in the context of the broader dialectic, the struggle between Marxist-Leninist socialism and capitalism.

The dialectic is international. Internationally, the Soviets will continue to develop links with non-Communist movements and religious organizations which oppose war. These connections will assist in propagating Marxist-Leninist ideology and in the quest for disarmament. The Communist Party acts as both the political and moral vanguard of Soviet society, and it has the responsibility of perfecting the ideological education of Communists, whom the Party expects to master the traditions of Bolshevism and education in these traditions.[70]

In its greater context, the dialectic is the struggle between capitalism and Communism. Within this international struggle, there exist lesser struggles, in each of which the dialectic operates between components of the two systems. Marxists expect each of these component struggles to yield a new thesis, historical progress, contributing to the ultimate goal of pure Communism in a single civilization, one world of a classless society.[71]

"Tell them what they want to believe."

NOTES

1. Gorbachëv, *Perestroika*, 11.

2. Ibid., 134.

3. Ye. Primakov, "New Philosophy of Foreign Policy," *Pravda*, 9 Jul. 1987.

4. Gorbachëv, *Perestroika*, 123, 148; Gorbachëv, "Holiday Reception in the Kremlin," *Pravda*, 8 Nov. 1989; Gorbachëv, "The Socialist Idea and Revolutionary *Perestroika*," *Pravda*, 26 Nov. 1989.

5. Gorbachëv, *Perestroika*, 40; Gorbachëv, "Report at the CPSU Central Committee Plenum 5 February 1990," *Pravda*, 6 Feb. 1990.

6. Gorbachëv, *Perestroika*, 257; *Pravda*, 25 Oct. 1989; Gorbachëv, "Report at the CPSU Central Committee Plenum 5 February 1990," *Pravda*, 6 Feb. 1990.

7. Gorbachëv, *Perestroika*, 20-21, 23.

8. Ibid., 37.

9. Ibid., 34-35.

10. Ibid., 205.

11. For specific examples, see Quentin Crommelin, Jr., and David S. Sullivan, *Soviet Military Supremacy: The Untold Facts About the New Danger to America* (Los Angeles, California: The Defense and Strategic Studies Program, University of Southern California, 1985), 137-147.

12. *Perestroika*, xi, xii, 3-8.

13. Ibid., 183.

14. Ibid., 151.

15. Ibid., 123, 148.

16. Ibid., 125.

17. Gorbachëv, *CPSU Central Committee Political Report, 25 February 1986, FBIS Daily Report*, (Supplement), 26 Feb. 1986, 1-42.

18. Gorbachëv, *Perestroika*, 147-152.

19. Ibid., 127; *Pravda*, 21 Jan. 1990.

20. Lenin, *Selected Works*, vol. 1, 743, 746.

21. Stephen Sestanovich, "What Gorbachëv Wants," *The New Republic* (25 May 1987): 6-9. Reprinted by permission of *The New Republic*, (c) 1987, The New Republic, Inc.

22. Ye. Primakov, "New Philosophy of Foreign Policy," *Pravda*, 9 Jul. 1987.

23. A. A. Grechko, *On Guard Over Peace and the Building of Communism* (Moscow: Military Publishing House, 1971), 90.

24. *TASS*, 18 Jan. 1990; *TASS*, 19 Jan. 1990; *Izvestiya*, 22 Jan. 1990; *Pravda*, 23 Jan. 1990; Moscow World Service, 2 Jan. 1990, *FBIS Daily Report*, 25 Jan. 1990, 47-48.

25. Penkovskiy, *The Penkovskiy Papers*, 252-253.

26. Marshal Sergei F. Akhromeyev, upon his retirement for the post of Chief of the Soviet General Staff, served as a Deputy to the Supreme Soviet from Constituency number 697 in Moldavia; he also serves as an advisor to the Chairman of the Supreme Soviet, Mikhail S. Gorbachëv. Moscow Television Service, 2 Oct. 1989, *FBIS Daily Report*, 4 Oct. 1989, 53; *Krasnaya Zvezda*, 18 Oct. 1989. Marshal V. G. Kulikov served as Commander of the Warsaw Pact Forces.

27.   Chiefs of the Soviet General Staff
1948 - 1952   Army General Sergei M. Shtemenko
1952 - 1960   Marshal of the Soviet Union Vasiliy D. Sokolovskiy
     (Marshal Sokolovskiy suffered a heart attack in 1960)

1960 - 1963   Marshal of the Soviet Union Matvey V. Zakharov
1963 - 1964   Marshal of the Soviet Union S. S. Biryuzov
     (Marshal Biryuzov was killed in an airplane accident)
1964 - 1971   Marshal of the Soviet Union Matvey V. Zakharov
     (Marshal Zakharov apparently was a favorite of Marshal Malinovskiy, since Zakharov had served in the Far East in 1945 under Malinovskiy as his Chief of Staff when Malinovskiy was commander of the Transbaikal Front. While Malinovskiy was Defense Minister, he brought several other members of the "Manchurian bunch" into positions of prominence, a number of whom were involved in developing the Soviet strategy for the initial period of war.)
1971 - 1977   Marshal of the Soviet Union V. G. Kulikov
1977 - 1984   Marshal of the Soviet Union Nikolay V. Ogarkov
1984 - 1989   Marshal of the Soviet Union S. F. Akhromeyev
1989 -   General of the Army Mikhail A. Moiseyev

28.   Soviet Ministers of Defense
1955 - 1957   Marshal of the Soviet Union Georgiy K. Zhukov
1957 - 1967   Marshal of the Soviet Union Rodion Ya. Malinovskiy
1967 - 1976   Marshal of the Soviet Union Andrey A. Grechko
1976 - 1984   Marshal of the Soviet Union Dmitriy F. Ustinov
1984 - 1987   Marshal of the Soviet Union Sergei L. Sokolov
1987 -   General of the Army Dmitriy T. Yazov

29. P. Rotmistrov, "Historic Victory," *Moscow News*, 11 May 1963; A. A. Grechko, "V. I. Lenin and the Building of the Soviet Armed Forces," *Kommunist* no. 3 (February 1969): 23; A. A. Sidorenko, *The Offensive* (Moscow: Military Publishing House, 1970), 115, 134; A. A. Grechko, *On Guard for Peace and the Building of Communism* (Moscow: Military Publishing House, 1971), Chapter 2.

30. John M. Collins, *U.S.-Soviet Military Balance: Concepts and Capabilities, 1960-1980* (New York: McGraw-Hill Publications Co., 1980), 44.

31. Public Law 92-448, 86 Stat. 746, 30 September 1972. Collins, *U.S.-Soviet Military Balance: Concepts and Capabilities, 1960-1980*, fn 7, 18.

32. Collins, *U.S.-Soviet Military Balance: Concepts and Capabilities, 1960-1980*, 119.

33. N. Petrakov, "To Restore the Erstwhile Glory of the Ruble," interview by N. Zhelnorova, *Argumenty I Fakty*, no. 39 (30 September-6 October 1989): 5-6.

34. *TASS*, 11 Nov. 1989.

35. *Sovetskaya Rossiya*, 5 Oct. 1989.

36. Moscow Television Service, 31 Oct. 1989, *FBIS Daily Report*, 1 Nov. 1989, 64-65.

37. *Krasnaya Zvezda*, 18 Jan. 1990.

38. Rodin, Chief of the Strategic Rocket Forces Political Directorate, interview, *Sovetskaya Rossiya*, 19 Nov. 1989.

39. Gorbachëv, *CPSU Central Committee Political Report, 25 February 1986*, *FBIS Daily Report*, (Supplement), 26 Feb. 1986, 1-42.

40. Lenin, *Selected Works*, vol. 1, 743, 746.

41. In his explanation of the tax in kind, Lenin misquoted what Jesus Christ said in Luke 18: 11. The scripture says: "... God I thank thee, that I am not as other men are, ..." Lenin wrote: "I thank Thee, Lord, that I am not as 'these.'" Lenin, *Selected Works*, vol. 3, 548.

42. Deuteronomy 8:3; Matthew 4: 4; Luke 4: 4.

43. *Kazakhstanskaya Pravda*, 27 Sept. 1989.

44. *TASS*, 30 Oct. 1989.

45. *TASS*, 18 Oct. 1989.

46. Moscow Television Service, 17 Oct. 1989, *FBIS Daily Report*, 18 Oct. 1989, 88-89.

47. "Fostering Committed Atheists," *Pravda*, 28 Sept. 1986.

48. Mikhail S. Gorbachëv, Speech at the Vatican, *TASS*, 1 Dec. 1989.

49. Gorbachëv, *Perestroika*, 39.

50. Theodore Draper, "Soviet Reformers: From Lenin to Gorbachëv," *Dissent* (Summer 1987): 287-301.

51. *Pravda*, 28 Sept. 1965. Draper, "Soviet Reformers: From Lenin to Gorbachëv," *Dissent* (Summer 1987): 287-301.

52. *Sovetskaya Rossiya*, 25 Oct. 1989.

53. Moscow Television Service, 25 Oct. 1989, *FBIS Daily Report*, 1 Nov. 1989, 78-90.

54. *Pravda*, 28 Jan. 1990; Gorbachëv, "Report at the CPSU Central Committee Plenum 5 February 1990," *Pravda*, 6 Feb. 1990.

55. Gorbachëv, *CPSU Central Committee Political Report, 25 February 1986, FBIS Daily Report*, (Supplement), 26 Feb. 1986, 1-42.

56. Ibid.

57. Herbert J. Ellison, "United Front Strategy and Soviet Foreign Policy," *Problems of Communism* 34 (September-October 1985): 45-64.

58. Gorbachëv, *Perestroika*, 37.

59. Gorbachëv, "CPSU Central Committee Political Report," 25 Feb. 1986, *FBIS Daily Report*, (Supplement), 26 Feb. 1986, 1-42.

60. Gorbachëv, "The Socialist Idea and Revolutionary *Perestroika*," *Pravda*, 26 Nov. 1989.

61. *Radio Liberty*, RL 299/87, 13 Jul. 1987.

62. *Krasnaya Zvezda*, 30 Sept. 1989.

232 Glasnost'

63. *Krasnaya Zvezda*, 10 Nov. 1989; *Pravda*, 3 Nov. 1989; *Krasnaya Zvezda*, 29 Oct. 1989.

64. Gorbachëv, *Perestroika*, 227, 228.

65. By late 1989, Czechoslovakia, East Germany, and Poland had governments which were not dominated by the Communist Party. In Bulgaria, the people demanded non-Communist participation. In December 1989, the people in Romania deposed the General Secretary of the Romanian Communist Party, Nicolae Ceausescu, and executed him and his wife. The Baltic countries, which consider their annexation to the Soviet Union to be illegal, clamored for independence. *Pravda*, 21 Dec. 1989; *Pravda*, 22 Dec. 1989; *TASS*, 22 Dec. 1989; *Tass*, 24 Dec. 1989; Moscow Domestic Service, 25 Dec. 1989, *FBIS Daily Report*, 26 Dec. 1989, 1; *TASS*, 25 Dec. 1989; *TASS*, 26 Dec. 1989.

66. Gorbachëv, *Perestroika*, 282-283.

67. Ibid., 285-286.

68. Ibid., 104.

69. *Argumenty I Fakty*, no. 42 (21-27 October 1989): 1-3.

70. Gorbachëv, *CPSU Central Committee Political Report, 25 February 1986, FBIS Daily Report*, (Supplement), 26 Feb. 1986, 1-42.

71. Gorbachëv, "The Socialist Idea and Revolutionary *Perestroika*," *Pravda*, 26 Nov. 1989, 1-3.

XII

CONCLUSIONS

The West should approach Mikhail S. Gorbachëv's "new thinking," *perestroika*, *glasnost'*, and democracy with great caution. There is an old axiom which states that "actions speak louder than words," and Soviet history speaks with a loud voice. Historically, the Soviets have been highly conservative, and they have not shown a propensity for sudden change. Yet, during the tenure of Mikhail S. Gorbachëv, especially in the second half of 1989 and in early 1990, in rapid succession, the Soviets announced drastic changes in the Soviet Union and in East Europe. Some observers view these rapid changes as evidence that Soviet actions are speaking louder than Gorbachëv's words. To be sure, rapid, drastic changes are completely out of character for the Soviets. "Can ... the leopard change his spots?"[1]

Regardless of announced changes, Communism is still an international movement based on the principles of Marxism-Leninism.[2] The primary danger from Communism has always been, now is, and will continue to be ideological. Notwithstanding, the political and military threats are real. Every Soviet action, whether of a deleterious or of a constructive nature, is designed to achieve some intermediate objective in the ultimate Marxist quest for an international order in which the proletariat is the only class remaining on the face of the earth.[3] In the Communist concept of one world, all "class enemies" will have been eliminated through the action of the dialectic between the forces of capitalism and socialism.[4] The Soviets, who control the motherland of Communism, have assumed the responsibility for achieving Marxist-Leninist goals.

In his rhetoric of the "new thinking," Gorbachëv combined all of the objectives and slogans of the "do gooders" in the Western world. These objectives run the gamut from humanism to ecology and include everything between.[5]   The "new thinking" program is not of recent origin. The Soviets began planning the "new thinking" in the late 1950s or early 1960s, and they established agencies for the study and implementation of this program.   The plan was thorough, and the Soviets tested the "new thinking" theory and prepared a salesman to project the new Soviet image to the West. In implementing the "new thinking," the Soviets have shown few restraints.

Within the Soviet Union in the early 1980s Communist doctrine had lost its operational importance.[6]   Consequently, the Soviet dedication to Marxist-Leninist ideology is the elusive intangible that Gorbachëv is trying to recapture. In domestic affairs the Soviet Union is one of the most *status quo* oriented nations in the world.[7] Hence, the change in tactics depicted by the "new thinking" cannot be ephemeral. Gorbachëv maintains that Marxist-Leninist ideology plays a major role in the determination of Soviet intentions, policies, and behavior. No matter how much, if at all, Marxist-Leninist ideology may have changed over the past seventy years, Marxism-Leninism remains the core of Soviet ideology.[8] It is important that the West not forget this truth.

Of the dangers from Communism, the ideological threat is the most serious because it acts silently and indirectly, attacks the thought process, and gradually undermines the moral fabric of the Judeo-Christian ethic. Ideologically, Marxism-Leninism, Communism, can destroy Western civilization from within and substitute the atheistic dogma of "socialist democracy."   While professing to be tolerant of all religions, the Communists continue to wage a domestic campaign to promote atheistic thinking and discourage those Soviet citizens who profess to be Christians. The Soviets have large bureaucratic organizations dedicated to the propagation of their ideology, and they conduct continuous programs to instill Marxist-Leninist ideology in the minds of their people. The Soviets educate the ignorant in "good atheistic thinking." Given the opportunity, they will follow the same pattern internationally.

The political threat from Marxism-Leninism is serious. Historically, Marxist governments have been controlled by an oligarchy consisting of top ranking members of the Communist Party. Although the Soviets talk about restructuring the state to provide a division of powers and to give the Supreme Soviet more authority, the rhetoric has not produced much substance.[9] Gorbachëv and his cohorts have no intention of giving up their Marxist-Leninist system.[10] The Soviets talk profusely about democracy, free elections, multiple candidates for office, and the will of the people; however, a study of these terms reveals that the Soviet definitions are not the same as those of the West. Moreover, they "adjust" the application of these terms to suit their ends. The democracy about which Gorbachëv continues to expound is different from the Western concept of democracy. Soviet democracy is "from above," not from the people as Gorbachëv alleges. Furthermore, in October 1989 he reaffirmed the necessity to preserve the Leninist principle of democratic centralism.[11] The reforms proposed by Gorbachëv at the Central Committee meeting in February 1990 appear to be a submission to the will of the people; however, they were proposed from the top. Should political parties arise to oppose the CPSU, the Communist Party intends to maintain political control.[12]

Above all, in Marxist-Leninist states there has been only one party, the Communist Party; otherwise, the state was not Marxist-Leninist. The Communist oligarchy are not elected by popular, secret ballot; they are selected by the highest Party organs. Democracy to the Soviets has meant that the people participate in providing a "rubber stamp" for Party policy and actions. The people voted, but they voted "correctly" in conformity with good Party discipline. The "will of the people" has been determined by the "vanguard of the proletariat" - the Party. Should Gorbachëv succeed in implementing a multi-party system in which the people elect their leaders, there will be many problems. The superposition of popular democracy upon a totalitarian culture provides opportunities for the rise of a dictator. People inexperienced in freedom frequently cannot handle their new responsibilities.

One thing is clear; Gorbachëv intends to maintain the supremacy of the Communist Party in the Soviet Union. The Communist Party, as the only party in the Soviet Union, has been the guiding force in the Soviet Union, and it will continue to be so under Gorbachëv's *perestroika*.[13] There has been no official opposition. The Party formulates theory, corrects strategy and tactics, elaborates policy, selects and places personnel, and serves as the guiding force organizationally and ideologically for *perestroika*.[14] The Communist Party will remain the final authority, and Soviet Communism is still international in character.[15] Hence, the Soviets intend for the Communist Party, guided by Marxist-Leninist teachings, to continue as the vanguard of the proletariat at home and abroad.[16] In the Red Army, in the State Security Committee, in the Foreign Ministry, and in every government department, the Communist Party has exercised the greatest authority and had the decisive voice politically.[17] In Lithuania on 11 January 1990, Gorbachëv described the continuing importance of the Communist Party: "... under decentralization the Party remains the cementing, integrating force of the whole of society and of the country."[18]

War continues to be one of the greatest fears of the Soviets, both to the leaders and to the people. Over the centuries Russia has experienced invasions from the west by Sweden, Poland, Lithuania, and Germany. World War II and its devastation are especially imprinted on the minds of the Soviets. They do not want another war if it can be avoided, since the destruction wrought by war impedes the advance of socialism and delays the Party relinquishing control to the proletariat. If at all possible, they will inseminate the Western world with Communism peacefully, since they understand the old adage "he who is convinced against his will is not convinced still."

The threat to the West from the Soviet armed forces is real and serious, but it can be contained. Although not an ideal solution, containment, or deterrence, has been the solution to the military threat since the late 1940s. A major reduction in forces could be effective in reducing the threat; however, the Soviets do not have a record of observing international agreements. Of the three major threats, the military responds most readily to control from above. The key to control of a military force is money, or resources, and this is the medium by which Gorbachëv appears to be reducing the influence of the Soviet armed forces. The response time is short when resources are curtailed. On the other hand, because of technological requirements, the response time is long when building a larger force and training troops. The long lead time for the production of technical equipment dictates the maintenance of a large, combat ready armed force so long as a threat exists.

The security of the Soviet state, the motherland of Communism, must be preserved at all cost. The Soviets will never relinquish the interests of the Communist motherland nor the interests of their allies.[19] Gorbachëv wrote in 1985 that the Soviets will not permit the upset of the military balance between the Soviet Union and the United States or between the Warsaw Pact and NATO.[20] Gorbachëv wrote further that any course directed toward the attainment of military superiority over the Soviet Union and its allies is unacceptable and has no prospects.[21] The Soviets have alleged for over thirty years that their military doctrine and the military doctrine of the Warsaw Pact are defensive and have never changed. This allegation is a continuation of the Czarist rationale for a large army. Defense Minister Army General Dmitriy T. Yazov, writing in *On Guard for Socialism and Peace*, implies that military sufficiency means that the Soviet Union will maintain military forces capable of repelling an enemy attack and destroying the enemy. Such military objectives can be attained only by offensive action.[22]

The Soviet armed forces constitute one of the largest military establishments in the world. They are modern, well equipped, and trained. Soviet military strategy and tactics are sound, and they pose a formidable threat to the West. Their highest military leaders are well educated and trained, experienced professionals. Soviet military writings indicate that their global and continental strategic forces are ready to fight. Soviet continental strategy, oriented on NATO forces, is related to the Soviet global nuclear strategy, and a major component of Gorbachëv's program is to dismantle NATO.

The Soviet Strategic Rocket Forces, an offensive arm and the main component of the Soviet strategic nuclear forces, are highly trained, well equipped, are on a continuous alert status, and are prepared at any time to deliver a retaliatory attack. Retaliation would be directed against United States strategic missiles as the primary targets. With the increased strain imposed on the missilemen by their constant alert status, a continuing problem for the West is an ignorance of what real or imaginary act, event, or situation might trigger the launch of a global nuclear strike.[23]   The uncertainty concerning the Soviet perception of a hostile Western act preserves the Soviet doctrine of preemption.

The Soviets are sincere in their quest for disarmament and equality among nations. They are sincere in their desire that all people be permitted to have a political system and government of their own choosing. They are sincere in their desire to eliminate war from the world. They want all of these worthy goals on their own terms so that they will be free to disseminate Marxist-Leninist ideology throughout the world, and when target peoples are sufficiently indoctrinated, they will assist them in realizing their revolutionary objectives.   If the West disarms, the Soviets will be free to spread their Marxist-Leninist ideology at will.

In spite of improved Soviet relations with the West, Gorbachëv's rhetoric has not been accompanied by a significant slowdown in Soviet production of military hardware. The Soviet threat to the West has not been reduced. Within the last decade, the Soviets have continued to develop doctrine, organization, and equipment for the purpose of improving the Soviet ability to carry out rapid offensive operations with large units.[24] There has been no downward change to Soviet offensive capability. The Soviet military continues to improve, and the Soviets still place their greatest emphasis on achieving surprise.[25] The Soviets have not retreated from their reliance on military power as the basis of their political policies.[26]

In February 1986 during his speech to the 27th Party Congress, Gorbachëv alluded to the concept of "reasonable sufficiency" in military forces; however, neither he nor any other Soviet official has explained what he meant by this term. There is no valid reason to believe that "reasonable sufficiency" means that the Soviets have changed or renounced the offensive nature of their military strategy.

"Reasonable sufficiency" supports the Soviet goals to divide and dismantle NATO, slow Western military modernization, and lure the West to reduce its forces through disarmament and arms control talks for the purpose of granting the Soviet Union a respite from their economic difficulties. Such a respite would permit the Soviets to catch up with the West technologically and put their economic house in order. In the meantime, their long term goals remain unchanged.   During Gorbachëv's first three years in office, Soviet defense spending rose.[27]

A study of Soviet pronouncements in 1989 on the reduction in the size of Soviet military forces shows that they do not intend to reduce the effectiveness of their forces. Their emphasis is on slightly smaller but more effective and more capable military forces. Previous reductions in forces have not reduced Soviet military capabilities.

There is a fourth area which the Soviets have perceived to be a long-term threat to the West. The Soviets have asserted for many years that the socialist economy is far superior to anything that capitalism can provide, but their lengthy arguments are not supported by reality. The Soviet economy is no threat to the West; however, it is a serious threat to the Soviet Union. The Soviets are faced with a serious loss of international and domestic prestige if they do not revive their economy and improve it to a level that is superior to capitalism.

In the advancement of Marxist-Leninist objectives, the Soviets find it necessary to refurbish their economy and align it with their ideology. To overcome their economic desperation, their critical economic situation, the Soviets must allocate more resources to their general economy and less to their military sector. To use their resources effectively, they must adopt new management techniques and a workable economic theory. This change of priorities requires that the Soviets perceive a reduced threat to their security. If they can convince the West to reduce its armed forces to a level which the Soviets find non-threatening, the Soviets may reduce the size and effectiveness of their own military forces. Yet, the Soviets will not effect any major reduction in forces and combat effectiveness until after they are certain that the West has reduced its forces. Moreover, the size of the Soviet armed forces is such that any one-to-one reduction in forces will always leave the Soviets in a position of superiority.

The purpose of Lenin's NEP was to build Communism with non-Communist assistance.[28] Gorbachëv is following the same course, and he will use the West to build Communism not only in the Soviet Union but in the rest of the world, wherever the West cooperates. The NEP inaugurated by Vladimir I. Lenin in 1921 extended much more economic freedom to the people than do Gorbachëv's proposals. Furthermore, Lenin permitted economic freedom while simultaneously maintaining and improving his control over the populace.[29] One major contradiction in

Gorbachëv's objectives is his unrealistic quest to change the Soviet economy with the same people, the same ideology, and the same environment.[30]

The desperation which grips the Soviet Union pertains to all sectors of Soviet society. Although the economy appears to be most critical, there has been an erosion of Marxist-Leninist ideology among the Soviet populace with a concomitant relaxation in other areas. Their desperation is exacerbated by a rising crime rate, problems with drugs and alcoholism, corruption, dishonesty, and a general breakdown of discipline. Gorbachëv's program is designed to solve all of these problems.

In trying to convince the Soviet people that a solution to their problems requires hard work, dedication, and sacrifice, Gorbachëv has repeatedly referred to Lenin and called upon the people to return to Lenin's methods and ideas. A close examination of Lenin's words and deeds reveals that he employed terror, deceit, lies, disinformation, deception, and other unsavory methods to accomplish his goals. Lenin justified his actions on the basis of the necessity to preserve the revolution and to protect the interests of the proletariat. He explained that these macabre actions were taken only against "enemies of the people," the bourgeoisie.

Gorbachëv has complained that political thinking in the Soviet Union has been in a state of stagnation for the past fifty years, a period that began in the Stalinist 1930s, the decade in which he was born.[31] He stated that the 27th Party Congress demanded that the CPSU must be a Leninist Party in content and methods.[32] Accordingly, the CPSU Central Committee Institute of Marxism-Leninism, in its effort to renew the Party as the political vanguard of society, has been at work restructuring the style of ideological work.[33] The Soviets still adhere to the Marxist-Leninist class analysis of the causes of world problems.[34] In their view, Marxism-Leninism is the solution to world problems, since everything else has failed.[35]

The Soviets are experts in the methods and techniques of deception and have formulated an elaborate theory and applications for carrying out deception on a global scale. Their writings on deception indicate that they have developed in detail a "scientific" approach to deception. The major scientific components of Soviet deception include *maskirovka, dezinformatsiya, demonstratsiya,* and *stimulirovniya,* each of which has its own detailed implementing instructions. Well known examples of Soviet deception include The Trust, the WIN operation, and the missile crisis of the late 1950s.

Gorbachëv's "new thinking" is deception. The implementation of a long range plan, "new thinking" represents the ultimate in a grandiose Soviet scheme to rescue the Soviet Union from stagnation, lull the West into disarming, motivate further relaxation of Western opposition to Communism, and promote the spread of Marxist-Leninist socialism to all parts of the world. Mikhail S. Gorbachëv is the "tool" wielded by the Soviet leaders for the accomplishment of these objectives.

From a socially crude Kuban Cossack in 1950, Gorbachëv has advanced to the status of a world-renowned diplomat whose skill and finesse in the social graces and world politics astound the most skeptical Soviet watchers. Eager to please his superiors, he probably developed these skills following his return to the Kuban in 1954. Since his patron was Fedor Kulakov and his acquaintances included high ranking Party officials, he fit the early plans of the "new thinkers." As the "new thinking" planning made progress, Gorbachëv advanced. He and the "new thinking" developed in concert.

The Marxist-Leninist contention that Communists are peace loving is an example of the big lie - disinformation. Soviet support of revolution anywhere in the world negates the Soviet rhetoric about peace. Gorbachëv couches Soviet support for revolution in terms of the international fight for social justice.[36] Furthermore, he discusses Soviet support of revolution as humane assistance in the struggle of peoples for liberation from colonial oppression.[37] Even though the Soviet Union temporarily suspended arms shipments to Nicaragua,[38] the Soviets take credit for the success of the Communist revolution in that country.[39] Moreover, the Soviet Union has recently become more actively involved in the affairs of Central America.[40] The Soviet Union has also supported the national liberation struggle of African nations.[41]

Marxists explain the process by which Marxism-Leninism will triumph as the dialectic. The dialectic consists of a continuing struggle between Marxist-Leninist socialism and capitalism the final result of which will be international Communism, a classless society. In the struggle, Marxists perceive the dialectic at work in myriad components of the overall struggle. Among the struggles in which the dialectic operates are those between crime and law, Marxist-Leninist ideology and Christianity, nationalism and internationalism, and war and peace. Marxist theory predicts progress towards Communism in the outcome of each struggle. The Soviets believe in the inevitability of progress as they perceive it historically. The Marxian dialectic and the concomitant historical determinism are still integral parts of the Soviet mind set.

The Soviets are improving the education of the young, the aim of which is a proper Communist upbringing and the acquisition of adequate cultural standards.[42] According to Gorbachëv, Marxist-Leninist ideology brings with it the truly humanistic ideals of social progress, the development of the individual, of a world without weapons and wars, and without oppression and exploitation.[43] The Soviet allegiance to the policy of peace and freedom is permeated with the spirit of "true humanism."[44]

In spite of the castigation of Josef Stalin by Soviet leaders beginning with Nikita Khrushchëv, Gorbachëv gives Stalin credit for the industrialization and collectivization of agriculture, which were essential to the rehabilitation of the Soviet economy. On the other hand, he does not condone Stalin's mistakes, or his deviation from Marxism-Leninism. He acknowledges that the suffering and sacrifice of the 1930s were necessary to prepare the country for defense against the impending military threat.[45]

The Soviets have not changed their objectives in terms of ideology, policy, organization, and proletarian class character. Their purpose remains to lead "society's movement toward the ultimate goal of Communism."[46] The only things new are a new style of rhetoric, a new public relations style, new tactics, and a public relations man who knows how to appeal to the West. The entire "new thinking" package is part of a well-planned and rehearsed public relations campaign which has been long in the preparation stage and long coming to light. The Soviets had to wait until they found and trained the right salesman to push their new program on the West.

The bottom line on *glasnost'*, written by Gorbachëv himself, is a warning. "*Glasnost'* must not be used to the detriment of the interests of the Soviet state and society,..."[47]   *Glasnost'* to the Soviets means officially managed perceptions.   Maintaining control over the news media, the Soviets selectively permit more thorough reporting of negative domestic news as well as foreign policy issues.   Regardless of their rhetoric to the contrary, the Soviets monitor public discussions of topics such as the dominance of the Communist Party, the KGB, and certain abuses of human rights.[48]   Those authors, editors, or media means which exceed the officially sanctioned bounds are severely castigated.[49] The new method for control of the media is intimidation.

His rhetoric is convincing, his manner is charming, his stated objectives are humane, and he claims that the Soviets want peace, but wedged between the peaceful rhetoric of Gorbachëv's florid discourse, he states explicitly that there has been no change in the ultimate Soviet objectives. A careful reading of his speeches, articles, and books reveals that he does not disguise these objectives. Gorbachëv, like all official Soviet propagandists, understands that people, especially those in the West, tend to hear only what they want to hear. The Soviets also know that the West, especially the United States, has no unified ideology, it has no ultimate objective, there is no national determination, no national unity, and that most people in the West are apathetic about these intangibles. By submerging Soviet objectives in high sounding prose and peaceful propaganda, Gorbachëv has lulled many Westerners into forgetting Soviet objectives and the insidious nature of Communism. The Soviets, masters of the big lie, temper their propaganda with sufficient truth to make it appear credible. Accordingly, to people who are looking for a change in the Soviets, this apparent convergence is a welcome change from the traditional braggadocio they have heard from the Soviets.

Soviet leaders are intelligent, they have an ideology, they are clever, they are determined, and they know their ultimate objective. None of them will acknowledge that socialism is dead or will not work. So long as socialism is alive in the minds of these men, socialism is alive in reality, it is not on the decline, and it is dynamic. The Soviets have realized for several years that something has been wrong with the application of Marxist-Leninist socialism in the Soviet Union, since it has not been working. They attribute their problems to mistakes of the past and a departure from the teachings of Marx and Lenin. The solution, as expounded by Gorbachëv, is to reexamine the mistakes of the past, learn from those mistakes, make corrections, and move forward.[50]

The Soviets still adhere to their belief in historical determinism with its accompany doctrine of inevitable progress, and Gorbachëv expresses a firm resolve to develop and strengthen socialism to its fullest capacity. The Soviets have no schedule for their objectives, and for the end result, a Communist world, they are content to let history decide.[51]

Accordingly, the Soviet Union and the insidious Communism which it propagates continue to pose a threat to the West, ideologically, politically, and militarily.

"Tell them what they want to believe."

NOTES

1. Jeremiah 13: 23.

2. Gorbachëv, *A Time for Peace*, 96, 106; Gorbachëv, "The Socialist Idea and Revolutionary *Perestroika*," *Pravda*, 26 Nov. 1989.

3. Gorbachëv, "The Socialist Idea and Revolutionary *Perestroika*," *Pravda*, 26 Nov. 1989.

4. Ibid.

5. Ibid.

6. Seweryn Bialer, "Ideology and Soviet Foreign Policy," in *Ideology and Foreign Policy: A Global Perspective*, George Schwab, ed. (New York: Cyrco Press, 1978), 84.

7. Ibid.

8. Ibid., 86.

9. *TASS*, 30 Nov. 1989; *TASS*, 4 Dec. 1989.

10. Gorbachëv, *Perestroika*, 23; Gorbachëv, "Report at the CPSU Central Committee Plenum 5 February 1990," *Pravda*, 6 Feb. 1990.

11. *Pravda*, 30 Oct. 1989.

12. Gorbachëv, "Report at the CPSU Central Committee Plenum 5 February 1990," *Pravda*, 6 Feb. 1990.

13. Mikhail S. Gorbachëv, Moscow Television Service, 12 Dec. 1989, *FBIS Daily Report*, 13 Dec. 1989, 51-55; Gorbachëv, "Report at the CPSU Central Committee Plenum 5 February 1990," *Pravda*, 6 Feb. 1990.

14. Gorbachëv, *Perestroika*, 108, 273.

15. Gorbachëv, "The Socialist Idea and Revolutionary *Perestroika*," *Pravda*, 26 Nov. 1989, 1-3.

16. Gorbachëv, *Perestroika*, 264; *Pravda*, 30 Sept. 1989; Gorbachëv, "Report at the CPSU Central Committee Plenum 5 February 1990," *Pravda*, 6 Feb. 1990.

17. Gorbachëv, *Perestroika*, 114.

18. *Pravda*, 12 Jan. 1990.

19. Gorbachëv, *A Time for Peace*, 19.

20. Ibid., 108-109.

21. Ibid., 45.

22. Department of Defense, *Soviet Military Power*, 12.

23. Rodin, Chief of the Strategic Rocket Forces Political Directorate, interview, *Sovetskaya Rossiya*, 19 Nov. 1989.

24. John R. Galvin, "NATO: After Zero INF," *Armed Forces Journal International* 126 (March 1988): 54-60.

25. John R. Galvin, Interview, *Armed Forces Journal International* 126 (March 1988): 50-52.

26. Department of Defense, *Soviet Military Power*, 10.

27. Ibid., 12-13.

28. Lenin, *Selected Works*, vol. 3, 630.

29. Charles Krauthammer, "When to Call off the Cold War," *The New Republic* (16 November 1987): 18-21. Reprinted by permission of *The New Republic*, (c) 1987, The New Republic, Inc.

30. Galvin, Interview, *Armed Forces Journal International* 126 (March 1988): 50-52.

31. Sestanovich, "What Gorbachëv Wants," *The New Republic* (26 May 1987): 6-9.

32. Gorbachëv, *Perestroika*, 245.

33. *Pravda*, 6 Oct. 1989.

34. Gorbachëv, *Perestroika*, 134.

35. *Pravda*, 30 Sept. 1989.

36. Gorbachëv, *Perestroika*, 162, 174.

37. Gorbachëv, *A Time for Peace*, 19.

38. *Pravda*, 6 Oct. 1989.

39. *TASS*, 17 Oct. 1989.

40. *TASS*, 5 Oct. 1989.

41. Gorbachëv, *Perestroika*, 173.

42. Ibid., 85.

43. Gorbachëv, *A Time for Peace*, 31.

44. Ibid., 110.

45. Gorbachëv, *Perestroika*, 27; Mikhail S. Gorbachëv, "Promoting the Economic Reform," *Pravda*, 30 Oct. 1989.

46. *Pravda*, 30 Sept. 1989.

47. Gorbachëv, *Perestroika*, 293.

48. Department of Defense, *Soviet Military Power*, 10.

49. *Sovetskaya Rossiya*, 27 Oct. 1989.

50. Gorbachëv, "The Socialist Idea and Revolutionary *Perestroika*," *Pravda*, 26 Nov. 1989.

51. Gorbachëv, *Perestroika*, 23, 24, 28, 29; Gorbachëv, "Holiday Reception in the Kremlin," *Pravda*, 8 Nov. 1989.

SELECT BIBLIOGRAPHY

PRIMARY

Akhromeyev, Sergei Fedorovich. "Military Detente: The Demand of the Times." *Krasnaya Zvezda*, 2 December 1980.
_____. "The Great Victory and Its Lessons." *Izvestiya*, 7 May 1985.
_____. Interview. *Krasnaya Zvezda*, 6 July 1987.
_____. Interview. *Krasnaya Zvezda*, 6 October 1989.
_____. Interview. Moscow Television Service, 9 October 1989.
Andropov, Yuri V. "Leninism: The Inexhaustible Source of the Revolutionary Energy and Creativity of the Masses." *Pravda*, 23 April 1982.
Anureyev, I. I. *Weapons for Anti-Rocket and Anti-Space Defense.* Moscow: Military Publishing House, 1971.
Arbatov, Georgiy A., and William Ottman. *The Soviet Viewpoint.* New York: Dodd, Mead and Co., 1983.
Argumenty I Fakty, no. 42 (21-27 October 1989): 1-3.
Argumenty I Fakty, no. 46 (18-24 November 1989): 2.
Bondarenko, V. M. *Contemporary Science and the Development of Military Affairs.* Moscow: Military Publishing House, 1976.
Brezhnev, Leonid I. "Speech at the Celebration of the 50th Anniversary of the October Revolution." *Pravda*, 3 November 1967.
_____. "Tula Speech." *Pravda*, 19 January 1977.
Burlatskiy, Fedor M., and A. A. Galkin. *Sotsilogiya, Politika, Mezhdunarodnye Otnosheniya.* Moscow: Gospolitizdat, 1974.
_____. "A New Strategy? No! Nuclear Madness." *Literaturnaya Gazeta*, 2 December 1981.

Cherednichenko, M. I. "The Initial Period of the Patriotic War."
    Krasnaya Zvezda, 30 April 1961.
Chernenko, Konstantin U. "The Soviet Peace Program for the 1980s."
    Pravda, 23 April 1981.
Churchill, Winston S. *The Gathering Storm*. Boston: Houghton-
    Mifflin, 1948.
Clausewitz, Karl von. *On War*. Translated by O. J. Matthijs Jolles.
    Washington: Combat Forces Press, 1953.
Dash, Barbara L. *A Defector Reports: The Institute of the USA and
    Canada*. Falls Church, Virginia: Delphic Associates,
    Incorporated, 1982.
Department of State. *SALT II Agreement*, 18 June 1985.
Druzhinin, V. V., and D. S. Kontorov. *Problemy Sistemologii*.
    Moscow: Sovetskoye Radio, 1986.
Fedorov, G. A. *Marxism-Leninism on War and the Army*. 3d ed.
    Moscow: Military Publishing House, 1962.
Galvin, John. Interview. *Armed Forces Journal International* 126
    (March 1988): 50-52.
_____. "NATO: After Zero INF." *Armed Forces Journal
    International* 126 (March 1988): 54-60.
Gareyev, Makhmut Akhmetovich. *M V. Frunze: Voeynnyy Teoretik*.
    Moskva: Voyenizdat, 1985.
Goluba, P. A., Yu. I. Korableva, and M. I. Kuznetsova, eds.
    Encyclopedia of the Great October Socialist Revolution. Moscow:
    Soviet Encyclopedia Press, 1987.
Golovine, Nicholas N. "A Demoralized Army Spread Dissatisfaction
    Among the People." *The Russian Revolution and Bolshevik
    Victory*. Edited by Arthur E. Adams. Boston: D. C. Heath and
    Company, 1960.
Gorbachëv, Mikhail S. *A Time for Peace*. New York: Richardson &
    Steirman, 1985.
_____. *CPSU Central Committee Political Report, 25 February 1986*.
    FBIS Daily Report, 26 February 1986.
_____. *Report to the CPSU Central Committee Plenum, 27 January
    1987, TASS*, 27 January 1987.

_____. *Perestroika: New Thinking for Our Country and the World.*
New York: Harper & Row, Publishers, 1988.

_____. *Pravda,* 6 November 1989.

_____. "Holiday Reception in the Kremlin." *Pravda,* 8 November
1989.

_____. "The Cause of *Perestroika* Needs the Energy of the Young,"
Pravda, 16 November 1989.

_____. "The Socialist Idea and Revolutionary *Perestroika.*" *Pravda,*
26 November 1989.

Grechko, A. A. "V. I. Lenin and the Building of the Soviet Armed
Forces." *Kommunist,* no. 3 (February 1969): 23.

_____. *On Guard Over Peace and the Building of Communism.*
Moscow: Military Publishing House, 1971.

_____. *Armed Forces of the Soviet State.* Moscow: Military
Publishing House, 1975.

Gromyko, A. A. "A. A. Gromyko's Address." *Pravda,* 28 September
1984.

Grudinin, I. A. "The Time Factor in Modern War." *Kommunist
Vooruzhennikh Sil,* February 1966.

Hegel, Georg Wilhelm Friedrich. *The Philosophy of History.*
Translated by J. Sibree. Chicago: The Great Books Foundation,
1952.

Humanist Manifestos I and II. Buffalo, New York: Prometheus
Books, 1976.

Ivanov, S. P. *The Initial Period of War.* Moscow: Military Publishing
House, 1974.

Ivanov, S. P., and M. M. Kir'yan. "The War's Initial Period." *Soviet
Military Encyclopedia.* Vol 5. Moscow: Military Publishing
House, 1978.

Kerensky, Alexander. "Both Left and Right Betrayed the Provisional
Government." *The Russian Revolution and Bolshevik Victory.*
Edited by Arthur E. Adams. Boston: D. C. Heath Company,
1960.

Kesselring, Albrecht. *The Memoirs of Field-Marshal Kesselring.*
Novato, California: Presidio Press, 1989.

Khrushchëv, Nikita S. "Khrushchëv's Secret Speech." Washington: United States Department of State, 1956.

_____. *Disarmament is the Way to Strengthen Peace and Secure Friendship Between Nations.* Moscow: Gospolitizdat, 1960.

_____. "Disarmament for Durable Peace and Friendship." *On Peaceful Coexistence.* Moscow: Foreign Languages Publishing House, 1961.

Kir'yan, M. M., ed. *Voyenno-Technicheskiy Progress i Vooruzhennyye Sily.* Moskva: Voyenizdat, 1982.

_____. *The Element of Surprise in Offensive Operations of the Great Patriotic War.* Moscow: Military Publishing House, 1986.

Kosa, John. *Two Generations of Soviet Man: A Study in the Psychology of Communism.* Chapel Hill: The University of North Carolina Press, 1962.

Kulikov, V. G. "Curbing the Arms Race." *Krasnaya Zvezda*, 21 February 1984.

Larionov, Valentin V., and I. Glagolev. "Peaceful Coexistence and the USSR's Defense Might." *International Life*, no. 11 (1963): 43-46.

Larionov, Valentin V. "New Means of Fighting and Strategy." *Krasnaya Zvezda*, April 1964.

_____. "New Weapons and the Duration of War." *Krasnaya Zvezda*, March 1965.

Lefebvre, Vladimir A., and Victorina D. Lefebvre. *Reflexive Control: The Soviet Concept of Influencing An Adversary's Decision Making Process.* Englewood, Colorado: Science Applications, Inc., 1984.

_____. *Reflexive Controll II.* Greenwood Village, Colorado: Science Applications, Inc., 1985.

Lenin, Vladimir I. *On the Great October Socialist Revolution.* Moscow: Progress Publishers, 1971.

_____. *Socialism and Religion.* Moscow: Progress Publishers, 1976.

_____. *Selected Works,* 3 vols. Moscow: Progress Publishers, 1977.

_____. *One Step Forward, Two Steps Back.* Moscow: Progress Publishers, 1978.

_____. *Marxism and Insurrection.* Moscow: Progress Publishers, 1980.

_____. *On the Question of Dialectics.* Moscow: Progress Publishers, 1982.

Malinovskiy, Rodion Ya. *Vigilantly Stand Guard Over the Peace.* Moscow: Military Publishing House, 1962.

Marx, Karl. *Capital.* Vol. 1. Edited by Friedrich Engels. Translated by Samuel Moore and Edward Aveling. New York: International Publishers, 1967.

Marx, Karl, and Friedrich Engels. *The Communist Manifesto.* Translated by Samuel Moore. Middlesex, England: Penguin Books, 1977.

Marx, Karl, Friedrich Engels, and Vladimir I. Lenin. *On Dialectical Materialism.* Moscow: Progress Publishers, 1977.

Meretskov, Kirill A. *Serving the People.* Translated by David Fidlon. Moscow: Progress Publishers, 1971.

Michta, Andrew A. *An Emigre Reports: Fridrikh Neznansky on Mikhail Gorbachëv, 1950-1958.* Falls Church, Virginia: Delphic Associates, 1985.

Mil'shteyn, Mikhail. Interview. *International Herald Tribune.* 28 August 1980.

Moskalenko, K. "The Missile Troops Guarding the Security of the Motherland." *Krasnaya Zvezda*, 13 September 1961.

Mstislavskii, Sergei. *Five Days Which Transformed Russia.* Translated by Elizabeth Kristofovich Zelensky. Bloomington and Indianapolis, Indiana: Indiana University Press, 1988.

Nikol'skiy, N. M. *The Primary Contemporary Question: The Problem of Annihilation.* Moscow: International Relations Press, 1964.

_____. *Nauchno-Technicheskoye Revolyutsiya: Mirovaya Ekonomika, Politika, Naseline.* Moscow: International Relations Press, 1970.

Nikol'skiy, N. M., and A. V. Grishin. *Nauchno-Technicheskiy Progress i Mezhdunarodnye Otnosheniya.* Moscow: International Relations Press, 1978.

Ogarkov, N. V. "Guarding the Conquests of Great October." *Agitator* (January 1978): 25.

_____. "Military Strategy." *Soviet Military Encyclopedia*. Vol. 7.
Moscow: Military Publishing Company, 1979.

_____. *Vsegda v Gotovnosti k Zachite Otchestva*. Moscow: Military
Publishing House, 1982.

_____. "A Reliable Defense to Peace." *Krasnaya Zvezda*, 23
September 1983.

_____. "The Unfading Glory of Soviet Weapons." *Kommunist
Vooruzhennikh Sil*, no. 21 (1984): 25.

Penkovskiy, Oleg. *The Penkovskiy Papers*. Garden City, New York:
Doubleday & Company, Inc., 1965.

Petrakov, N. "To Restore the Erstwhile Glory of the Ruble."
Interview. *Argumenty I Fakty*, no. 39 (30 September-6
October 1989): 5-6.

Polsky, Yuri. *Soviet Research Institutes and the Formulation of Foreign
Policy*. Falls Church, Virginia: Delphic Associates, Incorporated,
1987.

Primakov, Ye. "New Philosophy of Foreign Policy. *Pravda*, 9 July
1987.

Prokp'ev, N. "Problems of War and Peace in the Modern Era."
International Life, no. 12 (1967): 82-83.

Reznichenko, V. G. *Taktika*. 1st ed. Moskva: Voennoye
Izdatel'stvo, 1966.

_____. *Taktika*. 2d ed. Moskva: Voennyoe Izdatel'stvo, 1984.

_____. *Taktika*. 3d ed. Moskva: Voennyoe Izdatel'stvo, 1987.

Rodin, Viktor Semenovich. Interview. *Sovetskaya Rossiya*. 19
November 1989. *FBIS Daily Report.*

Rotmistrov, P. "Historic Victory." *Moscow News*, 11 May 1963.

Rybkin, Ye. I. *War and Politics*. Moscow: Military Publishing House,
1959.

Shirman, A. A. "The Social Activism of the Masses and the Defense
of Socialism." *Filosofskoe Naseledie V. I. Lenin i Problemy
Sovremennoy Voyny*. Edited by A. S. Milovidov and V. G.
Kozlov. Moscow: Gospolitizdat, 1972.

Shtemenko, Sergei M. *The Soviet General Staff at War, 1941-1945*. Translated by Robert Daglish. Moscow: Progress Publishers, 1981.

Sidel'nikov, I. "Mirovoye sosushchestvovaniye i bezopasnost' norodov." *Krasnaya Zvezda*, 14 August 1973.

Sidorenko, A. A. *Nostuplenie* [*The Offensive*]. Moscow: Military Publishing House, 1970.

_____. *The Offensive*. Translated by the United States Air Force. Moscow: Military Publishing House, 1970.

Sizov, L. G. Interview. Moscow Domestic Service, 18 September 1989. *FBIS Daily Report*.

Smith, Gerard. *Doubletalk: The Story of the First Strategic Arms Limitations Talks*. Garden City, New York: Doubleday & Company, Inc., 1980.

Sokolov, S. L. "The Great Victory." *Kommunist*, no. 6 (1985): 65.

Sokolovskiy, V. D. *Soviet Military Strategy*. 2d. ed. Translated by Herbert S. Dinerstein, Leon Gouré, and Thomas W. Wolfe. Englewood Cliffs, New Jersey: Prentice-Hall, Inc., 1963.

_____. *Soviet Military Strategy*. 3d ed. Edited by Harriet Fast Scott. New York: Crane, Russak & Company, Inc., 1968.

Sokolovskiy, V. D., and I. M. Cherednichenko. "On Contemporary Military Strategy." *Kommunist Vooruzhennikh Sil*, April 1966.

Sovetskaya Voyennaya Entsiklopediya. Moskva: Voyenizdat, 1976-1979.

Strakhovsky, Leonid I. "Kerensky Betrayed Russia." In *The Russian Revolution and Bolshevik Victory*. Edited by Arthur E. Adams. Boston: D. C. Heath Company, 1960.

Suvorov, Viktor. "GUSM: The Soviet Service of Strategic Deception." *International Defense Review* 8 (August 1985): 1235-1240.

Talentsky, N. "Thoughts on Past Wars." *International Affairs*, no. 5 (April 1965): 23.

Trofimenko, G. A. "Some Aspects of U. S. National Security Strategy." *SShA: Ekonomika, Politika, Ideologika*, no. 10 (October 1970): 15-26.

Ustinov, Dmitriy F. "Averting the Threat of a Nuclear War." *Pravda*, 12 July 1983.

_____. "Six Heroic Decades." *Kommunist*, no. 2 (1978): 26.

Volkogonov, Dmitriy A. "A Strategy of Adventurism." *Zarubezhnoye Voyennoye Obozreniye*, no. 5 (1984).

_____. "War and Peace in the Nuclear Age." *Krasnaya Zvezda*, 30 August 1985.

Zhilin, P. A. "Past Lessons and Future Concerns." *Kommunist*, no. 7 (1981): 71.

_____., ed. *Istoriya Voeynnogo Iskusstva*. Moskva: Voyenizdat, 1986.

Zhukov, Georgiy. *G. Zhukov: Reminiscences and Reflections*. Vol. 2. Translated by N. Burova, R. Daglish, P. Garb, G. Kozlov, S Sossinsky, and M. Sidney. Moscow: Progress Publishers, 1985.

SECONDARY

Bialer, Seweryn. "Ideology and Foreign Policy." In *Ideology and Foreign Policy: A Global Perspective*, edited by George Schwab. New York: Cyrco Press, Inc., 1978.

Brzezinski, Zbigniew. "The Soviet Union: World Power of a New Type." In *The Soviet Union in the 1980s*, edited by Erik P. Hoffmann. New York: The Academy of Political Science, 1984.

Cohen, Richard, and Peter A. Wilson. "Superpowers in Decline? Economic Performance and National Security." *Comparative Strategy* 7 (1988): 99-132.

Collins, John M. *U. S.-Soviet Military Balance: Concepts and Capabilities, 1960-1980*. New York: McGraw-Hill Publications Co., 1980.

Colton, Timothy J. "Approaches to the Politics of Systemic Economic Reform in the Soviet Union." *Soviet Economy* 3 (April-June 1987): 145-170.

Crommelin, Quentin, Jr., and David S. Sullivan. *Soviet Military Supremacy: The Untold Facts About the New Danger to America*. Los Angeles, California: The Defense and Strategic Studies Program, University of Southern California, 1985.

Defense Nationale (October 1989): 57-71.

Department of Defense. *Soviet Military Power: An Assessment of the Threat, 1988*. Washington: United States Government Printing Office, 1988.

Draper, Theodore. "Soviet Reformers: From Lenin to Gorbachëv." *Dissent* (Summer 1987): 287-301.

Dziak, John J. "Soviet Deception: The Organizational and Operational Tradition." In *Soviet Strategic Deception*, edited by Brian D. Dailey and Patrick J. Parker. Lexington, Massachusetts: D. C. Heath and Company, 1987.

Ebenstein, William and Edwin Fogelman. *Today's Isms: Communism, Fascism, Capitalism, Socialism*. Englewood Cliffs, New Jersey: Prentice-Hall, Inc., 1958.

Ellison, Herbert J. "United Front Strategy and Soviet Foreign Policy." *Problems of Communism* 34 (September-October 1985): 45-64.

Epstein, Edward Jay. "Disinformation: Or, Why the CIA Cannot Verify an Arms-Control Agreement." *Commentary* 74 (July 1982): 21-28.

George, Alexander L. "The 'Operational Code': A Neglected Approach to the Study of Political Leaders and Decision-Making." In *The Conduct of Soviet Foreign Policy*, edited by Erik P. Hoffmann and Frederic J. Fleron, Jr. Chicago: Aldine Publishing Company, 1971.

Grant, Natalie. "Deception on a Grand Scale." *International Journal of Intelligence and Counterintelligence* 1 (1986): 51-77.

Hauslohner, Peter. "Gorbachëv's Social Contract." *Soviet Economy* 3 (January-March 1987): 54-89.

Heuer, Richards J., Jr. "Soviet Organization and Doctrine for Strategic Deception." In *Soviet Strategic Deception*, edited by Brian D. Dailey and Patrick J. Parker. Lexington, Massachusetts: D. C. Heath and company, 1987.

Hoover, J. Edgar. *Masters of Deceit*. New York: Holt, Rinehart and Winston, 1958.

Hough, Jerry F. "Gorbachëv Consolidating Power." *Problems of Communism* 36 (July-August 1987): 21-43.

Kennan, George, "X." "The Sources of Soviet Conduct." *Foreign Affairs* 25 (Summer 1947): 566-582.

Kennedy, Paul. "What Gorbachëv is up Against." *The Atlantic Monthly* 264 (June 1987): 29-43.

Krauthammer, Charles. "When to Call off the Cold War." *The New Republic* 199 (16 November 1987): 18-21.

Laue, Theodore H. von. *Why Lenin? Why Stalin?* New York: J. B. Lippincott Company, 1977.

Lenczowski, John. "Themes of Soviet Strategic Deception and Disinformation." In *Soviet Strategic Deception*, edited by Brian D. Dailey and Patrick J. Parker. Lexington, Massachusetts: D. C. Heath and Company, 1987.

Mandelbaum, Michael, and Strobe Talbot. "Reykjavik and Beyond." *Foreign Affairs* 65 (Winter 1986-1987): 215-235.

Mihalka, Michael. "Soviet Strategic Deception, 1955-1981." In *Military Deception and Strategic Surprise*, edited by John Gooch and Amos Perlmutter. London: Frank Cass Company, 1982.

Moorehead, Alan. *The Russian Revolution.* New York: Harper & Row, Publishers, 1958.

Pipes, Richard. *Survival is Not Enough: Soviet Realities and America's Future.* New York: Simon & Schuster, Inc., 1984.

_____. "Detente: Moscow's View." In *The Conduct of Soviet Foreign Policy*, edited by Erik P. Hoffmann and Frederic J. Fleron, Jr. New York: Aldine Publishing Company, 1971.

Sestanovich, Stephen. "What Gorbachëv Wants." *The New Republic* 199 (25 May 1987): 6-9.

Sharp, Samuel L. "National Interest: Key to Soviet Politics." *Problems of Communism* 7 (March-April 1958): 15-21.

Trotsky, Leon. *The History of the Russian Revolution.* Vol. 1. Translated by Max Eastman. New York: Simon and Schuster, 1932.

Tucker, Robert C. *The Marxian Revolutionary Idea.* New York: W. W. Norton & Co., Inc., 1969.

Ulam, Adam B. *Expansion and Coexistence: Soviet Foreign Policy, 1917-1973.* 2d ed. New York: Praeger Publishers, 1974.

United States Department of Commerce. *Military Strategy: A Comparison of the 1962 and 1963 Editions*. Washington: JPRS, 1963.

Yost, David S. "The Soviet Campaign Against INF in West Germany." In *Soviet Strategic Deception*, edited by Brian D. Dailey and Patrick J. Parker. Lexington, Massachusetts: D. C. Heath and Company, 1987.

NEWSPAPERS

Izvestiya, 1989.
Kazakstanskaya Pravda, 1989.
Krasnaya Zvezda, 1961-1989.
Literatura Ukraina, 1989.
Literaturnaya Gazeta, 1981.
New York Times, 1961-1987.
Pravda, 1965-1990.
Selskaya Zhizn, 1989.
Sovetskaya Rossiya, 1989.
Tanjug, 1989.
The News and Daily Advance (Lynchburg, Virginia), 1989.
Trud, 1990.

OTHER

AFP, Paris, 1989.
Moscow Domestic Service, 1989.
Moscow Television Service, 1989.
Moscow World Service, 1989.
Prague Domestic Service, 1989.
Radio Liberty, 1987.
TASS, 1987, 1989.

INDEX